February 13, 2010

Larry,

Thanks for a phenomenal tribute to Russ

Bill Finnie

Hands-On Strategy

THE GUIDE TO CRAFTING YOUR COMPANY'S FUTURE

D1411168

WILLIAM C. FINNIE

Grace & Company, P.C. • St. Louis, Missouri

Requests for permission or further
information should be addressed to
William C. Finnie, The Finnie Group,
12501 Glencroft Drive
St. Louis, MO 63128

ISBN 0-9678696-0-9

DEDICATION

I am blessed with both challenging work and a wonderful family. My parents, Thomas C. and Evelyn W. Finnie, gave me a firm foundation. This book is dedicated to my wife, Glenda, and my two sons, John and Steve. Glenda is one of the most talented and caring people I have known. It's been a great marriage for the last 32 years. While my father is a hard act to follow, my sons are a wonderful Act III. They and their friends give me confidence in America in the 21st century.

PREFACE

The strategy development process detailed in this book works. In our last 27 programs, over 97 percent of the participants rated the final vision, strategy, and implementation plan as eight or higher on a 10-point scale. The reason for its success is simple. It combines the most powerful strategy concepts with in-depth experience and a passion for superior performance.

Powerful strategy concepts: *Hands-On Strategy* shows you how to combine the brilliant strategy concepts of the 1980s (from Michael Porter and Russell Ackoff) and the 1990s (from Gary Hamel, C.K. Prahalad, and many others) so your company can achieve its full potential. In-depth knowledge of these techniques results from teaching strategy to Washington University MBAs since 1978, publishing the only subscription newsletter on strategy in the U.S., being executive editor of *Strategy & Leadership* magazine, and (most importantly) seeing how they work in the real world as a practitioner.

In-depth experience: Above all else, I am a businessperson. I have loved my 26 years at Anheuser-Busch (including 15 years in senior management), six years of running my own strategy consulting firm, and directing the Business Consulting Group of Grace & Company since 1998.

Passion for superior performance: Nothing compares with being part of a team that is working together to its full potential and winning big-time in the real world. I challenge my clients to develop a strategy that grows the value of their company dramatically--five or 10-fold in 10 years. As we show, however, such long-term growth can only be achieved if the strategy also provides superior benefits to employees and customers.

The great contribution of the first edition was to present a proven framework for strategy development. Its basic structure has passed the test of time. The only structural change in strategy development is the addition of chapter 9 on people-driven strategies.

Strategy implementation, however, is a different matter. No compelling approach to implementation had replaced the bureaucratic planning cycles that died by 1980. New ideas on implementation (including change management and leadership) in chapters 11 and 12 were the original reason for the second edition.

I thought that the second edition would require only light editing outside of chapters 9, 11, and 12. I was wrong! Over 90 percent of the book is new for two reasons:

1. As discussed in chapter 1, the extraordinary changes in the business environment in only six years produced major changes in the strategies of successful companies.

2. The second edition is much more pragmatic and goal-oriented. Gone are any "interesting" strategy concepts that have not helped clients produce results. Included are the real world examples that have most consistently sparked breakthroughs.

Hands-On Strategy is designed for goal-oriented business people. In the past, many CEOs stayed far too long with strategies that clearly weren't working. As we enter the "winner take all" Internet era, both the payoff from a superior strategy and the cost of a losing strategy increase. Fortunately, the Three-Cycle Process in *Hands-On Strategy* provides a clear road map for developing and implementing a winning strategy. Do it!

The Three-Cycle Process is designed so a knowledgeable, goal-oriented management team can develop a superior strategy. Yet, using an experienced strategy consultant to facilitate the process can lead to a better final strategy (and save immense amounts of management time). Complete and return the form on the last page to obtain no cost, no obligation information on how we can help your company develop and implement a strategy that produces exceptional results.

I plan to update *Hands-On Strategy* regularly so it reflects best practices. Your comments and suggestions are greatly appreciated.

Bill Finnie
The Finnie Group
12501 Glencroft Drive
St. Louis, MO 63128

wcfinnie@earthlink.net
(314) 849-4404

February, 2000

ACKNOWLEDGMENTS

The strengths of the 1994 edition of *Hands-On Strategy* rested on three foundations:

- Dr. Russell L. Ackoff, my doctoral advisor at the University of Pennsylvania and the most creative person I have known.
- August A. Busch III, Jack Purnell, and other senior executives at Anheuser-Busch, who consistently stretched me to 100 percent of my ability from the time I got a summer job in 1965 until I left the company to form my own consulting firm in 1991.
- Teaching strategy to second year MBAs at Washington University since 1978, which has honed my approach to planning and strategy.

The much more entrepreneurial focus of the new edition results from three new forces:

- I have received an incredible education (and intense satisfaction) from helping 60 management teams develop and implement breakthrough strategies since 1991.
- The rock solid values and total commitment to clients of the people at Grace & Company are a daily inspiration. The people in the Business Consulting Group are dedicated to becoming the "trusted solutions partner" to help our clients grow their companies' value dramatically. They are a great group of people with a great mission.
- The opportunity to publish my ideas allows me to meet fascinating business leaders and integrate the best new concepts into the Three-Cycle Strategy Process. I particularly want to recognize Ellen Sherberg (publisher of the *St. Louis Business Journal,* where my Marketing Trends column has appeared since 1991), Jim Fullinwider (who helped me with the first edition of the book and then worked with me to publish 14 issues of *The Real World Strategist* newsletter), and Marilyn Norris (who was a marvelous editor when I was executive editor of *Strategy & Leadership* magazine).

Finally, I want to thank Dr. Joseph Michlitsch, who edited this second edition of *Hands-On Strategy* while on sabbatical from Southern Illinois University-Edwardsville. Joe enhanced both the content and readability of each chapter.

CONTENTS

CHAPTER ONE

The Nature and Importance of Strategy

WHAT IS STRATEGY?

Strategy is concerned with developing a vision and a coherent set of action plans for making that vision a reality. The vision should be challenging but achievable. It should be instantly understandable and grab people in their gut—since motivated people are the essential element in implementation.

Both the vision and the action plans must reflect all of your business realities: customer wants, your capabilities, your competitors, and all of the climate forces. Designing your strategy to be consistent with these forces allows you to exploit change. You will be positioned to take market share away from competitors who are swimming upstream with strategies that fail to reflect their competitive realities.

Strategy is about change. Identify the opportunities on the horizon and develop action plans to exploit them. Identify and get rid of problems. Every hour and every dollar spent exploiting opportunities produces five or 10 times more payback than efforts spent on problems. Indeed, the PIMS data base indicates that incremental investments for companies in the weakest competitive position not only fail to return the cost of capital but lead to actual losses (Exhibit 5.6).

Strategy development is the responsibility of top management. Yes, the process should reflect inputs from customers, suppliers, and employees at all levels. Yes, the final strategy may be fine-tuned after communicating the preliminary vision throughout the organization. Most emphatically yes, strategy implementation is primarily bottom-up. Yet, senior management is responsible for developing an effective strategy and should be held accountable for its success. Their position, experience, and responsibilities dictate that they lead the strategy process.

Strategy is long-term, requires large commitments of resources, is hard to reverse, and cuts across all areas of the business. Strategy implementation requires investments in people, equipment, internal and external communications, and technology. Even in a small company, it will take a year before employees fully understand the strategy and two or three years before customers recognize the benefits. Hence, strategy must be built on an objective assessment of opportunities and realities so it lasts for seven to 10 years or longer. Changing your strategy every two or three years is a formula for disaster.

Most importantly, the purpose of strategy is to increase sales, profits, and company value. In order to do that, it must meet the needs of target customers so well that it gives the company an unfair (but not illegal or unethical) advantage over competitors. If this is to be accomplished, each member of the management team must sincerely believe that the final strategy is at least an eight on a 10-point scale. Examples of strategies producing such results include:

- Wal-Mart versus main street retailers,
- Enterprise Rent-A-Car versus Hertz and Avis, and
- Wintel (the combination of Microsoft Windows and Intel) versus Apple.

This book presents a process for development and implementation of strategies that can help your company develop such an unfair advantage.

Effective and Ineffective Strategies

Effective strategies must work for all key stakeholders. Southwest Airlines' CEO, Herb Kelleher, says strategy must work for employees, customers, and owners, in that order. If Southwest does a great job of selecting, training, and motivating its people, they will do a wonderful job of "wowing" the customer. Super-satisfied customers become loyal customers, and loyal customers are a solid foundation for superior financial performance and happy owners.

Exhibit 1.1 illustrates some effective and some ineffective strategies. Wal-Mart's experience shows that a well-executed low-cost strategy can work beautifully. Microsoft used a differentiation strategy to dominate the market for personal computer software. Both companies had a clear and relevant strategy and executed it well. The disastrous strategic error is being "caught in the middle." In the 1980s, Sears had neither low-costs nor products with distinctive appeal. It was "caught in the middle" and consistently lost share to competitors.

Exhibit 1.1 **Effective business strategies work for all three key stakeholders**

	WAL-MART	**MICROSOFT**	**SEARS** (IN 1974-92)
STRATEGY	Low-cost	Differentiation	"Caught in the middle"
CUSTOMER PERCEPTIONS	Great value, friendly, good variety, clean	It's the standard	Bad service, old fashioned, still good quality in durables
EMPLOYEE PERCEPTIONS	Good culture; glad I bought stock	Lets me do great work; rich from stock options	It's a job; I hope I don't lose it when they cut costs
STOCKHOLDER PERCEPTIONS	Great company	Great company	It's been a disaster

Frederick Reichheld[1] provides a six-step process which leads to a strategy that provides superior benefits for all three key stakeholders:

1. Develop a strategy that delivers truly superior value to a specific customer segment.
2. Focus all your efforts on these target customers.
3. Earn customer loyalty with the right pricing policies, product line, and service levels.
4. Find the right employees. Be selective. Look for people who share the company's values, and have the needed talents and skills.
5. Earn employee loyalty with compensation, incentives, training, benefits, and a positive working environment.
6. Gain cost and performance advantages through employee productivity.

The potential bottom-line benefits of superior customer-driven and people-driven strategies based on these six steps are amazing. This fact is illustrated by Southwest Airlines, Wal-Mart, Tyson Foods, Circuit City, and Plenum Publishing, which have three things in common. They are in tough industries. They have solid people- and customer-driven strategies. And they increased owner value an average of 18,360 percent from 1972 to 1992 (29.8 percent annually). The lesson is clear: investors receive superior financial returns in the long term only if the strategy is built on the solid foundation of superior benefits to customers and employees. Great strategies must work for all three key stakeholders.

Mediocre strategies are eventually disastrous for all key stakeholders. At some point, a weak strategy produces below average value to customers. The inevitable result is declining sales and profits. Without a strategy that adds value, management responds by cutting costs. The best employees, recognizing the lack of opportunities in both the short term and long term, leave. Sales and profits decline further. This downward spiral continues until a new strategy (usually from new leadership) provides superior customer value. The turnarounds of American Express under Harvey Golub and IBM under Lou Gerstner are classic examples.

Whether employees or customers come first depends on the particular company. For many decades, "the customer comes first" was a truism. This belief continues to work for strategy consulting giant McKinsey & Company. At McKinsey, the long-term customer relationship comes first, McKinsey comes second, and the individual consultant comes third. McKinsey is able to attract and retain the best new consultants by promising lavish rewards for those who do a superior job of meeting the needs of customers and the firm. An increasing number of companies, however, believe everyone benefits if "the customer comes second." They agree with Southwest Airline's Herb Kelleher that what is delivered to the customer is much better if you first take care of your employees.

Stockholders are not myopic. The value of a company reflects profits today and the current growth rate of profits. Also, as reflected by General Electric's price/earnings ratio of 42, a company's value reflects the quality of management and infrastructure investments to ensure continued growth. Hence, I believe the company itself should be regarded as a key stakeholder. A balanced scorecard of goals should include growth in the company's human capital and capabilities since they are the source of future benefits to the other three stakeholders.

For certain companies, other stakeholders must be considered in crafting strategy. Increasingly, society and the environment demand explicit recognition. In the past, only certain industries (e.g., alcohol, tobacco, and petroleum) had to worry about such issues. Today, however, healthcare, biotech, and even relatively small businesses such as pig farmers have had to be very sensitive to such issues. Importantly, corporate social and environmental responsibility is becoming more important in attracting and retaining the best younger employees. As part of a balanced life, they only want to work for companies that are socially responsible.

Additional stakeholders will command attention in strategic planning due to such trends as the growth of outsourcing and global business. Outsourcing allows companies to focus on their core competencies. Success, however, requires trusted partners. Outsourcers such as United Parcel Service (in logistics) and information technology consultants must earn the right to be considered stakeholders. Global companies such as Boeing and Royal Dutch Shell must often explicitly recognize governments as stakeholders in their strategies.

THE VALUE OF STRATEGY

Russell Ackoff has devised four approaches that organizations have traditionally followed for planning and strategy (Exhibit 1.2).

Exhibit 1.2 **Types of planning**[2]

	ATTITUDES TOWARDS CHANGE	PERCENT ACHIEVING POTENTIAL
INACTIVE	Avoid Change	8%
REACTIVE	React, don't plan	17%
PROACTIVE	Predict and prepare	53%
INTERACTIVE	Create your own future	67%

- Inactive organizations are bureaucratic and avoid change. Classic examples include government, schools, unions, and such corporate staff departments as human resources and information systems
- Reactive companies accept change. They believe the key to success is to be close to the customer and respond quickly to problems and opportunities. Many small company entrepreneurs are reactive. They are very goal-oriented and focused on increasing sales and profits. They don't believe, however, in such academic concepts as planning and strategy.
- Proactive organizations take the quantitative predict and prepare approach. Most large companies were proactive through the 1970s.
- Interactive companies take the strategic thinking approach developed since 1980. They believe that nothing is inevitable but that you can understand the forces of change and create your own future with a strategy that is consistent with the forces of change.

For the last several years, I have taken my evening MBA students at Washington University in St. Louis through these four approaches to strategy in the first class of each semester. These students are 30 to 35 years old and work full-time. Most are middle managers. A lot of hands go up when I ask them if they have ever worked for an organ-ization that was primarily inactive. Over 90 percent of those hands go down, however, when I ask them to keep their hand up if that organization did a reasonable job of achieving its potential while they were there. The amazing result is that five out of six reactive companies fail to achieve their potential. The reason these organizations fail is simple. People at a company whose strategy is to respond quickly to problems and opportunities spend 95 percent of their time dealing with problems. The big payoffs in this world, however, come from exploiting opportunities.

Exhibit 1.2 indicates that proactive companies are over three times as likely as reactive companies to achieve their potential, and interactive companies are four times as likely. On at least an annual basis, these companies try to identify the opportunities on the horizon. They then systematically develop plans and find the resources for sup-porting those plans to exploit the opportunities. These companies have a two to five year head start over the reactive companies. As a result, reactive companies will have a hard time surviving in the 21st century.

A Bain & Company survey[3] (Exhibit 1.3) also quantifies the effectiveness of strategic planning. Companies were placed in one of four clusters based on how they used strategic planning tools. The survey also asked each company how satisfied it was with its financial performance on a five-point scale (5 being very satisfied). Average financial results were then computed for companies in each cluster.

Exhibit 1.3 **Use strategy tools systematically**

	CHARACTERISTICS	FINANCIAL RESULTS (5 = Very Satisfied)
LEADERS	Use new tools systematically	3.78
SKEPTICS	Avoid planning	3.16
FOLLOWERS	Wait for a tool's track record	2.96
FADDISTS	Adopt latest tool as a panacea	1.56

- **Leaders** were early adopters of new tools. They integrated useful new tools into their overall approach to managing their company and had significantly higher financial performance than other companies.
- **Skeptics** are like Ackoff's "reactive" companies. They believe in the basics rather than planning and strategy.
- **Followers** are late adopters of new strategy tools. Skeptics and Followers have similar financial results that are between Leaders and Faddists.
- **Faddists** were also early adopters, but they tended to grasp at new tools

such as total quality management or reengineering as a panacea. After disappointing results, a few years later they drop that tool and seek salvation in a more recent tool. Faddists have much lower financial results than other companies. Strategy tools are a means to an end, not the ultimate objective. Don't be a Faddist!

The Bain survey results are consistent with my less formal survey results. Companies can use strategy and planning to significantly increase performance. Antiplanners suffer. The Bain survey demonstrates, however, that naïve use of strategic planning tools is especially destructive.

This book uses the "create your own future" tools of interactive planning in developing strategy. It uses a combination of quantitative "what gets measured get rewarded" proactive planning tools and "softer" tools from leadership and change management to drive implementation. Together, they provide a roadmap so your company can develop and implement a strategy for achieving its full potential. (People-oriented strategic planning tools are increasingly important for success. Referring to them as "soft" is not meant to diminish their importance.)

THE EVOLUTION OF STRATEGIC PLANNING

Developing a solid approach to strategy benefits greatly by looking at the evolution of planning and strategy over the last 50 years. Exhibit 1.4 summarizes this evolution by decade. Modern planning began with operations research and management science during World War II. The most famous case of wartime planning brought to business was Robert McNamara and the other "whiz kids" at Ford Motor Company.

The methodical "predict and prepare" approach worked great during the 1950s and 1960s. Smooth growth and the mass market characterized this post-war era. There were three television networks, one flavor of Coca-Cola, and the Big 3 car companies owned 90 percent of the market with relatively few models. Planning departments allowed large companies to determine with a fair degree of accuracy the "inevitable future" and develop plans to fully exploit it. Companies that obtained financing, built plants, hired production workers, and created marketing departments to grow at five or 10 percent a year based on these plans had an unfair advantage over those who reacted on a quarterly basis.

This approach to planning died in the 1970s from multiple attacks. The rise of global competition, with high quality competitors from Europe and Japan and ultra low cost competitors from developing countries, accelerated the rate of product innovation. Shocks to the system, such as quadrupling of oil prices in 1973 and again in 1979 and 20 percent interest rates in the late 1970s, made the concept of a long-term forecast as a foundation for strategy laughable. Finally, the movement from the mass market to fragmentation as marketing entered the segmentation and positioning era in the late

Exhibit 1.4 **The evolution of strategy**

	PRIMARY CHARACTERISTICS	APPROACH	OBJECTIVE
1950s	Budgeting and management science	One-year, bottom up	Improving efficiency; providing top-management control
1960s	Long-range planning	Five-year "predict and prepare" planning	Bottom-up functional plans based on corporate planning forecast
1970s	Formula planning	Financially-driven formula planning	Experience curve and low cost strategy; growth-share matrix for managing business units
1980s	Strategic thinking (static)	Market-driven	Develop strategy consistent with 5 Cs (customers, competitors, climate, culture, and capabilities)
1990s	Strategic thinking (dynamic)	Design a desired future and develop a strategy to achieve it	A dynamic framework that favors speed and vision over size
2000s	Strategic action	Combine market-driven strategy with leadership	Develop an unfair advantage and implement aggressively

1970s mandated the movement from "predict and prepare" planning to "strategic thinking."

The new era of strategic planning began with Michael Porter's *Competitive Strategy* (The Free Press, 1980) and Russell Ackoff's *Creating the Corporate Future* (Wiley, 1981). These books shifted from the forecast-based approach to understanding the forces of change and creating a strategy consistent with those forces. Their basic philosophy is that nothing is inevitable but that we can develop a strategy for achieving breakthrough results based on action plans consistent with our competitive realities.

In retrospect, the 1980s were a "static strategic thinking" era. Porter's five competitive forces (customers, competitors, suppliers, potential entrants, and substitutes) were believed to largely determine what your ROI (return on investment) could be. Similarly, the laws of marketing warfare said big armies beat little armies, and small companies should never aspire to overtaking large ones. The success of Japanese consumer electronics and automobile companies versus the American giants, however, revealed the flaws in static approaches. Companies with superior "strategic intent" and sharpened capabilities could accomplish amazing results.

The 1990s had a flowering of dynamic strategic thinking. The leading strategists of the 1990s, such as Gary Hamel and C.K. Prahalad, showed how companies with superior strategies could attract the best people and move faster than larger, slower-moving competitors. Unlike earlier static approaches, these approaches to strategy explain how Microsoft can grow from 11 employees in 1978 to become the most valuable company in the world in 20 years. In the information age, size is no longer destiny. Instead, victory goes to the company with the superior vision, strategy, and systems.

The 1990s also saw breakthroughs in strategy implementation. *The Balanced*

Scorecard by Robert Kaplan and David Norton (Harvard, 1996) provided guidance on the quantitative side of implementation: What gets measured and rewarded gets done. *The Balanced Scorecard* showed how to put together a foundation of measurements and link them to an overall management system. *Leading Change,* by John Kotter (Harvard, 1996) addressed the softer side of implementation. It provides the eight steps that the CEO must take in order to make permanent, major change in an organization. *Results-Based Leadership* by David Ulrich and others (Harvard, 1999) shows how to combine hard and soft strategy tools.

The World of Business Has Changed Since 1994

The world has changed—quietly but dramatically—since 1994. In October 1994, I asked my evening MBA students to raise their hand if they were having fun at work. No hands were raised. My probing revealed a lot of anger. One said, "My company has down-sized and eliminated two-thirds of its middle managers. I'm doing the work of three people. It used to be blue-collar workers who had drudgery jobs. Now it's us." Another student said, "The yuppies have all of the good jobs. We were born 15 years too late." There were lots of murmurs of agreement to these statements. I was shocked that every one of the 45 students in the class was unhappy at work.

In 1995, I asked the same question, and was pleased when a third of the students indicated they were having fun at work. In 1996, 55 percent were enjoying their jobs. In 1997, 75 percent said they were having fun. To go from zero to 75 percent of students enjoying their jobs in three years is absolutely amazing. Here are four drivers of major change since 1994:

1. **Big companies have changed their focus from cost reduction to growth.** The U.S. had back-to-back recessions in 1979 and 1981. Japan dominated the consumer electronics industry and the Big 3 U.S. car companies were on the ropes. U.S. quality was lousy and costs were out of control. From 1980 to 1995, most big companies focused internally on getting costs down and quality up. It was the era of corporate raiders, reengineering, downsizing, and early retirement programs. Cost reduction isn't fun. Lack of job security causes stress. There is guilt about those who have lost their jobs. Survivors work longer hours, and the work is routine and boring.

   Since early 1995, most big companies have shifted their focus to growth. After 15 years of cost reduction and total quality management, the United States now has the highest productivity of the 15 advanced economies in the world. Big companies realized they could no longer get the profit increases Wall Street demands through cost reduction. Instead, except for industries like healthcare and banking, the path to increasing bottom-line profits has shifted to increasing top-line revenue. Bob Shapiro launched 50 "growth initiatives" when he became CEO of Monsanto in early 1995. Emerson Electric now has "growth conferences" with its business units instead of planning conferences.

2. **We have incredible prosperity.** The U.S. has moved to a position of prosperity and international leadership unmatched since the Roman Empire. Capitalism is triumphant and threats to peace come from only small, renegade states. While the rate of change continues to accelerate, uncertainty is much lower. After the oil shocks and 20 percent interest rates of the 1970s, inflation has declined smoothly to the point where some are more concerned about deflation. Meanwhile, the economy has grown smoothly except for the recession of 1991-92 that cost George Bush re-election. The Dow-Jones Industrial Average increased from an average of 3,785 in 1994 to over 11,000 in 1999, 24 percent annual growth.

3. **We have entered the information age.** The big winners in the last five years have been technology companies and the largest 100 of the S&P 500 companies. Internet stock prices indicate that investors believe e-commerce will transform many industries.

   The information age has certainly transformed economics. As noted by Stanford economist Paul Romer[4], the foundation for wealth has shifted from the land, labor, and capital of Adam Smith to hardware, wetware, and software. Hardware is plant and equipment. Wetware is brains and human capital. Software is the recipe for Starbucks coffee and the patent for a Merck drug as well as Windows from Microsoft. Software is the real foundation for wealth since it has basically no marginal cost. Starbucks sells a nickel's worth of the commodity coffee for $2.00. And, once you become the standard, you own the dominant market share worldwide. The information age and the rise of global commerce has created a "winner take all" economy. The key to huge business success is developing processes that transform wetware into software.

4. **Global commerce continues to expand.** Imported products have grown from less than four percent of manufactured goods in 1960 to over 20 percent in 1999. With telecommunications, programmers in India illustrate how we can now import services as well as products. Global competition has been a major force in holding inflation down. Global commerce benefits consumers with greater variety and lower prices. But it is both an opportunity and a threat to business. It represents an opportunity for industry leaders who want to dramatically increase their potential market. Businesses who do not move internationally, however, will suffer in three ways: from lower margins, from lower market share from international competitors, and from tougher competition from domestic companies that have responded to the international threat.

Business Strategies Have Also Changed

Part of the success of the economy may well be due to better strategic management. Large U.S. companies did an outstanding job of improving quality and reducing costs from 1980 to 1995. They also recognized when the time had come to shift to an external focus on increasing revenue. Finally, many companies did a solid job of integrating new management tools into their overall approach to business. Here are six of the ways in which the strategies of corporate America have changed in the last five years:

1. **People come first.** Having the best people is the foundation for success in a growth economy. (You must also have the management processes in place to transform superior "wetware" into superior "software" and products.) For service companies, loyal employees lead to loyal clients, ... and loyal clients are the foundation for superior growth and profits. It is increasingly a "winner take all" economy. You need the best people to develop and market mega-successful new products and services. Soft aspects of strategy are much more important (e.g., teamwork and leadership designed to eliminate functional chimneys).

2. **Companies are moving faster.** The bureaucratic planning cycle is dead. Many companies have embraced time-based competition. Detroit has reduced the development time for new cars from 60 to 30 months. Strategy has moved from static (Porter's five forces) to dynamic (strategic intent and other concepts of Hamel and Prahalad) to reflect the information age.

3. **Companies are more focused on their core competencies and core customers.** Successful companies have increased focus by divesting non-core businesses. Anheuser-Busch closed Eagle Snacks, sold the St. Louis Cardinals baseball team, and spun off Earthgrains bakery so it could focus on domestic and international beer. Monsanto spun off its commodity chemicals into Solutia so it could focus on transforming itself into a growth-oriented biotech and pharmaceutical firm. In both cases, both the parent company and the divested companies benefited from increased focus.

4. **Partnering and other forms of alliances are accelerating.** Companies have downsized and want to remain lean. They would rather partner with a world class supplier than do it internally. Outsourcing of information systems departments reflects the desire of management teams to rely on partners for areas unrelated to their key success factors. Large companies but not smaller ones have aggressively moved to consultants. Relationships with such partners have two benefits. The partner can do the job better, faster, and cheaper since it is expert in its niche. And the company gets to focus its resources on its area of expertise. Indeed, some strategists have argued that the focus of business is shifting from the individual firm to the network of firms (e.g., the Wintel ecology of Microsoft Windows and Intel, along with the hundreds of companies that supply related hardware, software, and services).

5. **Differentiation strategies increasingly beat low cost strategies.** Companies

with low cost strategies such as Wal-Mart and Southwest Airlines were the big winners through 1994 as we were still emerging from the 1991-92 recession. With the strong economy, the emphasis has now shifted to unique products such as Starbucks coffee, $45,000 Lincoln Navigator sport utility vehicles, and a host of Internet services.

6. **Functional strategies are having major strategic impacts.** For example, finance may directly focus on shareholder value with pay for performance and open book management. Information technology and marketing may work together to implement e-commerce solutions. Operations and marketing may increase customer satisfaction with mass customization or cycle time reduction. Human resource departments that help senior executives attract, develop, and retain the best people and help implement policies for getting everyone to work together can become the key to corporate success.

The changes in the world of business show that we are now entering the era of strategic action. The strategy development tools of the 1980s and 1990s and the implementation tools of the 1990s provide the raw materials. This book combines the best of these tools into a step by step approach that has been successfully implemented by companies of all types and sizes.

The Critics of Strategy Are Wrong

There is a significant group of business executives, academics, consultants, and speakers who simply do not like the disciplined approach to strategy development and implementation. *The Rise and Fall of Strategic Planning* by Henry Mintzberg[5] is one of the more notable books on the type. Amazingly, writing in 1994, he spends 408 pages to attack the "predict and prepare" approach to strategy that died by 1980. He rarely takes note of any of the powerful "strategic thinking" tools developed since then. He begins, reasonably, with an attempt to define strategic planning. At length, he comes up with – in bold type – a definition he claims to have extracted from strategic planners' own words, **"strategy formation is a planning process designed or supported by planners, to plan in order to produce plans."** That is on page 32. By page 321, he has arrived at the planning schools' grand fallacy: **"because analysis is not synthesis, strategic planning is not strategy formation"** (again his bold type).

After 322 pages, Mintzberg states that his "highly critical" tone will now become "constructive". He proceeds to define a new role for planners. Strategy is to be left to top-management thinkers. Planners are mostly to be information gatherers and number crunchers. Since that is not much different from the 1960s-style planners he attacks, I wonder what the point of the book is.

A 1996 survey of senior executives by *CFO Magazine* does a better job of explaining why companies have too often failed to implement strategy effectively (see Exhibit 1.5).

Exhibit 1.5 Views of senior executives on strategy[6]

1. Does your company have a clearly articulated statement of its mission?	Yes No	91% 9%
2. How important a role should a clear vision play?	Significant Some Little	79% 20% 1%
3. What percentage of people in your organization clearly understand the vision?	Senior executive team Primary operating managers General employee base	71% 40% 3%
4. How important a role does your strategic planning process currently play in your company's overall success?	Significant Some, little, or none	31% 69%
5. To what extent are the priorities of your long-range strategy reflected in your annual budget?	Strong Some or small	43% 57%
6. To what extent is the incentive compensation of your employees linked to long-term business strategy?	Executive management Middle management Line employees	47% 24% 8%

- **Strategy and vision is important.** Over 90 percent of the respondents say their company has a clearly articulated statement of its mission (question #1) and 79 percent believe that vision has a significant role to play in their company (question #2).
- **Unfortunately, this vision is not effectively communicated throughout the organization.** Nearly 30 percent of senior executives do not clearly understand the vision. Even worse, 60 percent of the operating managers, who have responsibility for strategy implementation, and 97 percent of the general employees fail to clearly understand the vision (question #3).
- **Planning processes are too often ineffective.** Nearly 70 percent of the senior executives surveyed say that the planning process currently has less than a significant role in the company's overall success (question #4).
- **Budgets usually fail to reflect the strategy.** Significantly less than half of the executives state that the priorities of the long-range strategy are reflected in the annual budget (question #5).
- **Finally, compensation isn't closely linked to strategy.** Less than half of executive management, less than 25 percent of middle managers, and less than 10 percent of line employees have incentive compensation linked to long-term business strategy (question #6).

Objective information indicates that companies without effective strategic planning will flounder. Companies with effective strategic planning processes are much more likely to thrive. Extremely powerful strategy development techniques have been developed since 1980. Equally powerful strategy implementation tools have been developed since 1990. As indicated by the 1996 *CFO Magazine* survey, however, far too few companies have exploited the potential of these tools. The rest of this book provides a roadmap so senior management can develop and lead implementation of strategies that allow their company and all of its employees to achieve their full potential.

Does Your Company Need a New Strategy?

Four situations create the need for a new strategy:

1. **A new chief executive officer:** Even if everyone feels the old strategy is on target, a new CEO will want to make sure the strategy reflects his or her vision. The strategy process also leads to a consensus for making major changes which would be harder to implement without a strategic review.

2. **A major internal change in the business:** A change in ownership, a restructuring, or a downsizing requires a new vision for growing value. Major growth or a major acquisition can also call for a new strategy.

3. **A major change in the industry or business environment:** A new competitor with a "new rules" strategy (e.g., e-commerce competition for a wholesaler or retailer), international competition, or deregulation (e.g., airlines, telecommunications, farming) often call for major change. Better, be the one who identifies the opportunity in these events to give you the potential for a breakthrough strategy. Anticipate the need for a new strategy when you see these threats or opportunities on the horizon. In the Internet age, it is often too late if you wait until a direct competitor has taken action.

4. **Organizational inertia:** Finally, it's time for a CEO to initiate a new strategy whenever the organization is performing significantly below its potential. It's time to focus people externally on a strategy that beats competitors in meeting customer wants if excessive energy is spent on internal issues or people are working at cross-purposes.

If the time has come for a new strategy, this book offers a process that works. Your management team, however, must focus on developing a strategy that will produce results. Exhibit 1.6 shows that excessive focus on process and insufficient focus on results led to disengaged planning "rain dances" in the 1970s. However, the results were equally unacceptable when highly results-oriented top executives met without a process that moved from broad review of issues to focused strategies. The first meeting or two often produced exciting discussions. Additional meetings, however, led to frustration when they failed to produce closure. Too many management teams then decided to eliminate strategic planning. This "head in the sand" approach simply leads to decline. Although it seems obvious, only now are companies combining solid strategic planning processes from outside consultants with a focus on results from top management.

Exhibit 1.6 **Effective strategy requires a solid process and a focus on results**

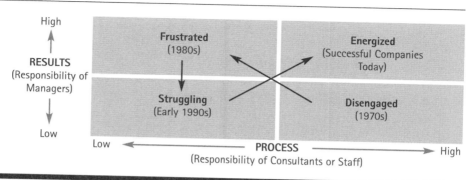

Source: Rath & Strong Management Consultants, Inc.

This book has a very simple goal: To provide a process that allows a goal-oriented management team to develop a strategy that leads to superior performance. Because strategies must make sense from every perspective and because mediocre strategies don't work, I strongly recommend that the management team make the following commitment at the beginning of the process: We will develop a strategy that each participant believes is "at least an eight on a 10-point scale."

CHAPTER TWO

The Three-Cycle Process for Strategy Development and Implementation

Strategy development is a responsibility of top management and requires strategic thinking. Implementation is the responsibility of everyone and requires leadership and predict-and-prepare proactive planning. Strategy development is glamorous. It's like the passing game in football. Implementation is more disciplined and quantitative. It's the ground-control, running game. Successful football teams have both a solid passing game and a solid running game. And successful strategy requires both strategic thinking and proactive planning.

Winning in the real world with superior strategy development and implementation is what this book is about. This chapter provides an overview of our proven Three-Cycle Process for strategy development and implementation:

- Cycle 1: Strategy development and strategic objective,
- Cycle 2: Departmental strategies and goals, and
- Cycle 3: Detailed performance measures and action plans.

The Three-Cycle Process differs in six ways from most current approaches:

1. Cycle 1 combines the most powerful strategic thinking concepts since 1980. Hence, it allows a management team to move systematically from a broad situation analysis to a compelling vision and strategy.
2. The Three-Cycle Process is both top-down and bottom-up. Top management provides broad direction. Department heads and lower level staff then propose detailed goals and specific action plans for achieving them.
3. It produces goal-oriented action rather than just strategic "thinking." The purpose of strategy is to help organizations increase sales and profits, not to produce intellectually appealing paradigms. Action is the result of (1) top-down/bottom-up accountability and (2) combining both objectives and action plans for achieving objectives in each cycle.
4. It recognizes that developing solid departmental strategies and goals is necessary before generating detailed individual performance measures and action plans.
5. Cycles 2 and 3 address strategy implementation. Cycle 2 assures departmental goals and strategies consistent with the overall strategy. Cycle 3 produces individual performance measures and action plans linked to budgets and departmental strategies.
6. The same Three-Cycle Process (greatly simplified) allows mid-course corrections each year while avoiding the excessively bureaucratic focus of 1970s-era planning.

OVERVIEW OF THE THREE-CYCLE PROCESS

The Three-Cycle Strategy Process, shown in Exhibit 2.1, incorporates both strategic thinking and proactive planning for superior strategy development and implementation. Each cycle includes developing both a clear objective and strategies or action plans for achieving them. The result is solid strategies and implementation plans for every type of organization:

- Small and large organizations,
- Makers of industrial products, suppliers of consumer goods, and service providers,
- Industry leaders and followers,
- High-growth, mature, and declining industries, and
- Businesses, nonprofits, and government organizations.

Exhibit 2.1 **Three–Cycle Strategy Process**

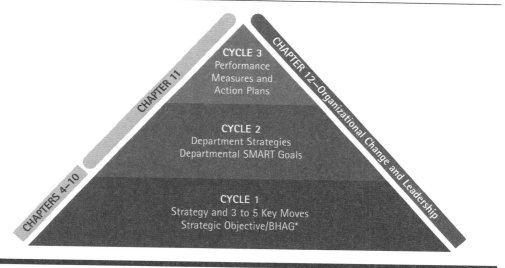

*BHAG is the acronym for Big, Hairy, Achievable Goal. James C. Collins and Jerry I. Porras developed the term BHAG in *Built to Last: Successful Habits of Visionary Companies* (Harper Business, 1994). They used "Audacious" instead of "Achievable." While we believe a BHAG must be a major stretch, we also believe it must be realistic.

The Three Cycles

Cycle 1 uses the most powerful strategic thinking concepts of the last 20 years to develop a strategy that is market driven and consistent with your capabilities. The goal is a strategy that gives your company an unfair advantage over competitors in meeting the needs of your target customers. The result is superior value for employees, customers, and owners. Our Cycle 1 approach to strategy development works. Since 1988, my students have used the approach to develop strategies for over 350 organizations. Since 1991, I have used it to facilitate strategies for over 60 organizations.

Cycle 1 begins with a situation analysis and tentative strategy and concludes with a solid vision and strategy for achieving the company's full potential. This strategy includes a two to six word vision and a three or four paragraph mission statement that explains how everyone will work together to make the vision a reality. It also includes three to five key moves and broad action plans for each key move. Importantly, all managers should focus at least 80 percent of their discretionary time and resources on these key moves. The strategy developed in Cycle 1 provides a foundation for decision making and actions for seven years or longer. It also provides clear direction for developing Cycle 2, departmental strategies and SMART goals—goals that are Specific, Measurable, Achievable, Results-oriented, and Time-based.

Cycle 2 is the missing link in effective strategy implementation. Each department must develop a solid strategy that is consistent with the company's strategy and key moves. Each departmental strategy reflects both qualitative considerations and quantitative SMART goals. Failure to develop solid departmental strategies often leads to adoption of a less than coherent set of tactical departmental action plans or implementing a popular management fad that does not fit with achieving the organization's vision. Hence, skipping Cycle 2 may be the leading cause of poor strategy implementation.

Cycle 3 produces performance measures and detailed action plans from each manager and supervisor. The Three-Cycle Process assures that detailed action plans reflect departmental SMART goals and the key moves of the company. By including the resources necessary to implement these action plans, the Three-Cycle Process links strategy with the annual budgeting process.

Pragmatic Considerations

The importance of objectives relative to action plans for achieving the objectives changes over the three cycles. Accordingly, the names for objectives and action plans change over the cycles. In Cycle 1, the firm's strategic objective or BHAG (Big, Hairy, Achievable Goal) must follow from consideration of the 5 Cs: Customers, Competitors, Climate (all of the competitive and environmental forces), and the firm's internal Culture and Capabilities. Hence, some strategic analysis must come before developing the BHAG. Strategy and goals have about equal importance in Cycle 2. Each department must develop its strategy based on its opportunities and the needs of its internal and external customers. Equally important, however, departmental SMART goals must be set so that achieving them allows the business to achieve its BHAG. Finally, in Cycle 3, setting performance measures comes before action plans. Detailed action plans must then be developed so each department will achieve its SMART goals if each person and group achieves their performance measures.

Cycle 1 uses largely qualitative analyses to develop a strategy that "fits" with the 5 Cs. The emphasis shifts increasingly to a balance of qualitative and quantitative measures in Cycle 2 and a predominately quantitative Cycle 3.

Developing a new strategy requires a major commitment of time and effort for any organization. It often takes smaller companies six months to go through all three cycles. Strategy development is harder for larger companies since the challenges increase with the size of the company.

Fine-tuning the strategy each year takes much less time than developing the new strategy in the first year. Most companies should go through the same three cycles annually. Executives of mid-size companies may spend a day in meetings for each of the three cycles. Preparation and follow-up take additional time. Bureaucratic processes in big companies once absorbed amazing amounts of time. Most, however, have greatly simplified their planning processes. The key is to develop a process that fits your realities while minimizing the unnecessary rain dance rituals. While the descriptions of this process sound complex, the final result must strip away the bureaucratic aspects so each person focuses on the linkages between the company's needs, their own actions, and the hard and soft rewards.

A solid strategy should last for seven to 10 years or longer. The only exception is a turnaround, in which case you will want to get the pain over as quickly as possible. Turnaround strategies may take two or three years for a mid-size company and five years for a large company. Once the company has completed the turnaround and figured out how to survive, it needs to develop a long-term, market-driven strategy to thrive. Even in a fast-changing industry like personal computers, strategies can last for seven years or longer. Compaq, for example, maintained the same differentiation strategy for nearly 10 years from its founding in 1982 until a price shakeout required shifting to a new CEO and a low-cost strategy in 1992. By 1999, Compaq had muddied its strategy (due in part to the acquisition of Digital Equipment), lost momentum, and gained a new CEO. After seven years with a low cost strategy, developing a more focused strategy must be a high priority of the new CEO.

Some strategies last much longer. Wal-Mart has had the same low-cost strategy since the first store opened in 1963. During that time, Wal-Mart has constantly evolved. It has moved from small stores in the south to larger Wal-Mart stores everywhere, introduced Sam's Club warehouse stores, moved into the grocery business with its Supercenters, and is now expanding internationally and moving onto the Internet. Throughout all of these changes, however, superb execution of its "every day low price" strategy has been the key driver of customer satisfaction and superior performance.

Deciding when a new strategy is necessary is the responsibility of the CEO, with counsel from a few trusted advisors and approval from the Board of Directors. The need for a new Cycle 1 may become clear during an annual planning "environmental analysis" or an accumulation of evidence or a single major event. Sometimes industry trends and its life-cycle phase point to an "inflection point,"[1] even though current results seem satisfactory. The necessity for a new Cycle 1 nearly always comes from one of four precipitating events:

- A new CEO, who will almost always want to make sure everyone is focused on achieving a common vision using a common strategy,
- Major internal changes, such as growing from $10 to $50 million (or a large company that has downsized to survive and now needs a growth strategy to thrive),

- Major external changes, such as the rise of global competition or the Internet or the graying of the population, or
- Your employees seem focused internally on petty issues and need a new market-driven strategy to get them working together to 100 percent of their ability.

Gaining support for changing to a new strategy requires "unfreezing" the organization from its current strategy. Sometimes the need for a new strategy is painfully clear to everyone in the organization. If the need is less obvious, the CEO faces a major education and selling job. In one form or another, a reference forecast[2] can show that the current strategy will lead to disaster (or at least to performance far below the organization's potential). A clear demonstration of the opportunity to exploit a window of opportunity can "unfreeze" many in the organization. Research showing competitors have lower costs or superior customer loyalty is also effective for mobilizing support for change.

Unfreezing Organizations to Achieve Consensus on the Need for a New Strategy

Analytical studies are less effective in unfreezing a company than approaches that grab people in the gut. In the 1970s, Xerox's share of the copier market fell from 80 percent to 25 percent. Benchmarking studies proved Japanese competitors were developing new products in half the time, had 50 percent lower costs, and 90 percent fewer defects. Action only came, however, when teams of Xerox workers videotaped a Japanese plant, which clearly showed 50 percent fewer workers on the production line. Worker involvement and the power of the video made the need for major change indisputable.

In late December 1976, CEO August Busch III brought together the top 25 marketing people at Anheuser-Busch. The meeting lasted a total of 10 minutes. Busch put a transparency on the overhead that showed flat Anheuser-Busch volume while sales of Miller Brewing Company were only 30 percent lower and growing dramatically. After looking each person in the eyes, Busch said that a lot of the people would not be in the room in 12 months unless the graph was a lot different. He then took the transparency and left. A month later, there was a new chief operating officer for the domestic beer company. By 1987, A–B's stock price had increased 945 percent and its sales were twice Miller's.

CYCLE 1: STRATEGY DEVELOPMENT

Cycle 1 is designed to help companies develop a new strategy. It has five parts, as shown in Exhibit 2.2:

- Situation analysis, which provides an understanding of your strengths, weaknesses, opportunities and threats, and the gaps between your potential and current performance,

- Tentative strategy, which provides broad direction for strategy analysis,
- Strategy analysis, which provides in-depth understanding from six distinct perspectives (from business definition through employee-driven strategies),
- Vision and Mission statement, which moves the process from complexity and analysis towards simplification and implementation, and
- Key moves and broad action plans, which provide sufficient direction for developing bottom-up departmental strategies consistent with the overall strategy.

Exhibit 2.2 **Overview of Goal–Oriented Strategic Planning**

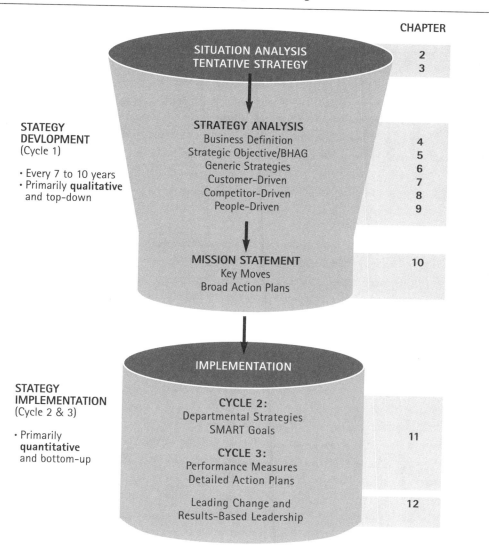

		CHAPTER
	SITUATION ANALYSIS	2
	TENTATIVE STRATEGY	3
STATEGY DEVLOPMENT (Cycle 1)	**STRATEGY ANALYSIS**	
	Business Definition	4
· Every 7 to 10 years	Strategic Objective/BHAG	5
· Primarily **qualitative** and top-down	Generic Strategies	6
	Customer-Driven	7
	Competitor-Driven	8
	People-Driven	9
	MISSION STATEMENT Key Moves Broad Action Plans	10
	IMPLEMENTATION	
STATEGY IMPLEMENTATION (Cycle 2 & 3)	**CYCLE 2:** Departmental Strategies SMART Goals	
· Primarily **quantitative** and bottom-up	**CYCLE 3:** Performance Measures Detailed Action Plans	11
	Leading Change and Results-Based Leadership	12

The **situation analysis,** detailed in chapter 3, provides the management team with a foundation of information to determine directionally what the new strategy should look like. Traditional sales and financial analysis provides solid indications of strengths and weaknesses. Customer and employee satisfaction surveys, competitive intelligence, and market research surveys provide more detailed insight into the causes and cures of problems and, more importantly, strengths that you can use as a foundation for your strategy. We use 10 climate and competitive forces to identify external threats and opportunities. Again, huge success results from identifying and fully exploiting opportunities rather than focusing excessively on threats.

The **tentative strategy,** also covered in chapter 3, is essential in assuring that a solid strategy evolves by the end of Cycle 1. Failure to do a tentative strategy often leads to major shifts in strategic thinking through each step of strategy analysis. As a result, the final vision and strategy are less than compelling. Success then requires another pass through each of the six steps of strategy analysis.

A tentative strategy developed by an external consultant or junior executive can provide fairly detailed suggestions for each step in Cycle 1. If developed by the CEO or other senior executive, however, it should be brief and contain three parts:

1. Key elements of the old strategy and why it was effective in the past,
2. Internal, competitive, and climate changes that require changes in the strategy, and
3. A general discussion of elements of the new strategy. Excessive detail in this final part will inhibit discussion and creativity since few people are willing to question the CEO.

Strategy analysis, covered in chapters 4 through 9, involves six basic steps:

Step 1: Business definition (chapter 4),
Step 2: Strategic objective, or BHAG (Big, Hairy, Achievable Goal, chapter 5),
Step 3: Generic strategies (chapter 6),
Step 4: Customer-driven strategies (chapter 7),
Step 5: Competitor-driven strategies (chapter 8), and
Step 6: People-driven strategies (chapter 9).

The **business definition** tells you how to focus your business so you have an unfair advantage in meeting targeted needs of a specific, attractive customer segment. The strategic objective, or **BHAG,** states the single critically important goal you are trying to achieve over the next seven to 10 years. **Generic strategy** states how you will achieve your BHAG. **Customer- and competitor-driven strategies** turn the generic strategy into marketplace strategies for beating competitors in meeting customer wants. **People-driven strategies** make sure that your company attracts, develops, and retains the people you need to implement your strategy—and that they work together to 100 percent of their potential. Developing each of the six steps of strategy analysis must be customized to exactly reflect your company's five Cs: Climate, Customers, Competitors, Capabilities, and Culture. They provide a solid analytical foundation for developing a strategy to achieve your company's full potential.

The **vision and mission statement** (chapter 10) moves strategy from complexity to simplicity, from analysis to action. It uses a process called "idealized design" to help the organization make a creative leap to a vision of a challenging but achievable future. The vision is two to six words that grab people in the gut and summarize what the organization is trying to achieve. The mission statement is three or four paragraphs that describe how people will work together to achieve the vision, and how achieving the vision will benefit employees, customers, and owners. Together, the vision and mission are the public statement of your strategy that will guide and motivate everyone in the organization for seven to 10 years.

While motivating, the mission statement does not provide sufficient direction for developing departmental strategies and bottom-up action plans. Hence, the final element in strategy development is identifying the **three to five key moves** for achieving the vision (also covered in chapter 10). Top management has not reached a shared vision until they agree on these key moves and a few broad action plans for each move. All managers should focus at least 80 percent of their discretionary time and resources on these key moves. Top management must not accept departmental strategies, bottom-up action plans, and budgets that inadequately reflect these key moves.

CYCLE 2: DEPARTMENTAL STRATEGIES AND GOALS

Solid departmental strategies are the missing link in strategy implementation. In the 1980s and early 1990s, gurus such as Tom Peters and Henry Mintzberg argued that formal strategic planning didn't work and was a waste of time. Their belief was disproved with the success of my Cycle 1 approach of systematically combining the most powerful strategy ideas. Over 97 percent of all participants in my programs since 1995 have rated the strategy they developed as eight or higher on a 10-point scale.

But half of my clients in 1995-98 failed to implement the strategies they developed. They never developed and implemented detailed action plans consistent with the key moves and broad action plans. Something was clearly wrong.

Accordingly, my basic research in 1998-99 was devoted to implementation. I found an amazing and appalling lack of compelling implementation paradigms from large companies, academics, and consultants. The lack of solid articles and books on implementation was also reflected in personal discussions. For example, I moderated a program with 18 professional planners and strategists in 1998, and **none** knew of an approach that effectively linked strategy to action plans or budgets.

Eventually, I found that the root cause of the failure to implement was simple. The broad action plans developed at strategic planning retreats simply failed to provide the level of detailed guidance required to develop effective individual action plans. The result was frustration. People would often develop disjointed action plans or simply let strategic planning die.

Once the cause was identified, the solution was simple. After the department heads participate in the strategic planning program, they need to work with their people to develop departmental strategies consistent with the overall business strategy. This process begins with getting bottom-up understanding, involvement, and commitment to the corporate strategy. Participants know while they are developing the departmental strategy that they will have to develop personal performance measures and detailed action plans to do their share in its implementation.

The process works. The department head leads development of a solid strategy that has the commitment of his or her people. The top management team gets to review and modify the department strategies to make sure they are reasonable, cost-effective, and will work together to achieve the vision and BHAG. Most importantly, the process lays the foundation for developing realistic Cycle 3 performance measures and action plans.

Cycle 2 has two key elements:
- Departmental strategies, and
- SMART goals.

Departmental Strategies

Departmental strategies must be driven by the key moves. Sometimes the departmental strategy may be one of the key drivers of the overall business strategy:
- Finance: Chief Financial Officers directly impact shareholder value through rollups, consolidations, and other forms of mergers. They create an environment for others to increase shareholder value through such performance measurement and incentive systems as open book management, The Balanced Scorecard, stock options at all levels, and pay for performance.
- Information technology: In the early and mid-1990s, the largest companies spent hundreds of millions of dollars each for Enterprise Resource Planning programs (ERPs) from SAP, Oracle, PeopleSoft, and Baan. Now, IT departments are shifting their infrastructure budgets to Internet-based, e-commerce solutions, which promise to transform industry after industry.
- Marketing: The 30-second television ad was the key tactical weapon in marketing from the rise of TV in the 1950s through the mid-1980s. Today, Promotion/advertising is the least important of the 4 Ps of marketing (Promotion, Price, Product, and Place/distribution). The "graying of the population" makes value (the best combination of Product and Price) more important than a glitzy ad. Even more importantly, Place/distribution has moved from the least important to most important marketing variable. This trend began with the rise of Wal-Mart and other national accounts in the 1980s. The move to e-commerce is creating new distribution channels which threaten to

eliminate many traditional retailers and distributors, as reflected in the market capitalizations of Amazon.com and Charles Schwab compared to Barnes & Noble and Merrill Lynch.

- Operations: Quality programs allowed companies to get costs down and quality up from 1980 to the mid-1990s. Now, supply chain management, partnering with suppliers, and outsourcing are allowing companies to cut time and costs. Mass customization allows firms to exactly meet the needs of each customer (and increase loyalty by dramatically increasing switching costs).
- Human resources: Instead of being the bureaucratic executors of downsizing programs, HR departments in the most successful companies are now the CEO's partner for growth. They are responsible for helping senior executives attract, develop, and retain the best people and help implement policies for getting everyone to work together.

The best business strategies, however, recognize the wisdom of KISS: Keep It Simple, Stupid. Instead of each department having its own blockbuster strategy, the departments should work together to implement one or two major strategies. An e-commerce marketing strategy, supported by IT and operations, may be the driver for increasing sales. Finance may be the driver in a performance incentive program or cost reduction effort. Human resources and high performance teams, with representatives from several departments, are often key elements in successful programs.

SMART Goals

SMART goals are Specific, Measurable, Achievable, Results-oriented, and Time-based. They are an essential element in strategy implementation because there is a lot of validity in the maxim "what gets measured and rewarded gets done." Wisely setting SMART goals—and then linking their achievement to hard and soft incentives—can lead to solid departmental strategies and action plans. Consider, for example, what can happen when the purchasing department is given the following two conflicting goals:

1. Having sufficient inventories so 96 percent of orders (by dollar volume) can be shipped the next day versus 92 percent today, and
2. Achieving 14 inventory turns annually versus a current average of 12 turns.

The first goal is needed for customer satisfaction while the second goal reflects the company's need for cash flow. Once the purchasing manager accepts that both goals are non-negotiable, essential elements of a departmental strategy to achieve them become clear. The purchasing manager must partner with both large customers (to track their inventories and requirements) and suppliers (to rush shipments when inventories get dangerously low). Good computer systems are required to forecast demand and track inventories. The SMART goals would specify how next day shipments and inventory turns would move from their current levels to the target over perhaps three years.[3]

CEOs should require each department to develop a few essential goals for tracking whether the department is doing what is necessary so the company achieves its vision. After the department head and CEO agree on the measures, the department head must determine their values for the past few years and propose goals for the next three or so years. The final values of the SMART goals must be selected so that they are challenging but achievable. Also, they must be designed so that achievement of the SMART goals will lead to achievement of the company's vision and BHAG.

SMART goals must be linked to rewards. A great part of their value is that each senior executive knows that one piece of paper in the CEO's top drawer has the SMART goals of each direct report. More importantly, annual performance reviews, bonuses, pay increases, and promotions must be linked to achievement of these goals. Linkage of rewards to goals ensures that people will develop solid Cycle 3 plans—and make sure they get implemented.

Mechanics of Cycle 2

A meeting to review departmental strategies and goals should come about 60 days after the completion of Cycle 1. That allows enough time to develop a solid Cycle 2 without losing momentum.

The department heads who developed the Cycle 1 strategy should attend all of the Cycle 2 meetings for three reasons:

1. To assure the department heads that the strategies of other departments are adequate so they can achieve their own SMART goals,
2. To make sure their own strategies mesh adequately with other departments, and
3. To advise the CEO on whether the strategies are likely to be effective and reasonably efficient.

Also, the people from each department should attend the presentation of their own department so that they can respond to questions and get a feel for the concerns of senior management.

Senior management should not approve a department's strategy and SMART goals until they are strong enough to fulfill the obligations in achieving the vision. In the first year of a new strategy, the Cycle 2 meeting is often a real working session and may last twice the time needed in succeeding years. It is normal to schedule a follow-up meeting a week or so later so departments can respond to major questions or provide modifications to the goals and strategies.

CYCLE 3: DETAILED PERFORMANCE MEASURES AND ACTION PLANS

It's amazing what a poor job traditional planning systems do in linking strategy with detailed action plans and budgets! Most companies fail in one of two ways:

1. Strategic planning begins and ends with Cycle 3. Action plans and budgets are developed and approved without any linkage to the strategy.

    Even today, many small companies believe a strategic plan consists of a list of 20 or 30 specific projects. Each project includes a description of the project, the person responsible for implementation, its cost, its benefits, and implementation time table. The problem is that Cycle 3, without Cycles 1 and 2, fails to produce strategically focused action.

    This bottom-up approach to planning was the rule through the mid-1960s. Department heads would make a list of "problems" and estimate the costs and benefits of eliminating each problem. Projects with the best cost/benefit ratios would be implemented until the budget was exhausted. This approach only gets rid of problems. It does not identify and exploit opportunities, which is the key to major success.

    Because each project is seen as independent rather than strategically important, the approach also lends itself to excessive politics. The department head will inflate benefits in order to get additional projects approved. They may ask for a 30 percent budget increase and hope to get 15 percent. Similarly, senior management will assume department heads are playing games and arbitrarily reduce budgets.[4]

2. Strategic planning begins strategically and ends with budgets, but lacks linkage between the two systems.

    The worst examples of this are companies that do their budgeting prior to developing action plans. Even some Fortune 100 companies, however, go through Cycles 1 and 2 to develop approved departmental goals and strategies and then budget based on percentage changes from last year. Because they have not provided resources to fund the action plans for achieving the goals, they seldom link rewards strongly to the goals. In both cases, planning is simply a bureaucratic exercise that consumes time without focusing resources or producing major benefits.

Mechanics of Cycle 3

By design, the Three-Cycle Process links strategy with resource allocation/budgeting. The mechanism for assuring this linkage is a one-page format with five key elements for each Cycle 3 action plan:

1. A **project description** including key goals,

2. **Who is responsible** for implementation, including dates for achieving the goals,
3. Which corporate **key moves** it is linked to,
4. Which department **SMART goals** benefit from this project, and
5. The **cost** and **budget line item** for the project.

Everyone who participates in the departmental strategy development process is responsible for developing action plans and budgets for their projects. They are basically agreeing to implement specific action plans and achieve specific results by a specific point in time if they are given specific resources.

In the first year, a department's action plans are likely to be very rough and fit together poorly. Hence, I recommend that they be presented orally at a meeting rather than just submitted in writing. Many department heads will find it much easier to move towards coherence if all direct reports are working together to develop a set of action plans that are cost efficient and effective in achieving the department's SMART goals.

Initially, the process may be more difficult than the department head doing it alone. Three benefits provide great returns from insisting on bottom-up involvement:

1. It helps identify the people with superior ability,
2. It leads to commitment and superior project implementation from each person because it is their project, and
3. The process will be easier than doing it alone in future years.

Conclusion

The goal-oriented Three-Cycle Process makes sense for senior management. It gives the CEO control and helps him or her to lead and manage the business. It allows the CEO and senior management to anticipate and respond to external change, on the one hand, and to implement and control internal change, on the other.

Cycle 1 produces a superior strategy since it focuses on employees, customers, and competitors, and reflects industry and company realities. Cycles 2 and 3 ensure effective implementation. Using the Three-Cycle Process each year keeps the strategy fresh and action-oriented. Above all, it produces superior results for employees, customers, and owners.

CHAPTER THREE

The Situation Analysis and Tentative Strategy

This chapter provides a solid foundation for your strategic plan in two ways:

1. **Developing a situation analysis.** Each company is unique. Your strategy must reflect your company's specific Strengths, Weaknesses, Opportunities, and Threats (SWOT), and the gaps between its potential and current performance.

2. **Developing a tentative strategy.** As you read through this book, especially the material on Cycle 1, you will come across some fundamental issues and questions. You should apply each of these to your business, pausing as you go to jot down your answers to those questions. By the time you finish, you should have three to four pages that become the basic material for a tentative strategy. An example of a tentative strategy at the end of this chapter provides a format that will be useful in developing your tentative strategy.

SITUATION ANALYSIS

Climate and Competitive Forces: Threats and Opportunities

What are the forces impinging on your business? Every day you are beset by two sets of external forces, as shown in Exhibit 3.1, which is based on Michael Porter's discussion of competitive strategy.[1] Five "climate" forces are shown outside the circle. The forces inside the circle are five competitive forces you face daily. It's clear how the competitive forces affect business, but business leaders sometimes tend to slight the climate forces.

Exhibit 3.1 **Porter's competitive and climate forces**

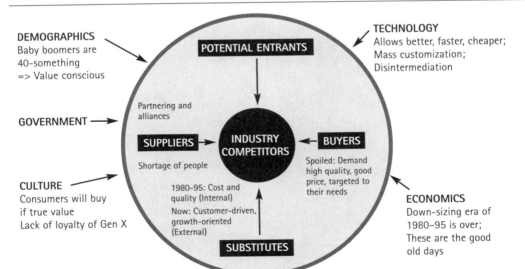

That's a mistake. Changes in the climate forces cause the changes in the five competitive forces.

A little thought will show how these climate and competitive forces affect your business. Use Exhibits 3.2 and 3.3 to identify some of the major "threats and opportunities" your company faces. Don't fill in all of the 20 cells. Instead, your work is just meant to help get discussion started with the rest of the management team. After about 20 minutes of discussion, people will start commenting that the current strategy isn't countering certain threats or exploiting opportunities. A little later they will start commenting on specifics that the new strategy should have. In short, the 10 forces are a great way to get your management team to use their detailed industry and company knowledge to begin thinking strategically.

Exhibit 3.2 **Threats and opportunities due to the five "climate" forces**

"CLIMATE" FORCES	THREATS	OPPORTUNITIES
Demographics		
Technology		
Economics		
Culture/Lifestyle		
Government		

Exhibit 3.3 **Threats and opportunities due to the five "competitive" forces**

"COMPETITIVE" FORCES	THREATS	OPPORTUNITIES
Industry Competitors		
Customers		
Substitutes		
Suppliers		
Potential Entrants		

Management and Customer Surveys: Strengths and Weaknesses

Nearly all companies believe they know what their customers want and do a fine job of meeting those wants. It's often very educational, however, to ask customers what is important to them. A customer satisfaction survey is a wonderful foundation for developing a market-driven strategy. Exhibits 3.4 and 3.5 show that tremendous insight can result from a very moderate investment.

A few years ago, the head of a library serving three Federal agencies asked me to talk to about 60 members of the Special Librarians Association. I agreed since I hoped some would subscribe to a strategy newsletter I was publishing at the time. But I needed a topic. After a little discussion, we agreed that I would do a customer satisfaction survey of his library and then use the results to talk about how librarians could develop a customer-driven strategy.

He called me at noon on a Friday. By the end of the day, we had agreed on Exhibit 3.4 as the survey instrument. On Monday, he wrote a cover letter and sent it to

Exhibit 3.4 "Importance" and "Satisfaction" survey for a government library

Rate the following on a 7-point scale	7 = Very Important	7 = Very Satisfied
	IMPORTANCE	SATISFACTION
Helpfulness/friendliness of staff	5.84	6.05
Technical knowledge of staff	5.69	6.00
Access to other libraries/sources of information	5.50	5.81
Electronic data bases - usefulness of searches	5.17	5.39
Electronic data bases - availability	5.09	5.41
Hours of operation	5.04	5.83
Reference books and research reports	4.80	5.27
Purchasing of books and periodicals	4.74	5.65
Electronic data bases - speed of surveys	4.67	5.19
Routing of business-oriented periodicals	4.25	5.37
Routing of technically-oriented periodicals	4.17	5.61
Back issues of periodicals	4.08	5.41
Quarterly list of recent materials	4.00	5.41
Routing of general information periodicals	3.91	5.56
Circulating books	3.83	5.11
Availability of legal publications	3.77	5.00
Overall, on the same 7-point scale, ...		
How important is the library to you in doing your job?	3.98	–
What is your overall satisfaction with the library?	–	5.65

200 users of the library. In 10 days, he sent me the 30 responses. I entered the results in a spreadsheet, took the averages, and sorted the 16 scales from most important to least important. I then graphed the results to produce Exhibit 3.5.

Librarians tend to like books, magazines, and research studies. Exhibit 3.4, however, clearly shows that library users want information and people who can get them information, not books per se. The two most important scales are helpful, knowledgeable **staff.** The other four scales that average over 5.0 in importance all deal **with access to information** (including electronic data bases). The physical product of reference books, research reports, and periodicals are less important.

Without this survey, the librarian may have sought $100,000 to buy more books and publications, hire another librarian to handle them, and more room to put them in. With the survey, it is apparent that customer satisfaction would increase more with only $30,000 spent improving electronic data bases and buying some reference books (the four important measures below the regression line in Exhibit 3.5).

Exhibit 3.5 also shows that the library is doing a good job of setting priorities. It is strong in the areas that are important to customers (highly positive regression line).

Exhibit 3.5 **"Importance" and "Satisfaction" for a government library**

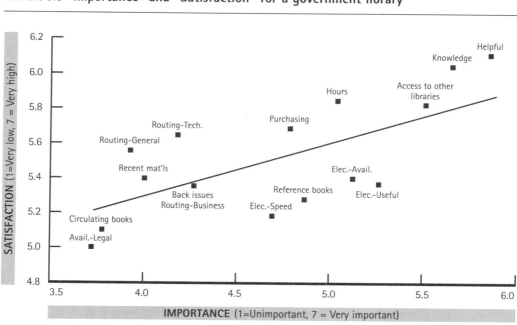

Exhibit 3.6 **Management "Importance" and "Performance" Survey**

Business: _____

Respondent: _____

Rate the following on a 7-point scale...based on their importance to the overall success of <u>your</u> business	1= Not at all Important; 7= Extremely Important Importance to Your Business Success	1= Very Poor; 7= Extremely Strong Your Company's Performance on Dimension	"Gap" Importance–Performance
Having a solid long-term strategy			
Purchasing (and managing suppliers)			
Keeping labor and other internal costs under control			
Developing new products and services			
Having a complete product line			
Maintaining product quality			
Maintaining good service			
Having a solid distribution system			
Effective customer segmentation			
Marketing: Awareness, attracting new customers			
Selling to current customers			
Offer superior value to each targeted segment			
Smart pricing			
Being innovative; exploiting change			
Hiring the right people			
Developing and retaining good people			
Getting rid of problems			
Focused on high potential products			
Internal communications			
Financial controls			
Information and computer systems			
Understanding and support from family members			
Clear goals and rewards for people at all levels			
Financial strategy (financing, acquisitions)			
Teamwork across all departments			
Bottom-up involvement and commitment to success			
Policies understood by all employees and customers			
Customer satisfaction			
Employee satisfaction			
Owner satisfaction (profitability)			

Exhibit 3.6 is a similar survey that I use as a foundation for surveying management prior to a strategic planning retreat. Of course, the scales are modified to reflect the specific industry and the company's situation. We show the results sorted by Importance, by Performance, and by "Gap" (the difference between Importance and Performance). The graph of Importance versus Performance always produces a spirited discussion of the important strengths to build on and important weaknesses that need attention. The absence of a significant positive correlation between Importance and Performance, for example, indicates a need for setting priorities.

"Gap" Analysis

As indicated in Exhibit 3.7, the situation analysis will often include financial analyses and sales analyses. Their purpose is to identify problems and opportunities and demonstrate at a gut level the gaps between potential and current performance. Compare key financial measures versus industry norms. Look at time series of profit and sales (or market share, if available) by product line, geography, and demographics. Each exhibit should have a clear purpose (e.g., motivate the desire to change or clearly identify a threat or opportunity).

You have now done your situation analysis. These materials suggest ideas for your "tentative strategy." They provide a solid starting point for developing a Cycle 1 strategy that gives you competitive advantage for seven to 10 years.

TENTATIVE STRATEGY

A three or four-page "tentative strategy" is your preliminary plan for how you can narrow the gap between your performance and potential. It makes the case for major change in direction. Exhibit 3.7 outlines sources of your tentative strategy.

The tentative strategy allows each successive step in Cycle 1 to build on a solid foundation. Without it, the following steps tend to be mechanical, and the final strategy is likely to be only a five or six on a 10-point scale. The whole process must then be repeated to get the strategy to eight or higher since mediocre strategies just don't produce results. However, the tentative strategy must be seen as provisional, so that further creative development and refinement occurs throughout the process. The tentative strategy often comes from an outside consultant since few executives are likely to aggressively question the CEO, and other senior officers can't afford to produce an off-target tentative strategy.[2]

When you start the task of strategy development, you will have prior notions about your business and your markets. These amount to a tentative strategy for how you will beat competitors in meeting customer wants. The better you articulate it at the start, the better your strategy will be in the end.

Exhibit 3.7 **Sources of gap analysis and tentative strategy**

SOURCE	BENEFIT OF SOURCE	RATIONALE
The previous long-term strategy	Provides overall strategy	It's the starting point
Employee and customer satisfaction surveys	Provides Strengths and Weaknesses	First half of a SWOT analysis
The five climate and five competitive forces	Provides Opportunities and Threats	Second half of a SWOT analysis
Financial analysis; Sales analysis	Provides factual foundation for gap analysis and strategy	Understanding current realities suggests strengths, weaknesses, and goals
Executive and employee interviews	Develop and test hypotheses	Helps consultants understand people issues; Builds trust
Studying company, competitors, industry	Develop preliminary strategy	Experience and knowledge of consultant is key

An Example of a Tentative Strategy: Grace & Company, P.C.

In late 1997, I helped Grace & Company develop a new strategy.[3] The following includes some of the key elements of the tentative strategy I developed for Grace prior to that meeting. As always, this tentative strategy was only meant to be a coherent approach that sparks ideas from the management team. Hence, the final strategy differed greatly from this tentative strategy.

Business Definition

Wayne Grace and seven others formed Grace & Company in 1983. By 1997, they had 120 people and were the third largest locally-owned CPA firm in Missouri. The business definition in Exhibit 3.8 was the foundation of its success.

Exhibit 3.8 **The business definition of Grace & Company in 1983–97**

Customer ··············▶ **Private companies**
Wants ··············▶ **Accumulating wealth**
Mechanism ··············▶ **One-stop shop for business services**

- **Customer:** From the beginning, Grace & Company focused on owner-CEOs: entrepreneurs.
- **Wants:** The foundation for its success was the recognition that the major goal of entrepreneurs was to accumulate and retain wealth and pass it on to the next generation, not low-cost financial statements.
- **Mechanism:** While Grace obviously provided audit, tax, and accounting

services, it differentiated itself from other CPA firms by being a solution provider—a one-stop shop for business services. Thus, clients could focus on making and selling whatever they did: the two things they liked to do and had to do to be successful. Grace could be their trusted business partner for strategic planning, information technology, human resources, and all of the other tasks they had to do but didn't particularly enjoy doing (including estate planning to pass it on efficiently to the next generation).

No strategy, however, lasts forever. By 1997, the strategy that had been so successful was not working as well. The Big 5 CPA firms were beginning to recruit CPAs from Grace and other mid-size firms instead of being a source of talent. Moreover, growth was slowing because other middle market CPA firms were getting more sophisticated in their marketing. The time had come to revise the strategy!

Strategic Objective or BHAG

The proposed strategic objective or BHAG (Big, Hairy, Achievable Goal) for Grace was to grow its value 10-fold by 2008 (26 percent annually) while growing from 15 partners and $10 million in revenue to 60 partners and $60 million. This strategic objective of major growth is consistent with:

1. Grace & Company's high quality, low share position,
2. The opportunity to consolidate a fragmented industry,
3. The threat of American Express and others consolidating the smaller firms and the Big 5 CPA firms targeting larger clients,
4. Clients' need for business assistance, and
5. Partners' desire for challenges and financial rewards.

Generic Strategy

Achieving such rapid growth in a mature industry requires a strategy that differentiates Grace from other professional service firms. A "customer intimacy" generic strategy was recommended because its definition includes:

- Personalized service and advice,
- Obsessions with helping the customer understand exactly what's needed, solution implementation, and relationship management, and
- A culture that embraces specific solutions and lasting relationships that produce results for carefully selected and nurtured clients.

A secondary low cost/operational excellence strategy should also have a high priority in the execution of audit and tax services, in part because low cost is always important in industry consolidation.

Customer–Driven Strategy

The resulting customer-driven strategy element was to position Grace as "clearly the best partner" to help privately held firms grow **their** value 5 to 10-fold over a 10-year period. This strategy required that Grace change a single word in its business definition. Instead of focusing on entrepreneurs who want to "accumulate wealth," Grace must focus on entrepreneurs with "fire in their belly" who want to "accumulate wealth **rapidly.**" This business definition, BHAG, generic strategy, and customer-driven strategy provided clear benefits to all three key stakeholders:

- **Clients:** Obviously, many entrepreneurs are interested in a professional service firm with the capability and commitment to help them grow their value by 17.5 to 26 percent annually (which leads to 400 or 900 percent growth in 10 years).
- **Partners/Owners:** Helping clients grow rapidly is the best foundation for Grace's profitable growth. Solid performance leads to loyal clients and new business. Many CPAs are not particularly good at sales. But, if you have helped a client grow 20 or 25 percent annually for a few years, it doesn't require great selling skill to ask for a referral. Finally, fees don't have to be cut as often for services that produce superior results.
- **Staff:** Growing from 15 partners to 60 provides obvious opportunities for attracting high potential people. For employees with families, quality of life is better at Grace than at Big 5 firms since many Big 5 people are on the road four nights a week. Moreover, they tend to work on very large projects for only two or three clients a year. Grace people get to make a larger impact with more clients. Limited travel is also a major benefit.

Key Moves
Successful implementation requires that everyone spend at least 80 percent of their discretionary time focused on three to five key moves. We proposed the following six candidates for Grace:

1. **People issues:** Attracting and retaining SWANs (people who are Smart, Work hard, Ambitious, and Nice) with the ability and drive to help clients grow value rapidly. The right people are the foundation of strategy for a professional service firm.
2. **Develop programs and systems to deliver on the promise:** Grace needed to significantly expand and strengthen consulting to deliver fully on its "trusted business partner for rapid growth" strategy.
3. **Sales and marketing:** To communicate its capabilities to the target market.
4. **Reducing costs for audit and tax services:** Companies are increasingly looking at these services as commodities, so using information technology and junior staff when possible are essential tools for doing these services better, faster, and at lower cost.
5. **Client relations:** Move clients with a poor fit with the new business definition to a low cost team so Grace can focus its resources on target clients.

6. **Geographical expansion strategies:** The business model provided the opportunity to increase profits per partner. Adding satellite offices and practice acquisitions provide opportunities for growing value.

The purpose of a tentative strategy is to give the management team something to tear apart. Its goal is to stimulate discussion of what makes sense for them. I personally enjoy developing a tentative strategy for a client after immersing myself in the company and discussing threats, opportunities, and alternatives with its senior people. Every time, I feel this strategy is really going to give them that "unfair advantage" in exactly meeting customer wants. But the clients always make major changes because they know their industry and company a lot better than I do.

The process works great. Because the final strategy was developed by them, they have ownership, involvement, and commitment. The odds of implementation are greatly increased.

Developing a tentative strategy ahead of time serves a second purpose. Without doing a tentative strategy, management tends to make major changes in its strategy with each new way of looking at itself. Then, at the end of Cycle 1, top management often feels the strategy lacks the coherence necessary to achieve its potential. The entire process must be repeated.

Conclusion

With your situation analysis complete and a feel for what a strategy looks like, you are now ready to go through the strategy analysis process in chapters 4 through 9. As you read through the chapters, wrestle with how each concept applies to your company. Sometimes you will be uncertain. That's OK. It allows good discussion, which will provide deeper insight into your company, customers, and competitive realities. Just make sure that everyone agrees the Cycle 1 strategy is at least an eight on a 10-point scale before moving to Cycle 2.

If you do the job right, you will develop a strategy that provides an unfair advantage for meeting the wants of target customers. The potential benefits to employees, customers, and owners are exceptional.

CHAPTER FOUR

Business Definition:
The Foundation for Strategy

A good business definition is the essential foundation for a solid strategy. A weak business definition is like building on sand. The strategy simply won't stand the test of time. This chapter covers five topics that will help you develop a winning definition for your business:

1. The nature and importance of business definition[1],
2. The three mandatory dimensions of business definition,
3. Two optional dimensions of business definition,
4. Key considerations in defining the business, and
5. Winning and losing business definitions and implementation.

THE NATURE AND IMPORTANCE OF BUSINESS DEFINITION

In his influential 1960 essay on marketing myopia, Theodore Levitt made the case, summarized in Exhibit 4.1, for the importance of a proper business definition.[2] If America's railroad executives had not had such a short-sighted product orientation, they might have seen that their customers needed transportation, not just railroads. Defining their business correctly would have allowed them to achieve major growth as they moved into automobiles and trucks and eventually into airlines. Being railroads, the business definition they selected, mandated decline.

Exhibit 4.1 **Business definitions based on "Product" versus "Wants"**

DEFINITIONS BASED ON:	RAILROADS	HOLLYWOOD
Product	Railroads	Movies (excludes TV)
Customer wants	Passenger and freight transportation	Entertainment

Levitt also found poor vision in Hollywood in the early days of television, which was centered in New York City. Defining their business strictly as movies, Hollywood moguls scorned TV and treated it as a threat, which it in fact was given their definition. However, if they had defined their business as entertainment, they would have seen TV as an opportunity. After losing the battle against TV through the mid-1950s, Hollywood belatedly redefined their business as entertainment. Since then, movies and television have formed a profitable relationship. If Hollywood had maintained its myopic business definition much longer, New York could have become the entertainment capital of the world.

Both the railroad and movie executives were fixated on product or technology, when their business success required a focus on the market. According to Levitt, the key consideration in a proper business definition is customer need, not just the product or service which satisfies that need.

Since the mid-1970s, the focus of marketing has moved from the mass market to segmentation and positioning. In the 1960s, GM sold two million Chevrolet Impalas a year and Ford sold 1.5 million Galaxy 500s. The largest selling cars in the 1990s were the Ford Taurus and Honda Accord with about 400,000 cars per year. Anheuser-Busch has gone from 2 1/2 brands (Budweiser, Michelob and—in 10 states—Busch) to over 50 brands since 1975. Success requires that you have products or services that exactly meet the needs of each targeted customer segment. Hence, the third key dimension of business definition today is exactly specifying your target customer.

THE THREE MANDATORY DIMENSIONS OF BUSINESS DEFINITION

Today, the concept of business definition usually includes three mandatory dimensions:
- Customer: *Exactly who* are you serving?
- Wants: Which *customer wants* are you meeting better than any competitor?
- Mechanism: *How* do you satisfy those wants (e.g., the products, services, or technology you sell)?

Together, dimensions 1 and 2 form the "served market," the demand side of the business definition. Dimensions 2 and 3 combined form the "product description," or the supply side of the business definition.

Too often, companies base their business definition only on their mechanism. This is a mistake! Saying you are in the banking, baking, or beer industry emphasizes what you have in common with your competitors. It mandates being a commodity. Instead, focus on exactly who your customers are and which of their wants you can meet qualitatively better than any competitor. This market-driven approach allows you to differentiate your company from competitors. It helps you to obtain the "unfair advantage" that leads to superior performance. The side-bar on "Commodities Versus Solutions and Experiences" shows that "commodity" business definitions are a formula for disaster.

Enterprise Rent–A–Car

In 1995, Enterprise Rent-A-Car passed Hertz to become #1 in the U.S. car rental business. How Enterprise became the leader in the car rental industry is a classic example of a wonderful business definition that leads to a strategy which produces major pay-offs to employees, customers, and owners.
- **Customer:** While the other major car rental firms focus on the business traveler with an expense account, Enterprise rents mainly to people who need a

car in their home town (see Exhibit 4.2). They often need a car because their car was in the shop or in an accident. Enterprise also takes care of a second customer, the insurance adjusters and auto repair shops. CEO Andy Taylor jokes that giving doughnuts to such referral sources is one of their biggest sales methods.

"Commodities Versus Solutions and Experiences"

Birthday parties show us how the U.S. economy has evolved from commodities to experiences.[3]

Commodities: In 1940, Mom would bake a cake from scratch. It would cost 25 cents for the eggs, flour, and sugar.

Branded Products: In 1960, she would buy a box of Betty Crocker or Duncan Hines cake mix and add two eggs. The cost was a dollar.

Services: In 1980, most Moms were working and didn't have time for baking. They called the bakery and asked for a chocolate cake with "Happy 10th Birthday, Jason" on top. It might have cost $10.

Experiences: In 2000, the birthday party might be held at Discovery Zone or Chuck E Cheese. The cost for 15 kids might total $100.

The importance of this evolution becomes clear when you ask yourself a simple question. Which business do you want to be in? Do you want to provide 25 cents of commodities or $100 of experiences? Successful business-to-business companies have made a similar transition from commodities to products to services and then to solutions (rather than experiences). Solution and experience providers have less competition and greater profit margins and growth since solutions and experiences are easier to differentiate than commodities.

Exhibit 4.2 **The business definition of rental car companies**

	HERTZ, AVIS, ETC.	ENTERPRISE RENT-A-CAR
Customer	Business People	Local renters, Referral sources
Customer Wants	Convenience, Speed	Local transportation, Low cost
Mechanism*	Airport	Lower rates, 4,000+ locations

* The product or service you sell or your technology

- **Customer wants:** While the business traveler wants to get from the plane to the rental car as fast as possible, the Enterprise customer is also concerned with price.
- **Mechanism:** Enterprise has rates up to 30 percent lower than rivals with expensive airport locations. Enterprise works mostly from store fronts and

shopping strips close to where its customers work and live. Its 3,600 U.S. locations are within 15 minutes of 90 percent of people in the U.S. It also provides greater convenience by picking up customers.

Since taking industry leadership in 1995, Enterprise has gone from success to success. Ernst & Young named CEO Andy Taylor and his father, Enterprise founder Jack Taylor, as Entrepreneur Of The Year. *Fortune* magazine included Enterprise in its list of "100 Best Companies to Work For." Jack Taylor was included in *Forbes'* 1999 list of the wealthiest Americans with an estimated worth of $2.8 billion. The success of Enterprise shows the power of developing a focused business definition that reflects your business realities—and then aggressively implementing the strategy.

The business definition of Enterprise Rent-A-Car also demonstrates the importance of focus. Targeting the key wants of a specific target niche can lead to strategies that give you an unfair advantage. The result can be clear market leadership and superior profitability.

We will now go through examples of each of the three dimensions of business definition. The objective is to spark ideas for a business definition that will lead to a superior strategy for your company. As you go through these materials, complete Exhibit 4.3. Determine what your company is implicitly using today for each dimension. Also make a first attempt at determining what your business definition should be.

Exhibit 4.3 **The business definition for your company**

	CURRENT DEFINITION	PROPOSED NEW DEFINITION	
		PRIMARY CUSTOMER	SECONDARY CUSTOMER (OPTIONAL)
Customer			
Customer Wants			
Mechanism			

Customer

The mass market died in the 1970s. Business success today requires developing products or services to exactly meet the wants of each customer segment. A classic example is being an attorney generalist in a metropolitan area. A formula for disaster is being one line in the 83 pages of lawyers in the St. Louis Yellow Pages. People want the best litigator or divorce lawyer. They go to the personal injury lawyer or estate planner whose visibility implies some combination of competence and fair prices. Following are a half dozen approaches that have produced a solid definition of the targeted customer.

- **Identify an under-served segment:** Sam Walton became the richest man in America in the 1980s by taking discount department stores to small towns. Even today, only the richest and poorest Americans use significant legal services. A Sam Walton is needed to bring legal services to the other 70 percent of Americans.

- **Focus on attractive current customers:** A manufacturer found that half of its volume had 25 percent margins while the other half had 5 percent margins. The high margin customers had high growth and high profits themselves. They were not price sensitive but demanded suppliers who were responsive and could be counted on to deliver products on-time and on-spec. The low margin customers were poorly organized with stagnant sales and poor profits. They could only stay afloat by squeezing suppliers. Increasing prices and reducing special services to the unprofitable segment greatly increased the profit margins from that segment. The lost volume freed up capacity so they could do an even better job with the profitable segment and accelerate their own growth.

- **Broaden the target market:** In the "mainframe age" through the 1960s, computer users were information technology professionals. Digital Equipment's glory years in the "mini-computer age" of the 1970s were due to allowing hands-on use by scientists and engineers. By 1999, Microsoft's market capitalization reached $600 billion by targeting everyone as its customer with its personal computer vision of "a computer on every desk and in every home."

- **Recognize you sometimes have two customers:** Temporary help companies must meet the needs of both the people who want temporary jobs and the companies who need their services. Successful temp firms have consistent strategies for both customers (i.e., focusing on low costs and minimal standards or higher prices and more demanding standards).

  Successful managed healthcare companies also have two customers, but their two customers demand different strategies. The first customer is the business, government, or insurance company that pays for healthcare. They require that healthcare suppliers be low cost. The second customer is the end user. Individuals want good healthcare in a patient-focused environment. The healthcare company that meets the wants of both customers may well be able to consolidate a trillion dollar industry and pass Microsoft in market capitalization. (Hint: The solution may be a percentage rather than a fixed dollar co-pay. Doctors and patients could then determine what services are required. Costs would decline for two reasons. First, it would eliminate layers of bureaucrats. More importantly, less expensive medical procedures would be selected when patients decide they aren't willing to pay even 10 or 20 percent of the cost.)

- **Recognize that your employees and suppliers are often customers:** Many companies have found that their most important Key Success Factor (KSF) is attracting, developing, and retaining good people and getting them to work together productively. Conversely, General Motors has declined in part because it took an adversarial approach to suppliers while Chrysler and Ford took a more win-win partnering approach.

- **Develop a business definition for all of your downstream customers:** Coca-Cola has three customers: bottlers, retailers, and consumers. Coke reaps the highest profitability because it has brand equity with the end users. Coke must also make sure that it rewards those bottlers that are efficient and effective in all of their distribution and local marketing efforts. Finally, it must work directly with its large "national accounts" retailers while leaving the smaller retailers to bottlers. Coca-Cola's business definition must place primary emphasis on the end user but it also must lay the foundation for optimizing the performance of the entire value chain.

Customer Wants

Wants are inseparable from the customer dimension, particularly if you seek a business definition that leads to a breakthrough differentiation or product leadership strategy. For premium products, success often requires seamlessly combining several wants. The success of Tommy Hilfiger clothing, for example, is due to premium price, good quality, and image.

- **Emotional and psychological wants:** Revlon has long acknowledged it is in the "hope" business, not cosmetics. Nike and Tommy Hilfiger focus on teenagers' desire for social acceptance. One marketer argued that Budweiser is in the business of facilitating male bonding.
- **Image:** In the 1950s, Harley-Davidson provided a macho, Hell's Angel image for young men. Small Honda motorcycles revolutionized the market by targeting clean-cut young people who wanted economical basic transportation. Micro beers, $45,000 sport utility vehicles, and $50,000 around the world tours via the Concord are contemporary examples of successful conspicuous consumption involving a new, premium price point.
- **Performance:** Fast cars, fast computers, and extreme sports are examples of products that result from focusing on the desire for cutting edge performance.
- **Experiences and memories:** Disneyland and other "major" vacations, Hard Rock Cafes, Rolling Stones concerts, and Star Wars movies are experiences that produce lasting memories. They also come with merchandising materials to help you remember the event (and show others what you have experienced through your T-shirts).
- **Solutions:** Companies of all sizes are moving from adversarial relationships with suppliers to win-win partnering approaches. Done right, it allows com-

panies to greatly reduce the size of their purchasing departments. More importantly, over time, it allows companies to reduce costs and accelerate innovation by focusing on their core competencies. The automobile companies, for example, have reduced the number of suppliers by 75 to 90 percent. The winning suppliers are solutions partners. They integrate their systems to reliably supply high quality products on time. They also have systems in place to consistently reduce costs and develop innovative, next generation products. The other suppliers lose 100 percent of their sales to the customer.

Implemented effectively, solutions offer both higher margins and higher sales. We have seen how Grace & Company positioned itself to be a one-stop solutions partner to help $10 to $100 million companies increase their value rapidly. Duke Manufacturing supplies a dozen different types of equipment to commercial kitchens. Its competitors, who offered a single product line, had an advantage over Duke because each focused on meeting a specific set of customer needs. Duke began to consolidate its industry, however, when it bundled its products together into systems that saved restaurants significant time and expense in designing a kitchen.

- **Offer the basics that the competition does poorly:** Focusing on more basic wants is fundamental to implementing a successful low cost strategy. McDonald's drove the greasy spoon, Ma-Pa restaurants out of business by indoctrinating all of its operators and employees in QSC&V: quality, service, cleanliness, and value. Consistent quality established with its brand reduced customer risk, which was increasingly important as travel increased. Faster service, clean premises and restrooms, and lower prices made McDonald's eventual victory inevitable.

  Similarly, after the oil shocks of the 1970s increased gas prices to over a dollar a gallon, Japanese cars provided reliability, low cost, and good mileage. Southwest Airlines designed its flights to affordably and reliably meet the wants of the non-business traveler. Home Depot was the first hardware store to offer both low prices and high service.

- **Recognize how wants are changing over time:** Through the 1960s, customers looked at supermarkets primarily as a place to purchase food for preparation at home. By the 1990s, however, the supermarket business definition had changed to "the one-stop shop for all frequently purchased consumer non-durables and services." Supermarkets include video rentals, greeting cards, flowers, health and beauty aides, and prepared foods that compete with specialty shops and fast food restaurants. The big winners were the chains that doubled the size of their stores because they recognized the high value working women placed on saving time through "one-stop shopping."

  Consulting firms have also responded to shifting wants. From 1980 through 1995, most large companies were focused internally on getting quality up and costs down. Consultants helped meet these wants with total quality programs and reengineering efforts while investment bankers and corporate raiders led the acquisition of laggard companies. Now, the fastest growing consultants are helping companies achieve their new primary goal of growth through development of Internet-based systems.

Mechanism: Products, Services, and Technology

Successful business definitions begin with targeting specific wants for specific customers. Only then do they design products and services that will give the customer superior value and generate superior profits. Declining companies begin their business definition with the products or services they offer (e.g., we are a greeting card company or bankers or an advertising agency). This product-based rather than market-driven business definition leads to staying with losing strategies long after the environment demands change.

Even commodity companies would be wise to consider customers and wants carefully in their business definition. Two of the most successful beverage can companies are Crown Cork & Seal and Metal Container Corporation (an Anheuser-Busch company). Metal Container's strategy is being the low cost, long-term supplier to very large customers. Half of its sales are to Anheuser-Busch and the other half to Pepsi-Cola. It achieves absolutely lowest possible costs by locating its plants close to customers and signing 10 year contracts for essentially all of its capacity. In its glory years, Crown also made superior profits, but with the opposite strategy of flexibility. It sold relatively small runs to smaller customers at premium prices.

Although the business definition should begin with identifying specific customer segments and their wants, it must conclude with developing products or services—the mechanism that produces superior value. Let's look at guidelines for developing a mechanism that gives you competitive advantage.

- **Change the mechanism to meet constant wants:** Exhibit 4.4 shows that, while the mechanism changed, successful retailers have focused on the same basic wants from the first department stores in the 1850s through the Internet era of today: lower prices, convenience, variety, and consistent if not high quality. Sam Walton became the richest man in America in the 1980s by wonderful execution of a century-old low-cost strategy. Walton simply changed the dimensions of customer and mechanism to take discount department stores to small-town and rural Americans. Now, a new generation of billionaires has emerged by using the Internet to combine more variety and lower prices with the convenience of never leaving the home.
- **Change the mechanism to reflect changing climate forces:** Exhibit 4.4 also shows how retailing has evolved to reflect changes in each of the climate forces. The Internet shows the power of **technology** to transform business defini-

Exhibit 4.4 **Industry evolution of retailing: 1850–2000**

ERA	RETAILERS	CUSTOMER BENEFITS	KEYS TO SUCCESS
Department stores	Wanamaker's, Macy's (1852-1910)	Low, known price, convenience, variety, good quality	Concentrated markets in metro areas, trolleys
Chains	A&P (1859), Woolworth (1879)	Low, known price due to mass buying, consistent procedures	Brought good strategy to neighborhoods
Mail-order houses	Ward (1872), Sears (1876)	Low prices and variety to people on farms and in West	Rapid expansion in West; railroads; literacy
Rural general merchandisers	J. C. Penney (1902)	Convenience of not waiting versus mail-order	Brought low prices to rural America
Supermarkets	King Kullen (1930)	Lower prices due to self-service and economies of scale	Depression created appeal
Discount department stores	E. J. Korvette (1948) Kmart (1961)	Lower prices	Beat "fair trade" laws to allow price discounting
Rural discount	Wal-Mart (1962)	Discount department stores for rural America	Brought good strategy to rural areas
Specialized catalogs and mall specialty stores	The Gap, Eddie Bauer, Victoria's Secret	Specialized merchandise with the convenience of the mall or home	Consistent with today's segmentation and positioning era
Internet	Amazon, eBay	Variety and low cost plus the convenience of the home	Permitted by technology

tions. **Economic** forces allowed low-cost supermarkets to emerge during the Depression. Working women (**culture**) have made convenience a key element of retail strategy. **Demographics** are reflected in mail-order catalogs to the West, the suburban mall after World War II, and successive transformations over the last 50 years as the Baby Boomers have grown up and aged. **Government** eventually enables changes that allow clearly superior benefits (e.g., rural mail delivery allowing catalogs; legislation allowing chain stores during the Depression, discount prices in the 1950s, and telecom competition in the 1980s).

- **Change the mechanism to reflect competitive forces.** The chapters on **customer-** and **competitor-**driven strategy demonstrate the importance of looking creatively at the five competitive forces in developing business definition. Partnering, out-sourcing, and supply-chain management demonstrate the growing importance of **suppliers** in business definition. Indeed, employee-driven strategies reflect the fact that employees are the most important supplier for many companies.

Why Not Begin Business Definition with "Mechanism"?

Some people disagree with our blanket condemnation of using product, service, or technology as the foundation of business definition. They point out that defining your business based on technological expertise often works. For example, Honda has moved successfully from motorcycles to cars and lawn mowers based on its expertise in small engines. And adhesives is the foundation for 3M's business definition and its reputation for constant innovation. These are great examples of solid business definitions, but they are based on capabilities or "core competencies" (an optional dimension of business definition discussed in the next section), not technology.

Critics will then point out the huge success of Coca-Cola in soft drinks, Anheuser-Busch in beer, Gillette in razor blades, and Philip Morris in cigarettes. Their focus on a specific product has been a key element in dominating their industries. In every case, however, the dominant brand is priced significantly higher than many competitors. The failure of "New Coke," despite its preference in blind taste tests, indicates that superior product is definitely not the deciding factor in brand equity. Industry domination requires focusing on the wants of each customer segment more than focusing on the product.

Finally, critics will cite the incredible success of IBM as a mainframe computer company and a host of other high tech companies that were renowned as the leaders in their product or technology niche. They are wrong for two reasons. First, IBM's success was due to meeting the customers' desire for safety and risk avoidance while it was IBM's unsuccessful competitors who were in the mainframe business. Second, success in a product category can lead to disaster when a substitute technology that is less complex, less powerful, and less expensive emerges. This is demonstrated by the decline of Digital Equipment, which was known as the mini-computer company, when personal computers emerged. Clayton Christensen[4] identifies industry after industry where such a "disruptive technology" led to a change in leadership.

In the next few years, the Internet will again demonstrate that companies which define themselves based on their product or service will find survival difficult when faced with competitors using radically different technologies.

TWO OPTIONAL DIMENSIONS OF BUSINESS DEFINITION

Core Competencies

Gary Hamel and C.K. Prahalad identified internal capabilities or "core competencies" as a dimension of business definition in their 1990 *Harvard Business Review* article. Indeed, many academics believe that looking at core competencies and other internal resources is the best foundation for building strategy. I disagree. While strategy must build on your strengths, most companies should focus externally on the wants of customers as the essential driver for developing (and implementing) strategy.

There is no denying, however, the importance of developing the detailed capabilities required for success in your industry. High tech companies must know their technology. Any leading consumer products company must know marketing. I simply argue that most companies should only identify the core competencies to focus on after selecting the three mandatory dimensions of business definition.

I do agree with the academics for industries experiencing rapid change. The reason is simple. Investing in your core competencies allows you to offer breakthroughs that greatly expand what customers want. Hence, many high tech firms should currently begin business definition with identifying core competencies. As the pace of change continues to accelerate, more firms will include core competencies as a primary dimension of business definition. Even in these cases, however, companies must partner with customers and prospects to make sure that they are developing products and services that will meet real needs. To survive and thrive, all companies must be market-driven.

Motorola shows the importance of capabilities to success in fast-moving industries. It started off in car radios (Motor-ola), but evolved into television in the 1950s, and eventually into telecommunications. The constant is its focus on state-of-the-art electronics. Similarly, Hewlett-Packard has focused on state-of-the-art electromechanical products, which led to the 1999 spin-off of its original testing equipment business. Combining two or three capabilities into your business definition can lead to superior performance. Canon has solid positions in cameras, copiers, and certain types of industrial equipment due to its expertise in precision mechanics, fine optics, and microelectronics. Since 1977, NEC's strategy has been driven by its vision of the ultimate convergence of computers and communications.

Vertical Integration

Vertical integration contributes less frequently to business definition, especially for smaller businesses. However, it can be an important dimension that helps drive strategy. Depending on your circumstances, vertical integration can be good or bad. Among potential benefits are the following:

- Backward integration generally can be important if you are seeking industry leadership with a low-cost strategy, such as Henry Ford with his Model T. If your suppliers have excessive market power and charge high prices, backward integration can encourage them to come into line.
- Vertical integration can reduce response time and cost when transaction costs are high. For example, Coke and Pepsi both acquired about half their independent bottlers during the 1980s. First, they modernized and consolidated inefficient operations and increased volumes. Second, they used the greater purchasing power to get lower prices on cans.
- Forward integration can improve your understanding of final consumers, but there's a risk here. You alienate your wholesalers or retailers, because forward integration puts you in competition with some of them. Merck learned this the hard way when it purchased pharmaceutical distributor Medco. Medco lost value because other pharmaceutical companies were reluctant to give profits to Merck,

their toughest competitor. Merck lost value because Medco's competitors didn't want to give preferential treatment to the parent of their largest competitor.

Most companies moved strongly away from vertical integration and diversification in the 1990s. "Focus" is one of the most important words in strategy today. Companies want to focus on making and selling whatever they do. They want to partner with other companies along the value chain rather than enter businesses beyond their expertise. Information technology has allowed development of supply chain management systems to allow such efficient coordination.

- Both Coke and Pepsi divested their bottling operations in the 1990s. They wanted to rid themselves of such highly capital intense operations and wanted a faster, more entrepreneurial culture among their bottlers.
- A low level of integration allows greater flexibility, since changing outside suppliers is easier than redirecting and retooling internal business units. This is why GM and Ford spun off their internal parts companies in the 1990s.
- External suppliers will usually be better at innovation, since they deal with customers of varying wants and usually have greater depth of expertise in their industry.
- Suppliers can often provide goods at a lower cost than you can internally, since they usually have greater economies of scale than you in their area of expertise.
- Forward integration usually results in serious conflict with your distributors or retailers.

Partnering, joint ventures, and other forms of alliances offer the best of both worlds. Done right, they provide the benefits without the drawbacks of vertical integration.

KEY CONSIDERATIONS IN DEFINING THE BUSINESS

The three mandatory dimensions—customer, customer wants, and mechanism—largely determine which served market you target, either the broad market or a specific niche, and which strategy makes most sense in that market. The following concepts help ensure that your business definition is right for your market:

1. **Strategic Business Units:** If your organization is large and complex, divide it into coherent and manageable units and develop a business definition for each unit.
2. **Key Success Factors:** Ensure that your definition is consistent with the essentials of your industry for high market share and profits. Your "KSFs" determine which core competencies you must develop.
3. **Competitive and Climate Forces:** Determine the forces that have the greatest impact on your business and account for them in your business definition.

Strategic Business Units

If you have a small or single-product company, you can probably manage it as a whole. Large organizations with multiple product lines, however, cannot be intelligently managed as a single unit. Nor are they likely to be adequately entrepreneurial and customer-driven. It's important, then, to subdivide the company into manageable smaller units commonly called Strategic Business Units, or SBUs. GE, for example, has 350 product lines, which it has organized into 13 SBUs.

Typically, each SBU is managed independently with
- Its own resources, costs, and profits,
- Its distinct and identifiable customers, competitors, and products, and
- Its own financial goals and business objectives.

Note that SBUs should be defined by external criteria. SBUs may share production facilities and staff services such as legal and human resources, but each SBU will have its own business definition and long-term strategy. However, the collection of SBUs must form a coherent whole to allow effective strategic corporate management. Don't repeat the failed strategy of conglomeration that was the vogue of the 1960s. Even with a diversity of products and business units, the corporation itself wants an identity, which requires a corporate business definition and long-term strategy.

Conglomerates tend to reduce the value of their SBUs in two ways. First, their overhead costs drain cash. Second, the extra layer of management increases bureaucracy and slows response time. A corporation should be structured so that the benefits of synergies among SBUs and corporate management expertise exceed the costs of corporate overhead.
- In the mid-1990s, Anheuser-Busch divested its baking subsidiary and sold the St. Louis Cardinals baseball team so it could focus on domestic and international beer. Performance of each affected company improved significantly in the following year.
- Monsanto spun off its commodity products into a new company, Solutia, so it could focus on high tech opportunities such as biotechnology. Both Monsanto and Solutia benefited from the greater focus of their management teams.

Key Success Factors

Next is the need to identify your industry's Key Success Factors, or KSFs. Every industry has its own unique set of KSFs; yet there are some variables common to the success of all businesses. You must consider both sets in your business definition.

A major research project begun in the 1970s has established correlations among hundreds of business variables and the relative weight of each in predicting the ROI of any business. Called PIMS (after Profit Impact of Market Strategy), this on-going program uses a massive data base compiled from the actual business experience of around 3,000 SBUs operated by 450 American and European companies.[5] Chapter 5 covers the

PIMS project in greater detail.

The PIMS project has collected empirical data on the following:

- Business position of SBUs, such as market share, relative quality, and degree of vertical integration,
- Industry attractiveness, such as rates of market growth, inflation, and distribution channels, and
- Performance measures of each SBU, such as pre-tax return on investment.

The PIMS data indicate that the most important factors for the success of any business are high quality, high market share, and low capital intensity. While there are many other critical correlations that have come from the PIMS analyses, these three should weigh heavily in developing your business definition.

In addition to the broad success factors identified by PIMS that apply to all businesses, every industry has its own unique set of success factors. These will influence one or more of the dimensions in your business definition, so you should take the two or three most critical of these into account.

For example, the KSFs for computer software are project management, efficient distribution channels, and after-sales support. The implications for business definition are (1) the customer dimension should include both your distributors and end-users, and (2) the wants dimension includes not only great product but also continuous improvement and personal service. The KSFs for management consultants are communicating with executive decision makers (customer dimension) and fully meeting the client's expectations (wants dimension).[6]

If you own a convenience store, your KSFs are location, product selection, pricing, and operating efficiency. For brewers, they are quality, distribution, and marketing. Fashion design and manufacturing efficiency are key for apparel manufacturing.[7] The list goes on and on, with KSFs varying from industry to industry. No single listing of industry-specific KSFs similar to the PIMS list exists for all businesses. You will need to do a thorough analysis of your industry to uncover those critical to your success.

Competitive and Climate Forces

Much of that industry analysis will emerge from a look at the competitive and climate forces affecting your business. A study of external forces should reveal much about where your industry is going and about what you must do in order to create a sustainable competitive advantage. The 10 climate and competitive forces discussed in chapter 3 (Exhibit 3.1) provide a useful schema for conducting this analysis. Test your tentative business definition in Exhibit 4.3 against your list of threats and opportunities from Exhibits 3.2 and 3.3. How should you modify your business definition to exploit your opportunities and defend against the threats?

WINNING AND LOSING BUSINESS DEFINITIONS AND IMPLEMENTATION

Winning business definitions lead to strategies that provide superior value—the best combination of product and price—to the target customer. For smaller companies, winning business definitions will target a narrow set of products, customers, and wants. Large companies can focus on dominating an entire industry with a single business definition (e.g., McDonald's) or by developing product lines positioned to provide superior value to each target customer (e.g., Anheuser-Busch with Natural, Busch, Budweiser, Michelob, and specialty brands at different price points).

Business definition provides the foundation for a strategy that gives you an unfair advantage by:

- Targeting a customer segment with poorly met wants,
- Understanding their wants and meeting those wants better than competitors,
- Developing and marketing products or services so they provide clearly superior value, and
- Developing core competencies that reflect the Key Success Factors in your industry.

Losing business definitions generally result from two management failings: Static minds in changing times and losing sight of the customer. Two final examples illustrate these shortcomings.

First, static minds in changing times is illustrated in Exhibit 4.5. Hallmark's card stores had been the foundation of its industry dominance through the 1970s. For 20 years, however, American Greetings has been growing its market share by focusing all of its efforts on Wal-Mart, supermarkets, and other mass merchandisers. Hallmark was reluctant to undermine its local card stores by offering its premium cards to mass merchandisers. Its card stores had become an albatross that prevented change.

Exhibit 4.5 **Business definition for Hallmark stores**

	CURRENT DEFINITION	INCREMENTAL INTERNET AGE DEFINITION
Customer	Women (age 25+)	Men and women (age 25+)
Wants	Demonstrating friendship by "Caring enough to send the very best"	Trusted, convenient, one-stop shop for products and services to celebrate special occasions (e.g., flowers, wrapped presents, cards for anniversaries, birthdays, Mothers Day, and Christmas)
Mechanism	Cards and momentos for every occasion	1. Database (past purchases and profile of recipient) 2. Internet connection to florists, restaurants, and all leading consumer product websites 3. Artificial intelligence capabilities that allow selection of the present, giftwrap, and card 4. Delivery nation-wide via FedEx or UPS

The Internet allows Hallmark to capitalize on its strength as the most trusted name in memorializing special occasions. In addition to offering cards, Hallmark could be an entry point for men and women to conveniently and quickly select and purchase complete solutions for memorializing special occasions. The incremental business definition solves a major source of stress for many men and for time-stressed working women. It allows Hallmark to move from selling cards and an occasional small gift to becoming the major U.S. intermediary for gift giving. Importantly, the database of past gifts and profiles of gift recipients, linked to a powerful artificial intelligence system for suggesting gifts, would lead to huge switching costs and very high loyalty.

Second, losing sight of customers and becoming internally focused is the most common characteristic of poor business definitions.

- Many suppliers to large companies will go out of business because they want to supply "products" while large companies today are demanding partners that provide "solutions" and are easy to do business with through integrated supply chain systems. Such suppliers should aggressively implement new strategies or sell out while they can.

- Many banks, traditional stock brokers, insurance companies, wholesalers, and retailers will be out of business in the next decade because the Internet will allow consumers to get better products and services, more conveniently, at a lower cost. Look at how the end user defines value and make sure your business definition gives you an advantage.

- If you define yourself as a "solution partner," make sure it is a solution that makes sense to the customer. Sears is not the only company to lose billions of dollars by trying to be a one-stop financial partner. Allegis Corporation thought bundling ownership of United Airlines, Hertz, and Westin Hotels would make it the leader in serving the traveler. Too often, the extra costs of the corporate bureaucracy reduce customer responsiveness and destroy value.

- Some companies combine businesses that appear to be related but require completely different core competencies. A classic example is Sony, which decided its BetaMax videotape format lost to VHS because it did not have enough BetaMax movies. To assure this never happened again, Sony paid $7 billion for Columbia Pictures and CBS Records. This was a strategic mistake. Sony has always been brilliant at technological creativity (hardware), but artistic creativity (software) is a fundamentally different business. As often happens with poorly conceived acquisitions, first the acquired company falters and then the parent company also declines as management attention shifts to the acquisition. Sony went on to lose $162 million in 1991.

Implementation of Business Definition

As with all aspects of strategy, even the most brilliant business definition is useless unless it is aggressively implemented. You must have the courage to do two things in implementing your business definition:

1. Divest or close down any business not consistent with your business definition, and
2. Invest in whatever is required so that you are the leader in meeting the needs of your targeted customers.

Divest Unrelated Businesses

Without a clear strategy, Sears declined consistently from the mid-1970s through 1991. It was a lousy place to work, a frustrating place to shop, and a disaster to own its stock. Yet, Sears had an amazing resurgence following the arrival of Arthur Martinez in 1992. Its turnaround was driven by the business definition in Exhibit 4.6: To offer superior value to middle-income families by focusing on its mall department stores. The business definition was consistent with Sears' competitive realities:

- It couldn't make any money from the poorest families and its image was too tattered to target the most affluent families. Women are the chief purchasing agents for U.S. households.
- Value, such as offering the exact same sweater for $38 that sold for $79 with a different label in other department stores, was important to the target customer.
- Sears' cost structure did not allow it to be competitive with Wal-Mart in small towns or strip malls but it could offer superior value compared to traditional mall department stores.

Exhibit 4.6 **Sears' business definition in 1992–96**

Customer	·············▶	Middle–income females
Wants	·············▶	Value: Good quality at a significantly lower price
Mechanism	·············▶	Mall department stores

Sears implemented its business definition with a vengeance because it realized that every dollar and hour of time focused on its strength in mall department stores would generate five or 10 times as much return as efforts devoted to turning around its weaknesses.

- It spun off or sold all of its other businesses (e.g., Allstate insurance, Coldwell Banker real estate, and Dean Witter Discover financial services) so it could focus on retail.
- It closed down 113 of its money-losing stores in small towns and inner cities.
- Most traumatically, it cut out its heart and soul: the 1,500 page catalog. With nearly everyone in America living within 15 minutes of a Wal-Mart, the general purpose "wish book" no longer served a purpose.

These efforts paid off. Sears had the second highest total return to stockholders of the Dow-Jones 30 Industrial Companies from 1991 to 1996.

Every company should identify the businesses and product lines that don't fit its business definition. They should be divested even if they produce good financial returns. They will be worth more to a company in which they are core products. Moreover, divesting them allows management to focus all of its energies on its keys to success. Finally, taking such tough actions demonstrates management's commitment to the new strategy. What is the "Sears catalog" that your company should divest?

Invest in Whatever Is Required by Your Business Definition

The key to business success is having an unfair advantage in meeting the wants of your target customer. The only way to make that happen is to identify exactly what actions are required to implement your strategy aggressively. Failure to do so allows competitors to move faster than you and signals a lack of commitment to your people. The following examples demonstrate that aggressively implementing a strategy based on a superior business definition can produce amazing results.

- State of the art information systems have long been key elements in the dominance of companies such as Wal-Mart and PepsiCo's Frito-Lay subsidiary.
- Jack Welch acquired over $20 billion of companies in 1981-86 to reach his goal of being number one or two in market share in every business.
- The Internet companies today are incurring huge losses in order to establish leadership in their niches (e.g., in 1999 quarter three, losses for Amazon.com exceeded 50 percent of revenue while Etoys' losses exceeded 300 percent of revenue).

CHAPTER FIVE

Determine Your BHAG
(Big, Hairy, Achievable Goal)

Business definition leads directly to the strategic objective of a business. It in turn leads to a goal-oriented strategy that beats competitors in meeting customer wants. The "evergreen" strategic objective of every business is to make its owners wealthier—to maximize shareholder value. The essence of business is to take one dollar in assets and create significantly more than one dollar in value. Whether an entrepreneur or an executive, a person who can do that consistently is very well rewarded.

But what does "maximizing shareholder value" mean for strategy and execution? With regard to execution, "maximizing shareholder value" doesn't motivate many people below senior management. That objective needs to be restated in more inspiring terms.[1] "Maximizing shareholder value" also gives little guidance on how to reach that objective. Hence, it needs to be taken to a lower level of abstraction and translated into objectives that are **actionable.** Strategically, you can take action on either **sales** or **profitability** (return on investment), or both, to increase shareholder value.

Your company's "strategic objective," however, is not the same as quantitative annual sales and profit goals, which are discussed in chapter 11. Instead, we are trying to identify **the single strategic, qualitative objective** that will guide decisions over the next seven to 10 years. It has a meaning more closely related to "purpose" than to "target."

A strategic objective might be, for instance, "profits today" as opposed to "profits tomorrow." "Profits today," which focuses on immediate profitability and cash flow, is often appropriate for businesses in weak positions or in unattractive industries. These businesses can increase shareholder value by achieving high free cash flows in the short term through such means as reducing costs, minimizing investments, and raising prices. "Profits tomorrow," which emphasizes sales growth, is appropriate for stronger businesses in highly attractive and growing industries (e.g., Internet companies in 2000). While short-term free cash flows are lower, the higher expected growth and lower risk (since greater consumer value makes competitive challenges less likely) increase the price/earnings multiple and create shareholder value.

As long as the strategic objective is appropriate to the business, stock price will reflect increased value. To select the appropriate strategic objective for your business, you will need to consider your capabilities, the 10 climate and competitive forces, and especially the characteristics of your industry and your strategic position within it. That's what this chapter is about—how to determine the strategic objective that will maximize the value of your business. It covers the following:

- The importance of your strategic objective in motivating your people,
- Quantitative factors affecting profitability,
- Qualitative factors affecting profitability, and
- Developing a single strategic objective as the focus of strategy for your company.

Strategic Objectives of Large U.S. Companies Since 1980

From 1980 to 1995, most large U.S. companies were focused internally on getting costs down and quality up. The U.S. had back-to-back recessions in 1979 and 1981. Japan had killed the U.S. consumer electronics industry, and Japan's fuel efficient, reliable cars were causing General Motors, Ford, and Chrysler to lose billions of dollars. *Harvard Business Review* and other business magazines reported that U.S. companies were no longer competitive. Costs were out of control and quality stunk.

The strategic objective for most large companies was obvious. They had to improve quality and reduce costs to survive and thrive in a world where international competition was accelerating. The key management tools of 1980 to 1995 were not subtle. Consulting firms helped firms reengineer and restructure themselves. In human resources, it was the era of downsizing and early retirement programs. Production, starting with Ford, began listening to Deming's principles of total quality management. Finance departments focused on shareholder value and Economic Value Added. Corporate raiders provided management with a sense of urgency, and did the cost cutting when the original management teams were not up to the task.

By 1995, after 15 years, the job of becoming competitive was largely over for many industries. The U.S. has been rated the most productive of the 14 developed countries every year since 1994. The CEOs realized that they were "lean and mean," and cost reductions could no longer deliver the 10 percent or so annual earnings growth demanded by stockholders. The July 5, 1995 *Wall Street Journal* had a front page article on "Lean and Frail: Some Companies Cut Costs Too Far, Suffer 'Corporate Anorexia.'" That same week, Mercer Management Consulting launched a series of full-page ads in business magazines with the headline, "You Can't Shrink to Greatness."

Cutting costs had become the equivalent of cutting meat and bone instead of cutting fat. It was leading to poor new product development, weak marketing, and lousy service. Cost cutting was hurting sales and reducing rather than increasing profits. The strategic objective for these industries shifted from an internal focus on costs and quality to an external focus on growing the top line of sales. CEO Chuck Knight of Emerson Electric shifted from "planning conferences" to "growth conferences" with his businesses.

USE A "BHAG" TO MOTIVATE YOUR PEOPLE

"Strategic objective" is MBA jargon. It conveys important information and allows productive discussion. Most importantly, it allows your management team to develop a single goal that will be the constant focus of your efforts for the next three to 10 years. But "strategic objective" will not motivate your people. Before you communicate your strategy to the company and begin the process of developing bottom-up understanding and commitment, you must translate the "strategic objective" into a BHAG, a Big, Hairy, Achievable Goal. Collins and Porras developed the concept of a BHAG in their landmark book, *Built to Last:*

> Like the moon mission, a true BHAG is clear and compelling and serves as a unifying focal point of effort—often creating immense team spirit. It has a clear finish line, so the organization can know when it has achieved the goal; people like to shoot for finish lines. A BHAG engages people— it reaches out and grabs them in the gut. It is tangible, energizing, highly focused. People "get it" right away; it takes little or no explanation.[2]

Collins and Porras provide five guidelines to keep in mind as you develop the BHAG for your company[3] :

1. First, and most importantly, the BHAG must be consistent with the company's core values. Motorola has a technical culture, and engineers love quantitative measures. Hence, Motorola's 1984 BHAG of achieving "six sigma quality by 1989" provided clear direction consistent with the corporate culture. Moreover, such a high level of quality was of great value during a time when customers were focused on poor quality from suppliers.

2. The BHAG should be so clear and compelling that it requires little or no explanation. President Kennedy's 1962 challenge to NASA—put a man on the moon and get him back safely by 1970—was unambiguous. From 1977 to 1985, although its senior management never said the words, the understood BHAG of Anheuser-Busch was "Kill Miller." All decisions were focused on obtaining clear superiority in every aspect of marketing. After its share lead over Miller fell from nearly 400 percent in 1971 to 50 percent in 1976, Anheuser-Busch again had a nearly 2 to 1 share lead over Miller by 1985.

3. While the BHAG should fall well outside of the comfort zone, requiring heroic effort and perhaps even a little luck, people in the organization should have reason to believe they can pull it off. (That is why I took the liberty to modify the Collins and Porras definition—Big, Hairy, Audacious Goal—to Achievable.) An achievable BHAG produces organizational commitment. An unachievable BHAG produces only cynicism.

4. A BHAG should be so compelling that it would continue to drive change even if the organization's leaders disappeared before it was completed. The 1963 assassination of President Kennedy had no impact on NASA's BHAG to put a person on the moon.

5. Have a follow-up BHAG since an organization can stagnate once its BHAG is achieved. NASA has floundered since the success of Apollo 11 because it lacked a BHAG beyond putting a person on the moon. Once Motorola's quality program was close to six sigma, CEO David Galvin maintained momentum by establishing an additional quantitative BHAG. He mandated reducing cycle time by 90 percent within five years (e.g., reduce the time for develop-

ing a new product from 30 months to three months or reduce the time from ordering a cell phone until it is operational from two months to less than a week).

A BHAG is often restricted to internal use. Grace & Company's "60-60" BHAG of moving from $10 million in revenue and 15 partners in 1998 to $60 million revenue and 60 partners by 2008 offers no direct value to the customer. It helps attract the best employees, however, because it promises a commitment to major growth and offers superior opportunities for becoming a partner.

Indeed, financial BHAGs can be very powerful even though they appeal directly to neither employees nor customers. As a consultant, one of my favorite BHAGs for a client is to grow the value of their company five to 10-fold in 10 years. That is, a company worth $5 million today will be worth $25 to $50 million in 10 years, or compound annual growth of 17.5 to 26 percent annually. Such a BHAG forces "out of the box" thinking. A company can only achieve such performance over a 10 year period if it really understands the wants of its target customer and develops a strategy that provides an unfair advantage in meeting those wants.

For example, many CPA firms would argue that the 20 percent annual growth required to grow from $10 to $60 million in 10 years is definitely not achievable in a mature industry like accounting. Once Grace & Company partners accepted 60-60 as non-negotiable, however, they identified a strategy that could lead to its achievement: Be recognized as "clearly the best partner" for helping mid-size, privately held companies grow their value rapidly. As detailed in chapter 3, this strategy leads to superior payoffs for customers, employees, and owners.

Use a "Catalytic Mechanism" to Drive Implementation

A BHAG can provide the foundation for strategy implementation in either of two ways. The traditional top-down approach is detailed in chapter 11. It begins with identifying the three to five "key moves" necessary for achieving the BHAG. It then leads to detailed goals, action plans for achieving the goals, and incentives so people work together to implement the action plans and achieve the goals. The approach can be spectacularly successful.

Jim Collins, one of the co-creators of the BHAG concept, has developed a less bureaucratic approach for achieving your BHAG. Collins argues that organizations should develop a "catalytic mechanism"[4] or system of catalytic mechanisms that causes all employees to work together to achieve the BHAG. Collins cites Granite Rock, a gravel and concrete company that adopted the outrageous BHAG of achieving a reputation for service that met or exceeded Nordstrom, the department store chain legendary for delighting customers.

Granite Rock's catalytic mechanism for achieving legendary service was not charismatic leadership and motivational programs. Instead, it simply added a phrase at the bottom of each invoice stating, "If you are not satisfied for any reason, don't pay us for it. Simply scratch out the line item, write a brief note about the problem, and return a copy of this invoice along with your check for the balance." This "short pay" policy provides feedback on service quality that is hard to ignore. Employees quickly respond to identify and correct the causes of service quality failure. The results have been spectacular. Granite Rock won the Malcolm Baldrige National Quality Award in 1992 and now commands a six percent price premium and a pretax profit of 10 percent.

According to Collins, catalytic mechanisms have five characteristics:

1. Catalytic mechanisms produce desired results in unpredictable ways. In 1956, 3M began allowing its scientists to use 15 percent of their time experimenting in any area of their choice. This catalytic mechanism has led to the constant stream of innovative products that have since driven its success.

2. Catalytic mechanisms push power down in an organization and reduce bureaucratic inertia. Since 1994, federal employees can take the initiative to overcome obsolete regulations. A "waiver-of-regulation request" must be acted on within 30 days or the requester can assume approval. Moreover, while lower level people can approve the waiver, only the head of an agency can deny a request.

3. Catalytic mechanisms have teeth. Nucor Steel has developed a system of catalytic mechanisms that leads to extraordinary productivity and superior compensation. The components include:
   - Base compensation below industry averages but bonuses that can double or triple the base depending on team productivity.
   - Losing the day's bonus if you are five minutes late to work and the week's bonus if you are 30 minutes late.
   - No bonus for poor quality work and no adjustment to the bonus formula if equipment breaks down.

4. Catalytic mechanisms attract the right people. Lazy people don't work for Nucor. The teams of 20 or 30 people won't tolerate members who bring down their productivity.

5. Catalytic mechanisms produce long-term impacts. Constant visibility and pressure change behavior. Eventually, it even changes the employee profile and culture.

QUANTITATIVE FACTORS AFFECTING PROFITABILITY

In the late 1960s and 1970s, planners and strategists moved beyond forecast-based predict-and-prepare planning and began to take greater notice of marketplace variables and business position in the market. This led to what became known as "formula" planning, since strategy consultants devised various formulas that told you just what strategic objective each business unit should pursue. Formula planning was particularly attractive in that era of conglomerates, offering strategic guidance to CEOs with a large number of businesses to manage.

"Formula" Planning

The best known and most influential proponent of formula planning was the Boston Consulting Group (BCG) with its "growth-share" matrix, shown in Exhibit 5.1. BCG assumed that the two most important determinants of profitability were size of market share and rate of industry growth. Your position on those two dimensions located you in a two-by-two matrix, and the appropriate strategic objective for your business depended on which quadrant your business landed in.

Exhibit 5.1 **Strategic objectives of businesses according to BCG's growth–share matrix**

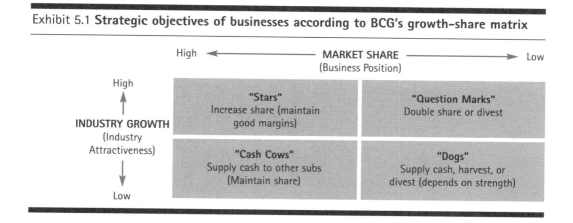

If your business is a "star," your goal is to grow. It should have a high ROI but it also demands a lot of investment to grow. That investment may be in the form of plant and equipment (traditional companies) or in marketing (in high tech firms such as America Online and Amazon.com). Therefore, its free cash flow may be negative.

A "cash cow" is put to pasture to generate large quantities of cash, little of which is reinvested. Some of it goes to fund the rising "stars" and the promising "question marks." Some also goes for dividends or stock repurchase.

A "question mark" requires additional analysis. Rapid industry growth provides opportunity, but its low market share means it's way behind the pack. If heavy investment can dramatically increase its market share and move its ROI from below to above your cost of capital, then its strategic goal might be to double its market share. If that's impossible, divest it.

A "dog" is not necessarily a loser, in spite of the name and the goal—divest—originally assigned to all "dogs" by BCG. If its ROI is below your cost of capital, BCG was right—harvest it for all the cash possible or divest it. However, some "dogs" are "hot dogs" with good ROIs. In fact, many businesses fall into this category. They should be treated as a cash cow and maintained rather than harvested or divested.

Selecting the wrong strategic objective can be a fatal blunder, as illustrated in Exhibit 5.2. To continue with the BCG bestiary, the proper goal of a "cash cow" is to provide the investment funds to turn today's "star" into tomorrow's "cow," and today's promising "question mark" into tomorrow's "star." That is the ideal sequence—"question mark" to "star" to "cash cow."

Exhibit 5.2 **Selecting the wrong goal is often a fatal strategy blunder**

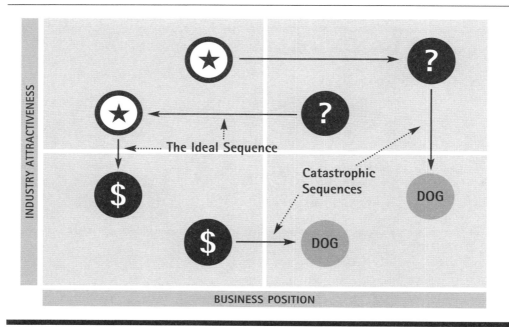

Source: Adapted from Arnoldo C. Hax and Nicolas C. Majluf, *Strategic Management: An Integrative Approach* (Englewood Cliffs, N.J.: Prentice-Hall, 1984), p. 136.

Catastrophe lurks in selecting the wrong sequence. Stuffing a "cash cow" produces waste, but starving it produces a "dog." Likewise, starving a "star" turns tomorrow's "cash cow" into a "question mark," which will become a "dog" as industry growth slows.

The problem with the BCG matrix is that it oversimplifies reality. There's a lot more to an attractive business environment than industry growth and market share. Sensitive to this fact, General Electric worked with management consultants McKinsey

& Company to develop a more realistic three-level matrix, shown in Exhibit 5.3, that plotted businesses along more comprehensive dimensions—"industry attractiveness" and "business position."[5]

Exhibit 5.3 **Strategic objectives of businesses according to the McKinsey/GE industry attractiveness/business position matrix**

INDUSTRY ATTRACTIVENESS	BUSINESS POSITION		
	HIGH	MEDIUM	LOW
HIGH	Grow aggressively	Grow	Double or divest
MEDIUM	Grow	Maintain	Harvest
LOW	Generate cash	Harvest	Divest

In this process, senior executives weighted and ranked a series of variables, such as market size, rate of growth, and market concentration to determine "industry attractiveness." Likewise, they determined "business position" by considering such variables as their current technology, marketing expertise, market share, and manufacturing efficiency. Based on their rankings of these variables, a business unit would fall into one of nine boxes, each of which called for a specific strategic objective.

PIMS—Profit Impact of Market Strategy

The question is, how do you determine which variables to include in "industry attractiveness" and "business position"? How should you weight them? Planners at General Electric, scholars at Harvard Business School, and others struggled with those questions, and their research ultimately led to a much better approach than BCG's arbitrary selection of industry growth and market share as the primary variables. The result was PIMS—Profit Impact of Market Strategy. This is a unique research program that provides quantitative guidance on what variables are important in determining the attractiveness of your industry and the strength of your position in the industry.[6]

PIMS is by far the most comprehensive and sophisticated empirical study ever of the correlation between ROI and those variables that relate to strategy, structure, and business position. The PIMS data base uses the experience of 3,000 business units in more than 450 companies. Drawing upon that mass of data, PIMS uses a regression model to show how 65 variables correlate with ROI and to calculate a "par" or expected ROI for any business unit.

The PIMS correlations indicate that the specifics of an industry and company are less important than certain variables common to all industries, whether industrial products, consumer durables, or consumer non-durables. For instance, a market share leader with high quality and low capital intensity will likely have a high ROI regardless of whether the industry is computers, steel, or financial services. Similarly, a company with low quality, low share, and high capital intensity will likely have a low ROI regardless of size, geographical location, or industry.

While the PIMS results establish correlations and do not prove causation, the fundamental PIMS findings demonstrate that **competitive strength** variables (e.g., market share, relative quality) and **industry structure** variables explain two-thirds of the variation in ROI. Your business definition should make sure these variables are as beneficial as possible. Still, the large residual variance of ROI indicates the importance of strategy in performance. As McKinsey & Company puts it, "strategy + structure = performance."

Business Position Variables

Relative market share, relative quality, and capital intensity (whether in the form of fixed capital or working capital) are critical influences on the pre-tax ROI of all businesses. In fact, these are the three most important business position variables in their impact on ROI, as shown in Exhibits 5.4 and 5.5[7].

Exhibit 5.4 **The effect of relative quality and market share on pre-tax ROI**

MARKET SHARE	RELATIVE QUALITY		
	BOTTOM THIRD	MIDDLE THIRD	TOP THIRD
BOTTOM THIRD <13%	10%	16%	18%
MIDDLE THIRD 14 to 27%	18%	20%	26%
TOP THIRD 28+%	26%	29%	37%

Exhibit 5.4 shows the combined relationship of relative quality and market share to ROI. For example, a business with a market share less than 13 percent but with very high perceived quality relative to competitors has an expected, or par, pre-tax ROI of 18 percent. Market share and relative quality combined can account for up to a 27 point spread in ROI (top third/top third 37 percent minus bottom third/bottom third 10 percent). Clearly, market share has a strong relationship to profitability, although using it as the sole indicator of business position greatly oversimplifies reality.

Capital intensity also has a strong impact on ROI, as you can see in Exhibit 5.5. Often, capital intensity is assumed to be a fixed industry characteristic, more or less beyond the control of an individual business. Certainly mining and steel demand heavy investment, but there is a lot of room for individual businesses to control their capital intensity relative to competitors. Some thoughts on this subject are presented in the accompanying sidebar.

Reducing Capital Intensity

Even in "capital intense" industries, individual firms have a lot of control over levels of investment. Here are some suggestions:

- Design all aspects of your company to minimize capital intensity and operating costs. Southwest Airlines achieves high aircraft utilization through highly motivated ground and gate crews, limited passenger services, avoiding connections with other airlines, and a dozen other tactics.
- Use recycled materials and avoid the investment in mining and primary production. Nucor Steel does this to position itself as a low-capital company in a high-capital industry. Nucor's 1998 market value was 25 percent above that of much larger US Steel.
- Buy bargains in plant and equipment during the "down" side of the business cycle. Jefferson Smurfit in paper making refused to buy capacity at prices above 50 percent of replacement cost.
- Sell or spin off the capital-intense parts of your company. Marriott franchises and operates hotels and timeshare resorts with its highly profitable management contracts but spun off its investment-intensive hotel buildings in 1998. Coca-Cola spun off its capital-intense bottling operations into Coca-Cola Enterprises in 1986.
- Smooth the business cycle. Increase capacity utilization rather than build capacity for peak demand. In the mid-1980s, Ford ran its plants over capacity and cut back on price promotions. Even if this reduced sales, it increased profits and ROI.
- Anheuser-Busch went from 75 percent to 95 percent capacity utilization by building up wholesaler beer inventories in refrigerated warehouses during off-peak winter months and reducing them in peak summer months. The result was an investment savings in plant and equipment of $3 billion.

Reducing your capital intensity, whether fixed capital or working capital, can have a dramatic impact on your ROI. As Exhibit 5.5 shows, the difference between the average ROI of a business with high capital intensity and the average ROI of one with low capital intensity is an incredible 34 points.

Exhibit 5.5 **The effect of capital intensity on pre-tax ROI**

FIXED CAPITAL/ SALES	WORKING CAPITAL/SALES		
	<20%	20 TO 30%	30+%
<25%	41%	28%	18%
25–50%	29%	23%	13%
50+%	18%	14%	7%

Source: Adapted and reprinted with the permission of The Free Press, an imprint of Simon & Schuster from THE PIMS PRIN-CIPLES: Linking Strategy to Performance by Robert D. Buzzell and Bradley T. Gale. Copyright © 1987 by The Free Press.

Additional analyses of the PIMS database provide clear direction for the appropriate strategic objective in various situations. For example, the actual ROI of Ralston Purina was about half what it should have been based on its quality, market share, and capital intensity when William Stiritz became CEO in 1982. The appropriate strategic objective was obvious: Double ROI by reducing corporate fat and shedding unwise acquisitions.

Similarly, Exhibit 5.6 shows that divestment is the right strategic decision for businesses with a very weak predicted or Par ROI. Additional investments in such businesses not only fail to get their cost of capital but actually earn negative returns. Trying to turn them around represents the triumph of hope over experience for simple reasons. First, they often have fewer opportunities (but this is not the main problem since few companies invest in projects projected to achieve returns below the cost of capital). Second, companies in such weak positions often lack the capability for successful imple-

Exhibit 5.6 **Get rid of problems so you can focus on opportunities**

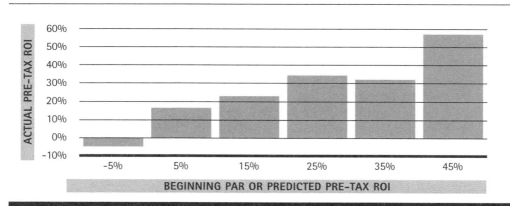

mentation. Finally, even when they muster the resources to implement a winning new product, competitors with stronger brand equity often copy the innovation and take over leadership. Bottom line, Exhibit 5.6 clearly demonstrates the wisdom of "getting rid of your problems so you can focus on your opportunities."

Industry Attractiveness Variables

PIMS also looks at industry- and market-related variables that determine industry attractiveness. Exhibit 5.7 lists the key industry variables in the order of their impact on ROI. This exhibit compares ROIs of those businesses in the most attractive quintile for each variable with those in the least attractive quintile.

If your products are big-ticket items (individual orders over $10,000) and they constitute a significant percentage of your customers' total purchases (more than five percent), then your customers will shop around for the best deal and they will negotiate hard from a position of strength. The result is that your expected ROI is going to be lower by 14.0 points (= 9.2 + 4.8) than it would be in an industry where purchase sizes are small and relatively less important to customers.

Exhibit 5.7 **Effect of industry variables on ROI**

| VARIABLE | PERCENTILE | | IMPACT ON PRE-TAX ROI | | |
	20TH	80TH	20TH	80TH	SPREAD
PURCHASE AMOUNT	$10K+	<$1K	-4.0%	5.2%	9.2%
PERCENT UNIONIZATION	75%	0%	-2.4%	2.9%	5.3%
PURCHASE IMPORTANCE	5+%	<1%	-3.0%	1.8%	4.8%
INDUSTRY GROWTH	-4%	+11%	-1.2%	1.1%	2.3%
INFLATION	4%	8%	-1.0%	1.0%	2.0%
OTHER			21.4%	23.9%	2.5%
AVERAGE ROI			9.8%	35.9%	26.1%

Source: Adapted and reprinted with the permission of The Free Press, an imprint of Simon & Schuster from *The PIMS Principles: Linking Strategy to Performance* by Robert D. Buzzell and Bradley T. Gale. Copyright © 1987 by The Free Press.

The degree of unionization in your industry affects profitability. An industry that is more than 75 percent unionized is less profitable than a non-unionized industry by an average of 5.3 percentage points. Which causes which? Perhaps unions make industries less profitable. Or perhaps they're low-profit to begin with, and workers feel they have to organize to get their "fair share" of the meager profits. As with all PIMS correlations, causality is a matter of judgment.

Inflation is also a factor. High inflation seems to allow price increases that also increase profitability. Industry growth is the fourth most important of the industry variables and certainly not the strongest indicator of industry attractiveness, which was the assumption in the BCG growth-share matrix.

The average pre-tax ROI of 80 percentile companies is 35.9 percent, nearly four times that of the 9.8 percent for the 20 percentile companies. The first five factors in Exhibit 5.7 account for all but 2.5 of the 26.1 point difference in ROI. Hence, consider being more aggressive in expanding your business opportunities that are attractive on these five factors.

"Soufflés" and "Opportunities"

Analysis of the PIMS database indicates that companies tend to move toward equilibrium ROI over time (see Exhibit 5.8). That means businesses with below-par ROI are "opportunities." Management effort and solid strategy can significantly increase ROI, thus making them attractive acquisition targets. Similarly, businesses with ROI above par are called "Soufflés." Eventually, their ROIs will collapse towards par. Acquiring a "soufflé" can be devastating to a CEO's career.

Exhibit 5.8 **"Soufflés" and "Opportunities"**

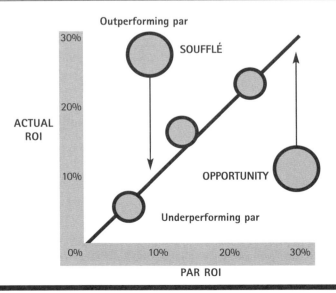

QUALITATIVE FACTORS AFFECTING PROFITABILITY

PIMS provides a quantitative foundation for selecting a strategic objective. The "Strategic Control Point Index" of Slywotzky and Morrison[8] (Exhibit 5.9) provides a qualitative, judgmental chart that shows the importance of achieving competitive advantage at a level that grabs CEOs in the gut.

Exhibit 5.9 **How profit happens: Strategic control point index**

PROFIT-PROTECTING POWER	INDEX	STRATEGIC CONTROL POINT	EXAMPLES
HIGH	10	Own the standard	Microsoft, Oracle
HIGH	9	Manage the value chain	Intel, Coca-Cola
HIGH	8	String of superdominant positions	Coca-Cola internationally
MEDIUM	7	Own the customer relationship	General Electric, EDS
MEDIUM	6	Brand, copyright	Many consumer products, Pharmaceuticals
LOW	5	Two-year product development lead	Intel
LOW	4	One-year product development lead	Mature consumer products
LOW	3	Commodity with 10 to 20 percent cost advantage	Nucor, Southwest Airlines
NONE	2	Commodity with cost parity	Countless
NONE	1	Commodity with cost disadvantage	Countless

Arguing with the specifics of the Index is easy. For example, truly having a 20 percent cost advantage in many commodity industries would allow complete market dominance and huge returns. But the basic reality of the chart is undeniable. Bill Gates is worth $100 billion because Microsoft Windows is the standard for the PC operating system and MS Office is the standard application suite. Coca-Cola, despite selling sugar water, had a market capitalization in 1999 of $200 billion because it has a 5 to 1 market share lead over PepsiCo in most countries and manages the value chain.

The commodity company at a cost disadvantage is worth a lot more to a competitor who can eliminate overhead costs and get other costs down. It should sell out quickly. As discussed in chapter 4, the commodity company with cost parity needs to focus. Concentrating all of its resources on a specific set of products and customers will increase its likelihood of becoming a market leader in a niche—and achieving Indexes 3 to 7 in the middle of the table.

Developing Your Strategic Objective/BHAG

The PIMS data and the BCG and GE matrices in Exhibits 5.4 and 5.5 provide a foundation for selecting a strategic objective that fits your strategic situation. Exhibit 5.10 summarizes these tools in a way designed to spark discussion of what makes sense for your company.

Exhibit 5.10 **What strategic objective makes sense for your company?**

SITUATION	EXAMPLE	STRATEGIC OBJECTIVE
Profits 50% below potential	Ralston in 1982	Increase ROI
Low quality, low market share	Pabst; Heileman	Sell out
Average quality, low share or Low quality, average share	Many companies	Increase quality, then increase share
High quality, low share	Many small companies	Increase share
Fragmented industry	McDonald's, Home Depot, Wal-Mart	Consolidate the industry, "Profits tomorrow" strategy
Low share, low ROI in an attractive industry	Eagle Snacks	Double share or sell out
Industry leader, mature industry	Anheuser-Busch in U.S.	Maintain share, generate cash
Industry leader, growing industry	Microsoft	Grow share; high ROI

Conclusion

Choosing the right strategic objective for your company requires a careful analysis of all the variables of your business position and industry that influence profitability. We know from PIMS that the most important variables are relative quality, market share, and capital intensity.

While we now know a great deal about these variables and appropriate strategic goals, many companies, including some market leaders, fail to adopt the right goals. Often the failure is one of timing—not changing goals when needed. An "improve ROI" goal is only a three- to five-year goal. Carried on too long, this goal can harvest a company and drive it into the ground. Don't stay with an "improve market share" goal once the market has matured; you'll waste money on unnecessary investment.

Of course, there are exceptions to the rules, none of which is absolute. If you are attacked by a powerful competitor in a mature market, an "improve market share" goal may be appropriate, since your competitor will take market share away from you if you don't take it away from him. If you are aggressively consolidating an industry, learn to live with a below-par ROI until the consolidation is complete.

Getting the strategic goal right can keep you from turning a "cash cow" into a "dog" or from acquiring a "soufflé" that collapses on you. "Soufflés" ... "cash cows" ... "dogs." The main thing is that you use some horse sense to determine the proper goal for your business. When you've done that, and then developed the right long-term strategy, you're in a position to beat competitors at meeting customer wants.

CHAPTER SIX

Generic Strategies:
Creating a Defensible Position

Strategies vary from industry to industry, company to company, and situation to situation. Your final strategy must reflect your specific internal and external realities. However, there is a small number of broad strategic approaches common to many businesses and situations. Michael Porter identified four of these, which he calls "generic strategies," in his landmark 1980 book *Competitive Strategy*.[1] This chapter also examines the three generic strategies developed in *The Discipline of Market Leaders*.[2]

A good generic strategy is the foundation for developing coherent functional strategies and action plans. In short, your generic strategy provides clear direction to competitive advantage, while failure to have a clear generic strategy—being "stuck in the middle"—is disastrous. It leads to political infighting and inefficiencies within the company. Worse, it leads to a confused image with customers. Being "caught in the middle" is a prescription for decline.

In this chapter, the discussion of three general topics will help you select and execute a generic strategy best for your business:

- Types of generic strategies,
- Product life cycles and generic strategies, and
- Selection and implementation of a generic strategy.

TYPES OF GENERIC STRATEGIES

A generic strategy is (1) a simply stated approach (2) for achieving financial and other objectives (3) by creating a defensible position in an industry. Your generic strategy should fit the stage of your product life cycle. It should also account for the forces affecting your business—the "5 Cs" of Company, Customers, Competitors, Capabilities, and Climate.

What are the generic strategies available to you? Porter identified four by asking two questions:

- What is your source of strategic advantage: low cost or differentiation (uniqueness)?
- What is your strategic target: the broad market or a niche?

The answers to these questions yield the four generic strategies shown in Exhibit 6.1. This table provides enough detail to help you see which generic strategy works best for your products or services.

Exhibit 6.1 **Porter's generic strategies**

	STRATEGIC ADVANTAGE: LOW COST	STRATEGIC ADVANTAGE: UNIQUENESS
Strategic Target: Total Industry (Broad)	**"Low Cost"** Comparable product at lower cost: Commodities (Oil, grain, cans, PCs, memory chips) Discount retailers: Wal-Mart #3 or 4 in a differentiation industry	**"Differentiation"** Appeal to customers based on image, quality, service: Beer, soda, cigarettes, clothes Real product or service attributes: Hewlett-Packard calculators, Maytag, Caterpillar, Microsoft, McKinsey & Co. Mass market lifestyle: Network TV, movies, pro sports, department stores
Strategic Target: A Customer Segment or Particular Product (Focus)	**"Cost–Focus"** A narrow product segment at a low cost: Nucor Southwest Airlines "Category killer" retailers (Circuit City, Home Depot) Small, low cost operators	**"Differentiation–Focus"** Clear superiority in meeting wants: Xerox in 1965, pharmaceuticals, small town drug store "Targeted" to relatively narrow segment: Luxury goods and services (Mercedes) Niche leisure/lifestyle (specialty magazines, cable TV) Mall specialty stores (The Limited)

The best way to explain these generic strategies is to look at their application to a specific industry. Exhibit 6.2 shows generic strategies in the retail industry.

Exhibit 6.2 **Retailers' generic strategies**

	LOW COST	DIFFERENTIATION
Broad Market	**Discounters:** Kmart, Target, Wal-Mart	**Full Service Stores:** Bloomingdale's, Dillard's
Focus	**"Category Killers":** Home Depot, Factory outlet malls	**Specialty Mall Stores:** The Limited, The Gap

Large department stores, often anchors in malls, typically follow a **differentiation** strategy. Companies like Dillard's and The May Company try to distinguish themselves through fashion, service, product variety, and store design. They do not strive to meet the low prices of the discounters.

Followers of a **low cost** generic strategy include discount department stores such as Wal-Mart, Dayton Hudson's Target Stores, and Kmart. These stores also carry a wide variety of products, but they appeal to customers through low prices.

Mall specialty shops tend to follow a **differentiation-focus** strategy. Each store carries a particular product category, such as women's clothing at The Limited and books at Brentano's. Most of these stores rely on convenience, variety, fashion, quality, and "good" value rather than low price.

"Category killers," such as Home Depot in home improvement, Office Depot in office products, and Circuit City in consumer electronics, relentlessly follow a **cost-focus** strategy. They are called "category killers" because small independent retailers and even local chains in a category tend to close up after one of these "killers" comes to town. They meet customer wants so well and have such favorable economies of scale at both the corporate and outlet level that direct competition is usually suicide.

Generic strategies should not be followed simplistically. A business following a differentiation strategy must offer reasonable prices. It may also strive to be the lowest-cost producer, thereby increasing margins and ensuring maximum strategic advantage in case of a price war. Similarly, a discount retailer such as Wal-Mart benefits from the friendliness of its associates (employees) and quality name brands. The trick is to offer "best value" for your strategy without becoming "stuck in the middle."

Sears was stuck in the middle in the 1980s. It wasn't low cost so it couldn't compete with discounters such as Wal-Mart and Kmart. Except for hardware, it wasn't high-quality. Sears seemed to develop a new strategy every few years. The result of an unclear strategy at headquarters was mediocrity in the stores. Customers left Sears and went to Wal-Mart for low prices and to mall stores for fashion.

A Newer Approach to Generic Strategies

In the 1994 best seller, *The Discipline of Market Leaders,* consultants Michael Treacy and Fred Wiersema developed the three generic strategies in Exhibit 6.3. Many CEOs find these strategies more intuitively appealing than Porter's. We discuss both approaches since Porter's approach works better for certain products.

Exhibit 6.3 **Strategies according to** *The Discipline of Market Leaders*

STRATEGY	EXAMPLES	CHARACTERISTICS
Product Leadership • Best Product • Focus-differentiation*	3M Microsoft, Intel Pharmaceuticals	Performance Uniqueness Industry standard
Customer Intimacy • Best Total Solution • Differentiation*	Nordstrom, Ritz-Carlton IBM Pre-1980 Most small companies	Personalized service and advice Trust Solutions
Operational Excellence • Best Value • Low cost*	Emerson Electric McDonald's, Wal-Mart Southwest Airlines	Lowest total cost Good service Dependability

* The correspondence with these generic strategies from Porter is only suggestive.

The **product leadership** strategy requires that the actual performance of your product or service be perceived as qualitatively better than competitors. Patents assure such superior performance for many pharmaceuticals and niche products, such as those made by 3M. The fact that Nike athletic shoes were perceived to be superior was important to its success in the 1990s, regardless of whether or not its products were technically superior.

Leading consumer product brands usually follow a customer intimacy strategy. People may pay 50 percent more for Coca-Cola, Budweiser, or Bayer aspirin than for a generic because they trust the brand. While product leadership rests on differences in performance, customer intimacy often depends on reputation and image.

Most smaller companies also follow a customer intimacy strategy. They aren't big enough to have the economies of scale and invest in all of the process reengineering required for operational excellence or the R&D for product leadership. But they do have personal knowledge of the customer. They know the importance of reputation so they will do whatever it takes to satisfy the customer.

As Emerson Electric CEO Chuck Knight loves to say, the operational excellence strategy means "best price" rather than "lowest price." Your customer wants the lowest total cost and is willing to pay for reliability. Image, non-functional packaging, and glitz, however, add no value. Operational excellence companies hire lots of engineers so they can produce huge quantities of products or services within tight specifications at low prices.

Unfortunately, fringe operators also claim they have an operational excellence strategy. If fact, many sell only on low price because they have poor quality and have not invested in the necessary systems and people to assure reliability.

Finally, companies can dramatically increase profitability if they can move from selling a relatively undifferentiated "product" with an operational excellence strategy to selling "solutions" with a customer intimacy strategy. As mentioned in chapter 4, Duke Manufacturing was at a competitive disadvantage because it sold products for commercial kitchens in a dozen different categories while competitors could focus on making products to exactly meet the needs of each niche. Duke converted its situation to a major advantage by positioning itself as the "solutions provider" for commercial kitchens. By providing trusted systems solutions, Duke now allows its customers to focus on preparing food rather than the details of kitchen equipment.

PRODUCT LIFE CYCLES AND GENERIC STRATEGIES

The product life cycle (PLC) is an important factor you must consider in selecting a generic strategy. The PLC concept postulates that products and industries all follow a similar, if not identical, course from birth to death, as illustrated in Exhibit 6.4.

Early proponents of the PLC treated this course as somehow pre-ordained, as if companies had little control over the life of a product. Clearly, this deterministic view is oversimplified, and the concept has been severely criticized.[3] Yet, the concept endures, and for good reason: So long as you appreciate its limitations, the PLC can be a useful

Exhibit 6.4 **Idealized PLC**

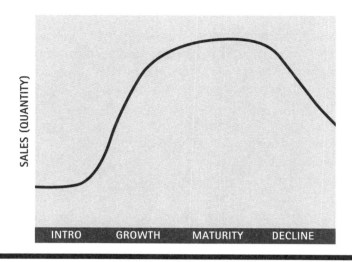

tool for understanding and explaining markets.

Companies with reactive managements who let events control them often do follow the idealized curve. However, life cycles often take different forms for leaders who attempt to control their destinies. The shape of the life cycle depends not only on uncontrollable market forces but also on your actions and those of your competitors. The future is controllable to a significant extent. That fundamental belief underlies this book.

Exhibit 6.5 **Strategy and tactics for the industry leader by PLC stage**

STAGE IN PLC	INTRODUCTION	GROWTH	MATURITY/DECLINE
Strategy	Product leadership	Customer intimacy	Operational excellence
Key Goal	Growth	Growth	Generate cash/Harvest
Profits	Negative	Strong	Weaken/Low
Costs	Very high	Declining	Low/Very low
Product	Narrow	Growing	Proliferation/Prune
Prices	High	High but declining	Price war "shake out" in early maturity/Low
Promotion	Very high for awareness	High to create brand equity	Shift towards price promotion/Very low promo
Distribution	Selective	Broad	Intensive; heavy "push" incentives/Prune in decline

Generic Strategy and PLC Stage

Different stages in a company's life cycle require different generic strategies. Exhibit 6.5 shows how certain generic strategies are more appropriate for the leader during certain life cycle stages than during others. Knowing where you are on the PLC curve helps you know which strategy is appropriate for you.

Introduction: During a product's introduction and its early growth, **product leadership** is usually the appropriate strategy. The product probably has no significant competitors at this stage, and customers are more interested in benefits than price. Overall costs are high since production experience is limited, production runs small, and distribution selective. Moreover, advertising and promotion costs are high because of the need to increase awareness. Classic examples are Polaroid, Xerox, the IBM PC, and pharmaceuticals.

Growth: During the growth phase, as a broad market emerges, the strategy should move to **customer intimacy.** High margins have begun to attract competitors, and the greatest concern of the leader is maintaining market share against the growing competition. In order to preempt competitors, the leader introduces product variations for most if not all niches in the broad market. Growing competition limits price increases. Still, margins remain high or even grow, since the market continues to expand while the experience curve and economies of scale reduce costs.

Maturity and decline: With maturity, leaders in some industries (e.g., beer, soda, cigarettes, clothing) may continue with a customer intimacy strategy. Leaders in most industries, however, will be forced into an operational excellence strategy. The market has ceased to expand. Any gains in sales must now come at the expense of someone else, and competition intensifies. Smaller competitors use lower prices to nibble away at the leader's market share, and the leader retaliates. Relying on a superior cost position due to greater economies of scale and production experience, the leader instigates a price war to "shake out" weaker competitors and to encourage the survivors to coexist in a "better state of peace." Prices may rebound a little when that "peace" is established. Still, competition remains price- and cost-driven. Even for "image" products, product differences become smaller, and price promotions increase at the expense of advertising.

During the decline phase, the leader's interest is to consolidate the industry and avoid excessive competitive warfare. Acquisitions can serve the dual purpose of reducing costs by spreading overhead and closing down excess capacity, which depresses prices. The company begins to "harvest" the business. It moves from "profits tomorrow" to "profits today," even if this means lower sales. It controls costs even more tightly. The company prunes the product line to get rid of marginal products and focuses only on those niches where it is dominant. An **operational excellence** strategy continues to be appropriate.

Objective analysis of the PLC can prevent major strategic mistakes. Make sure your strategic objective and generic strategy are right for your stage in the PLC.

Product Life Cycle for High Tech Companies

This sidebar serves two purposes. First, it is directly relevant to technology companies. More importantly, use this example to determine where you are in your PLC and what combination of generic strategies makes sense for your company over the next seven to 10 years.

Inside the Tornado by Geoffrey Moore[4] shows how the product leadership, customer intimacy, and operational excellence generic strategies should be applied to high tech companies. Exhibit 6.6 shows the five stages in the high tech PLC and the strategies appropriate for each stage.

Exhibit 6.6 **Generic strategies in each stage of the high tech PLC**

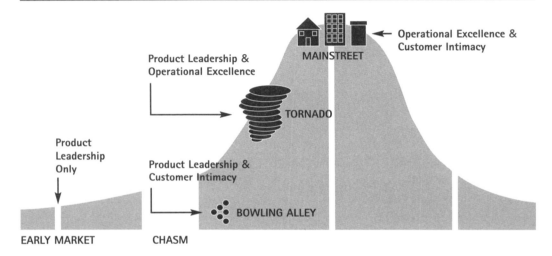

1. **The Early Market** is a time of great excitement when customers are technology enthusiasts and visionaries. Focusing completely on product leadership is the right generic strategy. In the earliest stage, your target customers are techies. Their budgets are small, so give them your product free.

   If the techies think it's cool, they will recommend it to the visionary, technology-enthusiast CEO, your target customer later in the early market. Such CEOs are a rare breed because this stage is the bleeding edge. CEOs will only invest in the new technology if they believe that it will give them enough of a permanent competitive advantage to compensate for the high risks. Your objective at this stage should be to do whatever it takes to make the product produce results. You need to be able to use these early victories to overcome the dreaded "chasm."

2. **The Chasm** is a time of great despair. The majority of CEOs and Chief Information Officers (CIOs) are pragmatists, not technology enthusiasts. They aren't comfortable with the imma-

turity of your solutions. Hence, they see the high costs and risks of implementing your product and discount the potential benefits. No sale!

3. **The Bowling Alley** targets the pragmatist CEO who will invest in new technology if it provides a long-term competitive advantage. Most CIOs will hate the idea because they have seen how difficult it is to implement new systems early in the PLC. Target a specific industry to cross the chasm and enter the bowling alley. Your strategy must now combine product leadership and customer intimacy. Product leadership gives the CEO the potential for breakthrough. Customer intimacy produces credibility that your system will work. It comes from in-depth industry knowledge and partnering with technology standards such as Microsoft and Oracle.

This stage is called the bowling alley because each project must "knock over" additional projects. A major objective in the bowling alley is gaining at least 40 percent of new installations. Being such a dominant leader allows you to set the industry standard, become the 900 pound gorilla, and enjoy outrageous profits.

Other CEOs and CIOs keep asking themselves if it's time to move yet. With each additional installation, the perceived risks go down and the benefits increase. When the lines cross, all the CIOs want to implement your system at once. You are in the tornado!

4. **The Tornado** is a period of mass-market adoption. Virtually overnight, demand outstrips supply. Each sale during the tornado represents an annuity for years to come. So what should your strategy be now? To be as succinct as possible: Just ship! Don't segment. Don't customize. It's like a sardine run. Don't bait your hooks; just stick in your bucket, pull them out, and go back for more. Operational excellence becomes a more important strategy than customer intimacy. You must have your systems down pat so you can double your sales force each year and manufacture and install your product to meet all the demand.

5. **Mainstreet** comes as a shock after the tornado. All of a sudden, no one in sales is meeting quota. Over half of target companies have installed the product. Only the most conservative, price sensitive, potential customers are left. Supply exceeds demand and price decreases accelerate. A classic example is personal computers in late 1991.

Your generic strategy must shift again. Operational excellence is now required in order to get costs as low as possible so you can cut prices. Engineer out your earlier partners to reduce costs and ease installation. Customers in the early stages were techies, CEOs, and CIOs. Now, for the first time, you target end users. Differentiate the commodity product with cool, high margin add-ons. Lend the credibility of your product by partnering with the latest product that is just crossing the chasm.

Note that Moore uses two (but never all three) of the generic strategies at each stage of the high tech PLC. Also, the same generic strategy may be used for very different reasons at different stages. Operational excellence is needed in "the tornado" to meet demand while in "Mainstreet" it has the more traditional purpose of keeping costs down. Most importantly, note the critical importance of changing the generic strategy at each stage in the PLC. For example, many high tech companies die because they fail to follow a customer intimacy strategy so they can cross "the chasm."

"Evolution" Versus Product Life Cycle

The metaphor of biological evolution complements the Product Life Cycle metaphor. The PLC was originally conceived of as analogous to an individual organism's life from birth through maturity to death—with clear limits on each stage. Many industries, however, can go on forever. A carefully nurtured brand can also live indefinitely, as illustrated by Budweiser and Coca-Cola dominating their markets for over 100 years. As with biological species, businesses and industries that adapt to environmental changes (climate forces) and other species (competitors) can avoid extinction.

Today, biologists are divided into two schools of thought on evolution. The "gradualism" school follows Charles Darwin's classic theory, arguing that evolution works continuously and gradually through the mechanisms of accidental variation and natural selection. A species variation survives and multiplies if it is better adapted to the environment than competing species.

The other school maintains that evolution occurs through "punctuated equilibrium." They cite the geological and fossil record as revealing long periods of little change in species, alternating with short periods of sudden and momentous change. Dinosaurs, for example, simply disappeared "overnight," if you're on geologic time. These short-lived periods of destruction and creation of species result from natural catastrophes, such as large meteorites smashing into the earth, or from the sudden release of steadily accumulated stresses.

The first ten chapters of this book focus on punctuated equilibrium: How to create a strategy that gives you an unfair advantage. The last two chapters, which focus on how to implement the strategy over time, reflect the "gradualism" approach of continuously adapting your strategy to the changes in the 10 forces and increasing your competitive advantages.

The evolution analogy has a couple of important implications for strategy. One is "strategic windows"[5]—those occasional periods of fit between market requirements and company strengths, which change more slowly than the marketplace environment. A company alert to external change and able to adjust its strategy quickly can exploit these opportunities as they occur. A classic example is the emergence of the Internet in the late 1990s. The Internet has already allowed startups like Amazon.com to overcome category killers like Barnes & Noble and Borders and companies like Charles Schwab to obtain a higher market capitalization than industry leaders like Merrill Lynch. Longer term, it will allow innovative companies who use this electronic channel to pass banking giants that stick with bricks and mortar and insurance companies that rely on armies of sales people.

Another implication for strategy is that looking outside your own company and your own industry will make you more "fit" and therefore more likely to flourish. You will be alert to developments or changes in technology and consumer trends that you can adopt to give you an advantage. If your product is sold through supermarkets, for example, you should "benchmark" it against Frito-Lay or other "best of store" vendors and not just against competitors in your category.

The evolution model should not be applied literally, of course. Biological evolution is mostly passive, while successful companies actively initiate and control change. Winning organizations monitor the horizon for threats and windows of opportunity and aggressively implement change.

SELECTING AND IMPLEMENTING A GENERIC STRATEGY

You are now ready to select and implement the generic strategy that will give your business a defensible position in the market. Your generic strategy depends upon your industry life cycle and your position in the industry, and the strategy must be consistent with competitive and climate forces. For brevity, we only discuss the three strategies from *The Discipline of Market Leaders*. For those who find Porter's four generic strategies more compelling, "product leadership" corresponds roughly with "focus-differentiation," "operational excellence" with "low cost," and "customer intimacy" with "differentiation."

Selecting a Generic Strategy

If you are the leader, you are free from some of the competitive constraints on the followers. You may focus on meeting customer wants, while smaller competitors must pay more heed to the competitive situation. That does not mean the leader can indulge in competitive complacency. Instead, it means that the leader's strongest competitive weapon is continual improvement of customer satisfaction, and the leader gets first choice of strategies most likely to do that. Exhibit 6.7 lists the factors that determine which strategy is most appropriate for the industry leader and the key to sales success for each generic strategy.

Exhibit 6.7 **Generic strategy for the industry leader**

	APPROPRIATE FOR INDUSTRY LEADER WHEN...	KEY TO SALES SUCCESS
Product Leadership	Consumers focused more on meeting their needs than price	Effectiveness (qualitatively better than other products)
Customer Intimacy	Lots of competitors Many dimensions to the product Image/reputation more important than price	Product features, image, trust Solutions
Operational Excellence	Commodities (i.e., small product differences) Major economies of scale or experience curve Strategy is to consolidate the industry	Low price, reliability, consistent quality

For reasons of competitive strategy, which are discussed in detail in Chapter 8, followers should rarely adopt a strategy similar to the leader's. That creates a head-on confrontation, and the follower will lose. Only a large "#2" competitor can sometimes mimic the strategy of the leader and get away with it. Followers must take into account the leader's strategy as well as customer wants. Competitive considerations are more important for followers.

Exhibit 6.8 **Generic strategies in the U.S. beer industry**

Product Leadership ················➤	Imports and micro-brewers (total share <10 percent)
Customer Intimacy ················➤	Anheuser-Busch, Miller, Coors (The Big 3)
Operational Excellence ··········➤	Pabst and other popular priced beers without premium image

---

In the American beer industry examples listed in Exhibit 6.8, leader Anheuser-Busch has adopted a customer intimacy strategy. No. 2 Miller has adopted a similar strategy, as has the third-place competitor, Coors. Anheuser-Busch and Miller have continually made gains at Coors' expense. Coors should have moved to a low-cost strategy years ago by acquiring the strongest popular priced brands (e.g., Stroh, Heileman, and Pabst). Imports and "micro-breweries," following a product leadership strategy, have found a niche where small volumes and very high prices prevail. This niche, however, accounts for less than 10 percent of the American beer market.

Implementing Generic Strategies

Implementing each generic strategy requires a significantly different marketing strategy. Exhibit 6.9 provides guidance on the relative importance of each marketing variable for each generic strategy. Exhibit 6.10 summarizes the skill, resource, and organizational requirements for each generic strategy. The likelihood of success increases as you match the profile for your selected strategy. For example, disaster is likely if you use the tight controls appropriate for an operational excellence strategy in implementing a customer intimacy strategy.

Exhibit 6.9 **Marketing profiles for generic strategies**

	PRODUCT LEADERSHIP	CUSTOMER INTIMACY	OPERATIONAL EXCELLENCE
Costs	Relatively unimportant	Somewhat important	Critically important
Promotion	Critically important Build brand equity	Critically important Build brand equity	Minimal Advertise specials
Price	Relatively unimportant	Low price can hurt image	Critically important
Packaging	Critically important	Critically important	Relatively unimportant
Distribution	Strategy sometimes increases logistics cost	Must reinforce differentiation	Minimize logistics costs

Exhibit 6.10 **Skill, resource, and organizational requirements for generic strategies**

GENERIC STRATEGY	SKILL AND RESOURCE REQUIREMENTS	ORGANIZATIONAL REQUIREMENTS
Product Leadership	Strong R&D and product engineering Understand underlying consumer wants	Strong coordination among R&D, engineering, marketing, operations Subjective measurement and incentives
Customer Intimacy	Strong marketing Reputation for quality Strong distribution channel	Able to attract strong marketing people Able to anticipate market changes Intense commitment to core values
Operational Excellence	Low-cost production and distribution Sustained capital investment Process engineering skills Intense labor supervision	Tight cost controls and control reports Structured organization and responsibilities Incentives based on meeting quantitative targets

Conclusion

The proper generic strategy gives you a defensible position and competitive advantage. Getting it right requires two things:

First, the strategy must be consistent with the external environment—the climate and competitive forces—and with the product or industry life cycle. Second, be alert to change. No strategy is forever—and you must be able to anticipate change and adapt your strategy as necessary. Through a new strategy every seven to 10 years, you can respond to major shifts in forces or to a new PLC stage. In addition, annual planning allows gradual adaptation to smaller external changes. It also allows you to seize "strategic window" opportunities when they present themselves.

Finally, don't be "stuck in the middle." Make sure that everyone in your company understands your generic strategy and acts consistently with the strategy. The right generic strategy for the times helps give you the power to beat competitors in meeting customer wants.

CHAPTER SEVEN

Customer-Driven Strategies

Do you know your customers' wants? Do you have products that satisfy those wants? Do you continuously strive to increase your customers' level of satisfaction?

The answers to those questions are at the heart of customer-driven strategy. You first have to know who your customers are and what they want. Next, you have to develop products and a marketing program that precisely meet those wants. And then you have to keep doing the first two steps better and better so that you continuously improve customer satisfaction. That's the focus of this chapter, which covers the following subjects:

- The "4 Ps"—the four controllable variables for meeting customer wants,
- Segmentation—knowing your customers and their wants,
- Positioning—designing the 4 Ps to precisely satisfy the wants of your target market, and
- Continuous improvement of customer satisfaction.

THE "4 PS" OF MARKETING

Since the mid-1950s, marketing strategies have been organized around four controllable variables: Product, Price, Promotion/advertising, and Place/distribution. The relative importance of these "4 Ps" has changed over time.

From the rise of television in the early 1950s through 1980, the most powerful marketing variable was **Promotion** (more specifically, the television ad). TV allowed major brands to be established in the market place through the convergence of three climate forces: (1) the power of the media (i.e., sight and sound, combined with the dominance of the three TV networks), (2) the mass market (which allowed enough potential demand to make TV affordable), and (3) the purchasing power of "baby boomers," who were young and more responsive to image advertising.

Place/distribution has moved from the least important of the 4 Ps to the most important. The move began with the rise of Wal-Mart and "category killer" retailers in the early 1980s. Suddenly, the right national accounts sales strategy could have a significantly greater impact (and much greater accountability) than the media budget. CEOs began to shift their focus from marketing to sales. The importance of the distribution channel is now accelerating as the Internet threatens older bricks and mortar retailers and traditional distribution channels and sales forces.

Finally, as the Boomers became "40-something," they responded less to glitzy TV spots and more to value, the best combination of **Product** and **Price.** During recessionary periods, low cost strategies from Wal-Mart and Southwest Airlines produce exceptional results. During the prosperous late 1990s, consumers are willing to pay premium prices for unique products. They are flocking to $45,000 Lincoln Navigator sport utility vehicles and paying $2.50 for a cup of Starbucks coffee.

The modern marketing system is based on **segmentation** and **positioning.** By the late 1950s, "segmentation" had emerged as a marketing concept that helped businesses divide the market into groups of customers with similar wants so that they could more effectively target their customers. In 1972, Al Ries and Jack Trout published a series of three articles in *Advertising Age* on "positioning," which they defined as developing an unassailable position in the mind of the consumer.[1] The era of segmentation and positioning had arrived.

This is not to say that segmentation and positioning had never been done. Alfred Sloan of General Motors beat Ford in the 1920s by segmenting the automobile market by price and then positioning a product for each segment. Lee Iacocca used segmentation and positioning to develop the Mustang. However, as late as 1976, Anheuser-Busch had only three brands of beer (versus 18 brands by the late 1980s and over 50 today), and Coca-Cola had only Coke and Tab.

The 4 Ps continue to be the key controllable variables of marketing. Success now, however, requires designing the 4 Ps to exactly meet the wants of each target market.

SEGMENTATION

Segmentation is the demand side of marketing. It precisely identifies customer wants by dividing the market into homogeneous groups—customers with similar wants, attitudes, buying patterns, and responses to marketing variables. Defining the segments is a critical process, and a difficult one. It's the classic problem of taxonomy—classifying "likes" with "likes." If you group all two-legged animals together, ostriches, apes, and corporate executives all belong in the same category. For most purposes, that classification will have somewhat limited usefulness. It's not hard to find a classification in which everyone is alike in some respects. The trick is to find a classification that is useful. Poorly done market segmentation in effect creates random classifications. You're worse off than you were before you started.

Requirements of Good Segments

To be useful, a segment must meet certain requirements, shown in Exhibit 7.1. First, customers that make up the segment must be **identifiable.** That was one of the problems with earlier attempts to segment by personality types.

Second, a segment must be **accessible.** If the customers are dispersed geographically, they'll be harder to reach than those that live close together. Their media habits will have a lot to do with how accessible they are. For instance, if you are trying to reach cardiologists, you'll pay less to reach more of them if they have a specialized journal, compared to an effort to reach them through a general publication that goes to all physicians.

A segment must be **substantial.** Don't define your target market so narrowly that

Exhibit 7.1 **Requirements of good segments**

REQUIREMENTS	EXPLANATION
Identifiable	Be able to classify customers into segments (problem with some personality theories)
Accessible	Be able to reach efficiently using media or sales people
Substantial	Offer adequate sales and profit potential
Homogeneous	Consumers in each segment should be similar in their wants, behavior, and responses to marketing stimuli (the 4 Ps)
Distinctive	Differ in wants from other segments

you will need a 500 percent market share to break even.

A segment must be **homogeneous.** Consumers in each segment should be similar in wants, behavior, and responses to marketing stimuli—the 4 Ps of product, price, place, and promotion. If the segment is not homogeneous, you will have to make compromises in developing the 4 Ps, which will lower the effectiveness of your marketing efforts.

Finally, a segment must be **distinctive.** It must be different enough from other groups to require meaningful differences in strategy.

Customer Characteristics for Segmentation

Marketers have used a variety of categories to identify customer segments, ranging from readily available industry classifications and demographic characteristics to personality types. Some time-honored approaches include copying the competition, based on the assumption that your competitor's customers are also your customers. This is not a good approach. It inevitably makes you a follower. It's appropriate only for a low-market-share competitor with a low-price strategy.

Price is the most pervasive basis of segmentation because it allows customers to select among "high, low, or middle" price points to maximize their value. For example, American beers segmented only on price for years, until Miller introduced a different type of beer, Miller Lite, in the early 1970s. Price segmentation applies to services (restaurants, clothing, credit cards, airline tickets, motels), consumer non-durables (nearly every product category in the supermarket), and consumer durables (from cameras to cars to houses). Two of the most powerful business strategies involve price: using an operational excellence strategy to offer consistent quality at a price competitors can't match (Wal-Mart and Southwest Airlines) and using a high price strategy to differentiate your product (Mercedes and Ralph Lauren).

Other useful analytical classifications are shown in Exhibit 7.2.[2] This Exhibit also makes a critical distinction between **identifiers** and **behaviors.** Marketers frequently use identifiers such as gender/age groups (e.g., males 18-34 years old), partly because their use has become conventional and partly because the data are readily available. However, their use can actually make targeting more difficult. For instance, segmenting an industrial product on four SIC codes, three customer sizes, and five geographic locations does not create a homogeneous segment but instead 60 segments that are not substantial, homogeneous, or distinctive. Identifiers are extremely useful for reaching customers once you have targeted them, but they should not drive your classifications.

Exhibit 7.2 **Customer characteristics for segmentation**

IDENTIFIERS	BEHAVIORS
Industrial markets: • Industry (SIC code) • Size (Sales volume, number of employees) • Profitability, growth, industry position • OEM versus end user • Geography (Country)	**Benefits sought or derived from the product:** • Product application or use occasions • Purchase behavior and loyalty • Volume and frequency of purchase • Switching among brands • Readiness to buy
Consumer markets: • Demographics (Age, sex, race, religion, family size) • Socioeconomic factors (Income, occupation, education) • Psychographics (Lifestyles, interests) • Media habits • Geography (Country; urban, rural)	**Sensitivity to the 4 Ps:** • Product features • Promotion • Price • Place/distribution channel

Source: Adapted and reprinted with the permission of The Free Press, an imprint of Simon & Schuster from Market Driven Strategy by George S. Day. Copyright © 1990 by The Free Press.

Far better are the behavior classifications. After all, it's behavior you're after. Customers purchase not because they happen to be male or 21 years old, but because they seek specific benefits. You want to identify them and then match your products to their wants so they will buy your products. Once you've identified those that will buy, then it is valuable for accessibility that they also fit into a demographic, socioeconomic, or some other identifier group.

A **use-occasion** classification is defined by the manner in which a product or service is used. For instance, within the larger category of shippers of parcels, letters, and documents is a subcategory of those who want rapid delivery. Thus, Federal Express targeted this segment and positioned its service to meet their key need: "If it absolutely, positively has to be there overnight ...."

Among beer drinkers there is a segment of more affluent drinkers who tend to buy beer for special occasions such as social entertaining. Anheuser-Busch successfully targeted this segment for its super-premium beer Michelob: "Weekends were made for Michelob." When Michelob tried also to go after the masses of regular beer drinkers through more convenient cans, price promotions, and the slogan "Put a little weekend in your week," sales declined, even among their original consumers. The new campaign made its positioning fuzzy in everyone's mind.

Purchase behavior segmentation is based on such variables as frequency of purchase, brand loyalty, and readiness to buy. ABB Electric had great success with a customer-driven strategy, the core of which was segmentation based on two of the purchase behaviors—those who were about to make major purchases and who were not loyal to any one manufacturer. By focusing their transformer sales efforts here, and not on those who were already loyal to ABB Electric or to some other manufacturer, they greatly increased sales success. Even as a new competitor going against giants like GE, Westinghouse, and McGraw-Edison, ABB Electric grew market share from 6 percent to 40 percent over a 14-year period.[3]

Purchase behavior has become increasingly easy to track with modern techniques and technologies, such as bar-code scanners. Retailers and consumer products companies increasingly rely on these for segmentation and marketing strategies.

Another way to use purchase behavior to identify and reach customers is to use a "geodemographic" system. The PRIZM system, for instance, has used large quantities of demographic data, primarily from census data, to identify 40 "lifestyles" clusters, which have been given such vivid names as "Pools and Patios," "Gray Power," "Blue-Collar Nursery," and "Shotguns and Pickups."[4]

Each of the 250,000 "census block groups" in the United States has been classified into one or another of these lifestyle segments. Because census block groups are subdivisions of postal ZIP codes, you can also determine the lifestyle composition of each ZIP code. This knowledge of ZIP code lifestyles allows selective and targeted advertising and direct mail campaigns. For instance, national magazines like *Newsweek* and *Time* ship different editions with different advertisements to different ZIP codes. Editions with luxury car advertisements go to "Blue Blood Estates" but not to "Norma Rae-Ville."

You can identify purchase-behavior segments and their locations by doing a small-scale, test-market mailing to all 40 lifestyle clusters. Then, by analyzing the sales response, you can determine the five or ten PRIZM segments for future mailings.

Of the behavior classifications, **benefits sought** works particularly well. "For strategic relevance," writes George Day,[5] "there is no other variable that is as revealing as the benefits the customers are seeking from the product or service." All other variables, both identifiers and behaviors, are retrospective and inferential. They are retrospective in that membership in a class depends on previously defined categories or previously observed behaviors. They are inferential in that you must assume from their membership in a demographic class, for example, that they want your product.

With a benefits sought group, you directly ask the consumers what their current and future wants are. There's no guesswork based on group membership or past behavior. This strength of a benefits group, however, is also its major drawback. Getting the special data you need costs considerably more than the readily available industry data you can use for other variables. The sidebar, "Segmentation Even Works for Small Companies," illustrates the power of segmentation based on benefits sought.

Benefits sought is usually inappropriate for segmenting image products such as soda and cigarettes. Consumers are often unable or unwilling to discuss their wants for such products accurately.

Segmentation Even Works for Very Small Companies

In 1994-95, Jim Fullinwider and I published 14 issues of *The Real World Strategist*, the only subscription strategy newsletter in the U.S. Before launching it, we surveyed 1106 Planning Forum members with the title of director or higher to determine what they would want in a strategy newsletter. This sidebar shows that even very small companies can afford to do market research that leads to a truly customer-driven strategy.

One part of the survey asked the respondents to give their "Desire for Coverage" on a 7-point scale for 19 possible content areas. We used a statistical package to "cluster" the respondents into three groups that were as similar as possible on their Desires. We did not specify the sizes of the segments. Exhibit 7.3 summarizes the results for the nine scales that had high Desires by at least one segment. We developed the names for the three segments to reflect our perception of each segment's overall approach to strategy:

- "Top Management" (39 percent): They average 5.79 or higher on "nuts & bolts" and "case studies" and rate everything else as 4.72 or lower. Their name reflects their pragmatic focus and aversion to theory.
- "Senior Practitioners" (39 percent): Averaged above 5.0 on five different scales related to strategy concepts and coverage of strategy books and articles. Very high involvement with the technical and professional aspects of strategy.
- "Low Involvement" (22 percent): These respondents did not rate any scale above 4.3. Apparently, they belonged to The Planning Forum because their company paid for it and it looked good on their resume. Not a target segment!

If there were other strategy newsletters, we would have had to position ours to exactly meet the needs of Top Management or Senior Practitioners. Being the only strategy newsletter, however, allowed us to examine whether we could effectively target both segments. As shown in Exhibit 7.4, we were able to allocate the eight pages of the newsletter so we included everything that was of high or very high interest to the two segments. Equally important, we excluded everything of below average importance and only included one item of average importance for each segment. *The Real World Strategist* was truly customer-driven! (We closed the newsletter when I was offered the position of editor-in-chief of *Planning Review*, the journal of The Planning Forum).

Exhibit 7.3 **Questionnaire for** *The Real World Strategist* **newsletter***

	DESIRE FOR COVERAGE IN A NEWSLETTER 1=No desire; 7=Strong desire		
	CLUSTER 1 "TOP MANAGEMENT"	CLUSTER 2 "SENIOR PRACTITIONERS"	CLUSTER 3 "LOW INVOLVEMENT"
Strategy concept articles	4.72	5.68	3.48
Strategy development case studies	6.02	4.41	3.89
Strategy implementation case studies	6.17	4.77	4.24
"Strategy book of the month"	3.08	5.11	3.55
"Strategy article of the month"	3.96	5.68	4.07
Book reviews and article summaries	3.42	5.19	4.28
"Nuts & Bolts" for ...			
• Practitioners (e.g., involving top management in planning)	5.79	6.02	3.07
• Top management (e.g., using strategy to lead change)	5.89	5.66	3.21
"The 5 or 10 most useful books and papers" regarding mission statements, implementation, TQM, etc.	4.21	5.49	3.97
Percent of respondents	39%	39%	22%

* A total of 208 respondents (18.8 percent) returned the questionnaire. The results above are based on 135 respondents who completed all of the questionnaire. This table omits 10 scales that had low Desire scores for all three segments.

Exhibit 7.4 **Contents of each issue of** *The Real World Strategist*

		RANKING FOR...	
SUBJECT	PAGES	TOP MANAGEMENT	SENIOR PRACTITIONERS
Strategy development/implementation case study	2	Highest	Average
"Nuts & Bolts" for top management	1+	Very high	Very high
"Nuts & Bolts" for practitioners	1+	Very high	Highest
Strategy concept article (connected to the case study)	2	High	Very high
Summary of "article of the month"	1+	Average	Very high

Targeting Segments

Once you've defined segments that are identifiable, distinctive, substantial, homogeneous, and accessible, you need to rank them in order of their attractiveness and your competitive position in them. To be attractive, a segment must offer adequate sales and profit potential to make targeting it worth your while. You need to look at each segment for its size, rate of growth, and the profit margins you can command. It must also be accessible through a reasonable mix of the marketing 4 Ps.

You should go after only segments where you can compete. Don't target an otherwise attractive segment that is firmly dominated by a strong competitor. As discussed in the next chapter, assaulting an industry leader head-on is generally disastrous. Before you target a new segment, take a look at the current level of customer satisfaction with existing products. If satisfaction is low, you have an opportunity. If high, someone else probably already owns that segment, and you will have a difficult time becoming competitive.

Obviously, you do not want to go after segments where you won't make money. Target those where you will make the greatest return on your marketing investment. The number of segments you target also depends on your industry position. If you are the industry leader, you will want to cover nearly all segments in order to defend your leadership position and to discourage potential competitors from gaining a foothold on your flanks. If you are a follower, you should move into only those attractive and accessible segments not well defended by a competitor.

POSITIONING

Positioning is the supply side of marketing. A fundamental belief of marketing is that you will achieve a dominant market share if you meet customer wants better than competitors. Segmentation divides the total market into large groups with similar wants. Positioning allows you to precisely meet the wants of each segment by using the 4 Ps of marketing.

Perceptual Maps

An extraordinarily powerful positioning tool is the perceptual map, which can tell you what the market looks like **as your customers perceive it.** Hence, you can locate yourself and your competitors in the current market, and you can detect opportunities for positioning yourself to meet unfulfilled customer wants.

Research–Based Perceptual Maps

To understand the explanatory power of a perceptual map, let's look at Exhibit 7.5. This is a **research-based** perceptual map. It was developed by asking a group of consumers to grade their city's seven hospitals according to how well each performed on a list of 16 health-care services.[6] The statistical sorting and correlation behind such a map can be complicated; you'll probably want to farm that process out to professional market researchers and statisticians.[7] But the result—the perceptual map—is a marvelously clear and revealing picture of how customers view the market. This one shows the following:

Exhibit 7.5 **Hospital Perceptual Map**

1. Certain niches are dominated: Hospital C controls the psychiatric segment, B the women's health segment, and G the specialized, higher-risk surgery segment. These hospitals should focus on serving these segments so well that potential competitors detect little opportunity.
2. Hospitals E and F are "community hospitals." If they are geographically close and thus competing for the same customers, they might consider merging. That way, they can maximize economies of scale and eliminate duplication.
3. Hospitals A and D are weak with no unique strengths. If they cannot find new segments where they have something special to offer, they remain vulnerable and a source of market share for the others.
4. In the areas of geriatrics, rehabilitation, and ophthalmology, no one has a strong position. These are "opportunity" segments. Hospitals A and D should consider targeting one of these segments.

Typically, a perceptual map "locates" customer wants and products, services, or suppliers in a two-dimensional space. Unless you have predefined the axes in your customer survey, the statistical analysis does not tell you what the x-axis or the y-axis means. The identification of these dimensions is left to you, based on the information gathered in the study and your own knowledge of the market. In the example in Exhibit 7.5, the x-axis appears to run from "specialties" to "general medicine" and the y-axis from "surgical/physical care" to "mental/psychological care."

Judgment–Based Perceptual Maps

This hospital example is just one kind of perceptual map, one based on hard research data. Another is the judgmental perceptual map. A judgmental map is simply one that is based on your own extensive knowledge and understanding of your market. Quite obviously, you cannot have the same degree of confidence in a judgmental map that you can in a research-based map. But judgmental perceptual maps can be a powerful tool for a variety of positioning issues.

The experience of Office Pavilion, a St. Louis Herman Miller office furniture dealer, illustrates the value of a judgmental perceptual map. Herman Miller had a unique capability in highly flexible modular work stations. Modular flexibility was their strength, providing the greatest value, distinguishing them from the competition, and returning the greatest unit profits. Previously, Office Pavilion had followed a product-driven strategy, perceiving their customers to be on a one-dimensional continuum that precisely paralleled their profitability and product strength, as shown in Exhibit 7.6.

Exhibit 7.6 **Office Pavilion's old scheme**

	DESCRIPTION	PROFITABILITY
Category 1	Customers willing to pay for both style/quality and flexibility	Higher
Category 2	Customers willing to pay for style and quality but not for flexibility	Medium
Category 3	Commodity buyers who are unwilling to pay for either style and quality or flexibility	Lower

With this view of their market, it seemed logical that their strategy should be to convert customers over time from being lowest-price commodity buyers (Category 3) into buyers willing to pay for style and quality (Category 2), and to convert those in turn into buyers willing to pay for flexibility in addition to style and quality (Category 1). This segmentation and positioning scheme simply did not produce the results they had envisioned. They had been trying without much success to move middle- and senior-management consumers in Category 2 (quality and style) to Category 1 (quality and style **plus** flexibility). They developed a perceptual map, shown in Exhibit 7.7, which helped them see that their old segmentation scheme did not reflect actual benefits sought by customers. Modular flexibility is valuable for technical professionals but not for management. Consequently, Office Pavilion redefined customer segments and refocused efforts and resources where they are most effective.

Exhibit 7.7 **Office furniture perceptual map**

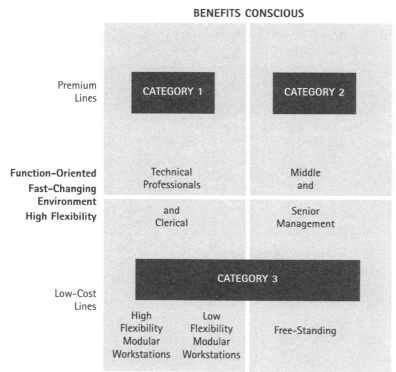

Perceptual Maps and Line Extensions

Judgmental perceptual maps are also useful for resolving the thorny issue of line extensions. Some people argue that you should never resort to line extensions. They believe a line extension almost always erodes the parent brand's market position.[8] But the fact is, many companies have had success with line extensions—Coke and Diet Coke, for example, or Budweiser and Bud Light. The most successful automobile makers have long used line extensions.

When using perceptual maps to position brands and line extensions, you should locate brand families along the most important customer dimension, the x-axis. Line extensions within each brand family then should be positioned along the secondary dimension, the y-axis.

Exhibit 7.8 is a perceptual map of the beer industry. For example, Anheuser-Busch has positioned the Natural, Busch, Budweiser, Michelob, and ultra-premium brand families along the x-axis (price and status). The y-axis (taste and body) allows each brand to have a range of products to meet the customer's desire for calories, alcohol, and taste. The Budweiser brand family, for example, includes Bud Light, Bud Dry, regular Budweiser, and Bud Ice. It no longer offers a Budweiser Malt Liquor, presumably because the high alcohol imagery of malt liquor is inconsistent with the desired positioning of the brand family.

Exhibit 7.8 **Perceptual map for the U.S. beer industry**

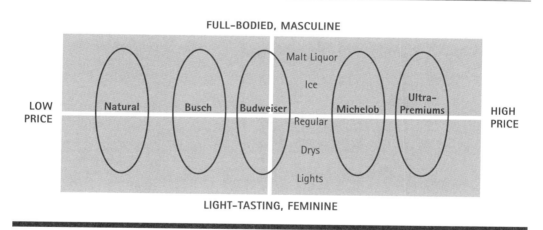

A similar judgmental perceptual map showing brand-family positioning strategy can be developed for other industries. General Motors' brand segmentation strategy began when Alfred Sloan segmented the market in 1923. From then until the first oil shock in 1973, however, nearly all cars were large. Cars had a one-dimensional map based on a price/status continuum. Exhibit 7.9 shows GM's brand families and line extensions in the 1980s. The x-axis is the same as the earlier price/status continuum. But now, GM has extended brands along another dimension, the y-axis, which is size and functionality. The Buick, for example, has become the Buick Park Avenue, Buick LeSabre, Buick Skylark, and so forth.

Exhibit 7.9 **Perceptual map for the U.S. car industry in the 1980s**

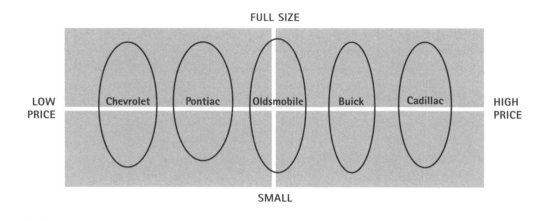

CONTINUOUS IMPROVEMENT OF CUSTOMER SATISFACTION

Customer-driven strategy doesn't stop with segmentation and positioning. In fact, they're just the beginning. The end is customer satisfaction. That's what delivers customer loyalty. A winning customer-driven strategy depends on a devotion to continuous improvement of customer satisfaction. Thus, you need some sort of program for tracking customer satisfaction and buying behavior. Without it, you won't know if your strategy is working.

You have to start with what customers really want. Use customer research to find the relative importance of their 10 to 30 key wants. Then track how well you are meeting those wants compared to your leading competitors. It's important that you use quantitative measurements so that you minimize subjectivity. Every company believes it is **the** high-quality, low-cost supplier—until it quantitatively compares itself to the competition.

One of the best systems for driving continuous improvement of customer satisfaction is the Maritz "Performance Improvement Planner,"[9] developed by Maritz Inc. of St. Louis. With this system, you first compile a list of all the attributes that influence customer satisfaction, such as price, after-sale service, courtesy of the sales force, and convenience of locations. Next, you obtain the following information from customers about each attribute: (1) How **important** is this attribute to them? and (2) How **satisfied** are they with your performance on this attribute? The results are plotted on the matrix shown in Exhibit 7.10.

Exhibit 7.10 **Maritz customer satisfaction**

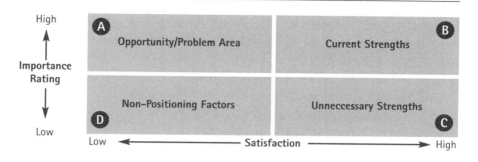

The objective is to increase satisfaction with your company's performance on those attributes customers consider important. If an attribute is high in importance and your customers are highly satisfied (Quadrant B), then it's a critical strength you must maintain. You may not need to invest more in it, but be sure to support it at its current level. If, however, customers are dissatisfied with your performance on an important attribute (Quadrant A), you are vulnerable to a competitor who does this better than you. The attribute is an "opportunity" that needs urgent attention.

If an attribute is not important to customers, you should use few resources supporting it. Since customers don't really care about it, a low level of satisfaction (Quadrant D) shouldn't be important to you. If customers are highly satisfied with an unimportant attribute (Quadrant C), you could safely move some of the resources you expend here to help improve performance on attributes in Quadrant A. But, be careful. Sometimes customers elevate the importance of an attribute in their own minds if they see too much or too quick an erosion of performance. Moreover, they might see slippage on that attribute as a reflection of a general decline in performance that affects other attributes they consider more important. Seek "excellence" on the key measures and "acceptable" on the unimportant measures.

With this analysis in hand, the Maritz customer satisfaction program proceeds as follows:

Step 1: Determine the relative importance of key customer wants.

Step 2: Track your performance on each key want compared to your competitors' performance. This quantitative measure is critical to objectivity.

Step 3: Assign responsibility for improving each dimension. If no one is accountable, no one will make it happen.

Step 4: Develop quantitative goals, a time table for achievement, action plans, and a budget. This creates top-down and bottom-up commitments and agreement on a plan for improvement.

Step 5: Track performance versus plan and reward accordingly.

Steps 3, 4, and 5 are discussed in more detail in Chapter 11.

The key to the satisfaction of final consumers often lies in superior performance by your distributors, store managers, salesmen, and other employees. Maritz has also developed the Excellence® System for continuous improvement of the performance of these key groups.

The Excellence® process has both strong similarities to and important differences from the Performance Improvement Planner. The difference is that the Excellence® criteria are designed by your most outstanding 10 or 20 store managers (or sales people or distributors). They first identify the 25 to 50 "Keys to Excellence" ("Best Practices") and then determine the relative importance of each by allocating 1,000 possible total points. The most important element, for instance, may receive a maximum of 75 points, the next most important 60 points, the next 50 points, and so on. Then, within its maximum number of points, each element is rated by level of performance. The most important element, with its maximum of 75 points, may receive 75 for excellent, 50 for good, and only 25 for adequate performance.

In a traditional sales contest, participants compete against each other and only a limited number can win a trip to the Caribbean, for example. With the Excellence® program, the participants compete only against themselves according to a set of objective standards. For example, they may receive bronze, silver, or gold awards if they receive over 500, 650, or 800 points. They can still earn awards, such as the Caribbean vacation, but now everybody is a potential winner. And if they win, you win.

Continuous improvement of customer satisfaction is the final step in effective customer-driven strategy. Quantitatively measured and verified, a continuous improvement program keeps customer-driven strategy fresh and relevant.

To make sure your customer-satisfaction system leads to constant incremental improvement, involve your entire organization. Provide performance feedback to everyone. Assign responsibility. Work with your managers to reach agreement on customer satisfaction objectives. Give them authority. Have them develop action programs that will achieve these objectives. Finally, reward performance. Tie pay, promotion, recognition, and non-cash awards to attainment of objectives.

Being "Customer-Driven" Can Lead to Disaster

"Be customer-driven!" If these words are the marketing gospel of the 1990s, Harvard professor Clay Christensen is committing heresy. His book, *The Innovator's Dilemma*,[10] shows when being superbly customer-driven can lead to corporate disaster.

Usually, industry leaders have huge advantages. Economies of scale and customer relationships allow industry leaders to stay in the lead. They can afford to invest in the current technology, continue to provide superior value, and widen their lead. Even technological breakthroughs often help the industry leader. Typically, customers want faster, bigger, more powerful products. Such new products have higher margins. Hence, industry leaders often perform incredible feats to simultaneously satisfy customers and increase margins. More powerful technologies allow leaders to thrive.

Leaders fail when the new technology is simpler, less powerful, and less expensive. Christensen calls these "disruptive technologies." Computer disk drives are a classic example. Leadership changed with each technology. Control Data was the industry leader for 14-inch disk drives for mainframes. Priam was the leader for 8-inch drives, Seagate for 5.25-inch drives, and Conner and Quantum for 3.5-inch drives.

The dynamics of this constantly shifting industry leadership are simple and clear. In the late 1970s, disk drives were only used on mainframe computers. They were 14-inches in diameter, held over 200 megabytes (MB), and had 50 percent profit margins. Both customers and management were angry when R&D developed 8-inch drives with 10 MB capacity. Customers said they needed more capacity, not 95 percent less. Management was upset because R&D was wasting time on products customers didn't want. Moreover, the poor price-performance ratio led to profit margins of only 35 percent. The R&D people left and eventually sold their 8-inch drives to Digital and other mini-computer companies. Because the capacity of 8-inch drives increased 40 percent annually, they took over the mainframe disk business by the late 1980s.

Around 1980, the story was repeated for 5.25-inch drives. R&D people figured out how to get 10 MB on a 5.25-inch drive. The mini-computer customers said they needed more capacity, not less. Management said it was absurd to waste time developing products with only a 25 percent profit margin that customers didn't want. The R&D people left, formed Seagate, and sold their small drives to PC companies. The capacity of the 5.25-inch drives increased 50 percent annually. By 1988, they replaced the 8-inch drives on mini-computers. Later, the same cycle was played out for 3.5-inch drives for laptops, with Conner replacing Seagate.

The same dynamics have transformed a dozen other industries. Steel minimills such as Nucor initially had such low quality that they could only make rebar, which had profit margins of only 8 percent. The integrated steel mills never responded effectively as minimills slowly improved their quality and took over other steel bars and rods, then structural steel, and are now targeting sheet steel. Similarly, with its Target stores, Dayton Hudson was the only department store giant to respond effectively to Kmart, Wal-Mart, and other discounters. The Swiss developed the first quartz watch but saw the number of people making watches fall 54 percent in the 1970s before responding effectively with Swatch.

The dynamics that allow disruptive technologies to change industry leadership are constant:

- Current customers reject the new technology because it is less powerful.
- Management rejects the innovation because margins are lower, current customers aren't interested, and initial volumes are small.
- New markets like it because it is cheaper, smaller, and simpler.
- The new technology eventually takes over because power requirements of users

increase much slower than the power of the new technology.

How can leaders prevent disaster from disruptive technologies? The answer is what Columbia University professor Michael Tushman calls an "ambidextrous organization." Create a separate group within the firm—with radically different cost structures, values, and culture—with authority and responsibility for developing and growing the new technology.

The business lessons of being too customer-driven extend beyond technology companies. Companies of **all** types face disaster from focusing on current customers and neglecting potential customers. Cadillac, for example, has had strong customer satisfaction scores from its current customers because it was so responsive to their desire for big cars with soft rides. But its future is clouded as current customers age and die and most younger customers find Cadillac irrelevant.

Disaster can be avoided. Budweiser has been incredibly successful since 1876 in attracting new customers while maintaining loyalty with current customers. Currently, its ads featuring frogs and lizards appeal to Generation X while Clydesdales and "heritage" ads featuring August Busch III and August Busch IV appeal to Boomers.

So what should be the marketing gospel for the 2000s? Be customer-driven. But also be driven by potential customers. Focus on what customers will want tomorrow as well as today.

Conclusion

Meeting customer wants is ultimately the only reason businesses exist. Doing it successfully requires at least the following:

- Profound knowledge of your customers,
- Accurate segmentation of your market,
- Selecting segments to target consistent with your capabilities,
- Using the 4 Ps to position your products in the market and offer superior value to your target customers, and
- A continuous improvement process to track and increase customer satisfaction.

Meeting customer wants better than competitors is the reason for a customer-driven strategy and critical for winning in today's competitive world. Once you get your customer-driven strategy right, you should then worry about your competitors. It's not enough for you to have great products. Customers must also believe your products provide greater value than competitive products. So if you are not worrying about your competitors, you had better start now. That's the subject of the next chapter.

CHAPTER EIGHT

Competitor-Driven Strategies

A solid customer-driven strategy is no longer enough. You also have to do a better job than your competitors of satisfying your customers. It's necessary to be both customer-driven and competitor-driven. Your business strategy must take into account the market positions and strategies of your competitors.

The modern era of competitive strategy began with the 1980 publication of Michael Porter's *Competitive Strategy*[1], which provided the broad framework for static strategic thinking. It led to a wave of breakthrough books focused only on competitive strategy.

The mid-1980s examined business warfare (cell A in Exhibit 8.1). Elting[2] showed how the laws of war that are taught at military academies around the world apply to business. *Marketing Warfare*[3] by Trout and Ries popularized the concept. Phil Kotler[4] gave it academic respectability. But peace is a lot more profitable than war. Axelrod[5] did the definitive research on how to move from the devastating lose-lose trench warfare of promoter's dilemma to peace through disciplined execution of a tit-for-tat strategy (cell B).

Exhibit 8.1 **A framework for competitive strategy**

	STATIC/EQUILIBRIUM MID–1980s	DYNAMIC/DISEQUILIBRIUM CURRENTLY
War: Required to achieve leadership	**A.** The laws of war taught at military academies	**C.** Strategic intent
Peace: More profitable	**B.** Tit-for-tat approach to promoter's dilemma	**D.** Alliances and co-opetition

The new era of dynamic approaches to competitive strategy began with Prahalad and Hamel's "Strategic Intent"[6] article, which showed that small companies with the right vision and strategy can out-innovate and beat big companies. Microsoft proved the point by moving from 11 employees in 1978 to becoming the most valuable company in the world (cell C).

The 1990s witnessed a revolution as businesses discovered that combining core competencies through alliances and joint ventures can produce superior value to customers and superior profits for themselves. *Co-opetition*[7] showed how Microsoft and Intel were "complementors:" success and innovation by one benefits the other. Similarly, the dominance of the Wintel "ecology" of Microsoft Windows and Intel microprocessors led academics to move the focus of industry analysis from the individual firm to the alliance of firms[8] (cell D).

Clearly, your strategy must take your competitors into account. This chapter takes you through these four stages of competitive strategy and shows how you can use these concepts for your specific competitive situation:

- The basics of business warfare,

- Strategic intent, a dynamic approach to business warfare that can lead to changes in industry leadership,
- How the leader can discourage war and maintain peace in a static environment, and
- Alliances and "co-opetition" in dynamic environments.

THE BASICS OF BUSINESS WARFARE

Obviously, the battlefield, the enemy, and the weapons of military conflict differ from those of business competition. Yet, it's remarkable the degree to which similar strategies lead to similar outcomes—victory or defeat. Business warfare provides a framework for determining how your company should seek competitive advantage. But don't carry the warfare metaphor too far. Competition among businesses, like competition among nations, should not always mean a state of war.

Success in business competition springs less from a theory of war than it does from a theory of war and peace. War in the short term is less profitable than peace and should not be an end in itself. Sir Basil Liddell Hart put it this way: "The object in war is to achieve a better state of peace." In business, the "better state of peace" is increased long-term profitability since that, not the defeat of your competitor, is the object of business. Thus, you should undertake war only for longer-term strategic reasons, with peace as your objective and peaceful competition the expected norm.

The Principles of War

Over the centuries, professional military strategists have developed a list of universal and essential principles of warfare.[9] Just as the 4 Ps of marketing are the foundation for customer-driven strategy, these laws of war are the foundation for competitor-driven strategy. While the 4 Ps were developed in the mass market era, the key to success in today's segmentation and positioning era is developing the 4 Ps to provide superior value **to each target segment.** Similarly, the new approaches to competitive strategy focus on how to avoid lose-lose competitive situations. But the principles of war still determine which company will win when facing a specific competitive situation.

The following principles of war are taught at military academies around the world. The first eight have been taught at West Point since 1921. Simplicity was added more recently. The last two laws are taught in the United Kingdom and some other countries but are not part of U.S. military doctrine. Most corporate disasters result from breaking these principles of war. Use them as a check list to make sure your strategy doesn't have the odds stacked against it.

1. **The objective.** The objective must be a clear, conclusive, and obtainable result. Otherwise, there is no basis for going to war. Likewise for a company,

the objective must be big enough and profitable enough to risk the struggle. A company can accomplish amazing results with the right BHAG (Big, Hairy, Achievable Goal) if it grabs people in the gut and gets them to work together to 100 percent of their ability.

2. **The offense.** Victory requires offensive action. Defensive operations only prevent defeat. To reverse a cliché, the best defense is a good offense. Seize the initiative and attack a market segment not well defended by your competitor. If you are a small company, this means dominating a small niche.

3. **Unity of command.** Forces must be under one commander with full authority and responsibility. Napoleon said, "It is better to have one incompetent general than two good ones." Clear responsibilities allow everyone to focus on meeting customer wants better than your competitor. The alternative is an internal focus that leads to political infighting.

4. **Mass.** Victory goes to the army with superior forces at the point of contact. This is the key law of marketing today. Focus your attack as narrowly as possible so you offer superior value based on the key wants of your target customers. You will increase your market share in the niche (and eventually dominate it) if (1) you offer superior value and (2) communicate that value effectively.

5. **Economy of force.** Allocate only the essential minimum of forces to areas of secondary importance. For business, this means keeping costs at a minimum while allocating resources where they will be most effective. Otherwise, "lean and mean" competitors will exploit your high costs and correspondingly high prices.

6. **Maneuver.** Forces must be deployed so they come together in the right place at the right time. Internally, it requires coordination and communication. Externally, it means integrating the 4 Ps of marketing and all other tactics so they work together smoothly.

7. **Surprise.** If you strike your enemy at a time or a place, or in a way he does not expect, you can often win your objective before the enemy even reacts. Speed to market and quick response systems are key sources of competitive advantage for many companies today.

8. **Security.** Surprise cannot exist without security. During war, an army must safeguard its own intentions and plans from the enemy. In business, security for the market leader means providing superior customer value and aggressively countering all competitive challenges. For the smaller company, it means keeping your intentions quiet lest they stir the leaders to action. Security through strength is also important in preserving peace. Countries seldom attack a strong foe. Similarly, companies seldom enter markets in which a strong competitor is doing an excellent job of meeting customer wants.

9. **Simplicity.** Objectives, strategies, and plans should be clear, concise, and simple. Simplicity keeps forces motivated, focused, and unified. Complex business strategies don't work. They don't motivate people, and the likelihood of good execution declines with complexity.

10. **Motivation.** Pride in capabilities and performance compensates for many weaknesses in other areas. Especially today, motivated people win wars. Employees who are well led, well trained, and confident in their strategies and capabilities achieve victory.

11. **Administration.** An army must be efficiently supplied and administered so total attention and resources are focused on the battle at hand. In business today, this means eliminating bureaucratic organization structures. Instead, information systems and incentives must create an environment that encourages people at all levels to sense and respond effectively to threats and opportunities.

Taken together, these principles of war can be stated this way: Hit the other guy as quickly as you can, as hard as you can, where it hurts him the most, when he isn't looking.

USING "STRATEGIC INTENT" TO GAIN INDUSTRY LEADERSHIP

Business war strategies discussed in the previous section are responses to current market and industry conditions. The discussion implicitly assumes that your strategy should have "strategic fit" with those conditions. However, gaining industry leadership sometimes requires truly long-term vision that transcends today's competitive situation. The dynamic concept of "strategic intent"[10] is more relevant than the static one of "strategic fit" to the small fry who wants to become a big fish—that is, to a small firm whose ambitions greatly exceed its current resources and industry position.

Indeed, one of the most important changes in strategic thinking in the 1990s was the movement towards dynamic strategies. The laws of war are still important (just as the 4 Ps of marketing are still relevant today because you must offer superior value in each niche). In addition to the static concepts, however, successful companies must move faster than their competitors. Exhibit 8.2 compares strategic fit with strategic intent.

Competitive Strategy Based on Strategic Intent

Strategic intent, as Gary Hamel and C. K. Prahalad define it, is the single-minded drive of companies "with ambitions out of all proportion to their resources" to become industry leaders over the long run. Strategic intent focuses on an ultimate goal, and it takes

---

Exhibit 8.2 **Comparison of "strategic fit" and "strategic intent"**

ISSUE	"STRATEGIC FIT"	"STRATEGIC INTENT"
Strategic approach	Trim ambitions to match available resources	Leverage resources to reach seemingly unattainable goals
How to achieve relative advantage	Search for advantages that are inherently sustainable	Accelerate organizational learning to outpace competitors in building new advantages
Competing against larger competitors	Search for niches or simply don't challenge the leader	Seek new rules to reduce leader's advantages
Corporate strategy	Allocate resources to independent SBUs	Invest in core competencies to produce synergy

advantage of all marketplace relationships, both warlike and peaceful. Just as most governments rely on diplomacy and economic policy more than on warfare to achieve national advantage, so should it be with a small company pursuing strategic intent. Strategy, then, should focus on developing your potential and avoiding direct confrontation with industry leaders.

But while it normally shuns direct war, strategic intent is profoundly competitor-driven. Hamel and Prahalad state that a company with the long-term goal of overtaking a much larger competitor "must fundamentally change the game in ways that disadvantage incumbents—devising novel approaches to market entry, advantage building, and competitive warfare." For smart competitors, "the goal is not competitive imitation but competitive innovation."

Hamel and Prahalad provide four approaches to competitive innovation:
1. Change the rules of engagement,
2. Attack undefended segments,
3. Compete through collaboration, and
4. Build layers of advantage.

Change the Rules

Don't fight the war on the leader's turf or with the leader's rules. By the 1980s, the name "Xerox" had become virtually synonymous with the word "photocopy" because Xerox so thoroughly dominated that market. Xerox had used its dominance to build huge barriers to entry in high-volume, high-quality copiers for big businesses. As Hamel and Prahalad put it, Xerox had built high barriers to "imitation." A frontal assault by any competitor would have been disastrous. But by changing the rules, Savin found a lower barrier point of entry into the photocopier market.[11]

Here's how Savin did it. First, Savin analyzed each step in the copier value chain and defined the Xerox advantage. Then Savin used those same steps of the value chain to develop a strategy that would give it a competitive advantage. That turned out to be a cost-focus strategy aimed at low-volume users—low initial cost, medium quality, and high reliability. Savin had defined a new segment on the periphery of the previously defined photocopier market.

Attack Undefended Segments

Look for not only *undefended* but also previously *undefined* market segments that can provide "an uncontested profit sanctuary" from which to launch later attacks.[12] A key to success with this approach is for you to position yourself close enough to the market leaders to have high-volume potential but sufficiently distant from their "served market" so that the leaders are reluctant to counterattack. In fact, bound by their conventional wisdom, the leaders sometimes do not even recognize how much of a potential threat you pose.

In this situation, appearances count. Loudly announcing your strategic intent to the world will only mobilize your competitors into action. Keep them ignorant of the threat you pose. Be like the television detective Columbo. His rumpled appearance and bumbling behavior made the bad guy feel superior to this obviously incompetent cop. The villain invariably let his guard down, and Columbo always won in the end.

The entry of Japanese competitors into the American automobile market was a classic case of attacking an undefended segment. The Japanese found a "profit sanctuary" in the low-price segment of the market. Detroit failed to counter them aggressively because doing so would have meant cannibalizing sales of their high-margin, high-volume cars. Besides, Americans wouldn't buy small economy cars, according to Detroit's conventional wisdom. From this base, the Japanese were able to develop core competencies and add on layers of advantage for a subsequent expanded assault on Detroit.

The disruptive technologies sidebar on page 110 elaborates on how attacking a specific type of under-defended flank is a major reason why industry leaders fail.

Compete through Collaboration

Collaboration is one of the most subtle means of winning without fighting. Joint ventures and OEM (original equipment manufacturing) arrangements are two forms of collaboration Japanese companies have used to become competitive and eventually achieve superiority in U.S. markets. In consumer electronics, Japanese companies used their initial low labor-cost advantage to make televisions for American companies at prices the American companies couldn't begin to match. The Japanese then offered to manufacture "next generation" products like VCRs, camcorders, and CD players for the Americans.[13]

The Japanese destroyed the U.S. consumer electronics industry this way. The high-volume manufacturing that resulted from these arrangements let them build experience, further reduce costs, and develop quality and reliability. Furthermore, they preempted the U.S. companies in technology development, since they were the ones making the advanced "next generation" products.

Of course, Americans have as much of an opportunity to exploit alliances and joint ventures as the Japanese. The advantage goes to the partner more willing to learn, the one less hidebound and more innovative. The 1990s saw explosive growth of partnering by U.S. firms as they focused on their own core competencies:

- Outsourcing of information systems by large firms is becoming the rule rather than the exception,
- The Big 3 car companies have reduced the number of suppliers by over 80 percent and required that their suppliers meet more challenging goals for cost, quality, and innovation than the Big 3 could internally, and
- Temporary joint ventures by large construction firms combine strengths and reduce risks on one project while they are competitors in other markets.

Build Layers of Advantage

Initially, a company must exploit whatever competitive advantage it has. Many companies stop there, but one with strategic intent takes a dynamic approach to competitive advantage, building layer upon layer of advantage as it moves from less defensible advantages like low labor costs to more defensible ones like global brands.

Again, take the case of Japanese television manufacturers. Their initial advantage was low labor costs. Competing on price, they became by the late 1960s the largest maker of black-and-white televisions. The resulting economies of scale allowed them to further consolidate their low-cost advantage. Next, they added new layers of advantage—quality and reliability—by moving into color televisions and becoming manufacturers for private American and European labels. Greater volumes allowed them to invest in new world-scale plants, further strengthening quality manufacturing and lowering costs through process improvements.

Knowing their cost advantage to be vulnerable to rising labor costs in Japan, monetary exchange rates, and international trade policy, the Japanese added an even stronger and more defensible advantage—their own global brands. Finally, they added a broad range of products to their lines. At that point, it was likely that the Japanese would dominate the U.S. television market. They had global brands with superior price, quality, reliability, and product choice, and they had preempted the technological lead through their manufacturing partnerships with the Americans.

Avoiding Surrender to Strategic Intent

Strategic intent provides guidance for the small company that wants to achieve industry leadership. This section provides guidance to the 900 pound gorilla that wants to retain industry leadership.

The key to profitability is to dominate your niche. Whether the market was a broad industry worldwide or a narrow regional niche, unseating the leader was a rare event through 1970. Yet, with increasing frequency over the last three decades, firms with superior strategic intent have toppled industry leaders. The lesson for the industry leader is simple: Be paranoid! Look at each of your competitors as having a BHAG to unseat you. In many industries that may take the 20 years that it took Wal-Mart to pass Sears. But information technology is collapsing the time required. To look at how well prepared you are to meet such a competitive challenge, ask yourself these questions:

- Do I have a long-term vision and am I developing the core competencies necessary to realize that vision?
- Does every person in my organization have clear performance measures and incentives? Do they have the skills and motivation to do their share in maintaining leadership? Are they moving faster and out-innovating our competitors?
- Do we understand the key wants of each customer niche? Do we offer superior value versus competitors to each customer niche? Are we expanding our lead in customer value over time?
- Do we aggressively exploit our opportunities and respond to challenges—not just from direct competitors but also from substitute products and potential entrants on the periphery of our market?

If you can objectively answer "yes" to these questions, you are prepared to fend off challengers armed with strategic intent.

This exercise should also serve as a warning to small companies excited about the concept of strategic intent. Many, but certainly not all, big companies are also well aware of the concept. Some will not only respond to a minor challenge, but also respond out of all proportion to the challenge. The reason is not just that they want you to back off. They also want to send a clear message to other potential challengers by crushing you: "Attacking us is a prescription for disaster."

HOW THE LEADER CAN DISCOURAGE WAR AND MAINTAIN PEACE

Blessed are the peacemakers—especially the industry leaders in mature markets. Too often, companies forget that the objective of business is to grow value. Instead, by default, they inappropriately adopt the military or sports goal of achieving victory.

- Mature industry after mature industry has gone through periods of devastating price wars. This section shows how companies in mature, consolidated industries facing strong competitors can avoid devastating price wars. This section applies, for example, to Coke versus Pepsi, the beer wars of the 1990s, airline price wars, and cars.
- Yet, the strategic intent of achieving victory makes sense if you have the potential of offering truly superior value and want to dramatically increase your market share. Wal-Mart, Microsoft, Southwest Airlines, and Amazon.com are

past and current examples of companies that would have no interest in this section. They clearly saw that war (holding prices below the level that maximizes short-term profits) would allow them to establish a dominant position and superior long-term profitability.

The Product Life Cycle and Warfare

In certain phases of a product's life cycle, competition can be so intense that profits of the industry leader fall below acceptable norms and smaller companies perish. Typically, warfare in these phases is conducted on price. Exhibit 8.3 summarizes the likelihood of business warfare during each stage of the product life cycle.

Exhibit 8.3 **Potential for business warfare during the product life cycle**

STAGE	PRICE	PRODUCT/ADVERTISING	POTENTIAL FOR WAR
Introduction	High to recoup costs	Little variety; high advertising	Very low
Growth	High demand leads to strong margins	Product variety to increase industry sales	Low; compete on product attributes
Early Maturity	"Shakeout" leads to low margins	Product proliferation to obtain marginal sales	High likelihood of war instigated by industry leaders
Late Maturity/ Decline	Pricing depends on industry strategy and structure	Reduce product line and ads to reduce costs	Warfare, instigated by followers, can be influenced by the industry leader

In the introductory stage, the likelihood of war is low. The company that developed and introduced the product has a near-monopoly. Without direct competition, the company sells the product more on benefits than on price. As costs decline, the manufacturer improves margins while reducing price to discourage the entry of competitors and to expand the market.

Margins are high during the growth stage. As the industry expands and cumulative volume grows, economies of scale and the experience curve drive down costs while margins remain high. The high margins now begin to attract competitors, but warfare is unlikely as long as the market grows faster than capacity.

The first wars take place in early maturity, as the industry leader instigates a "shakeout." High margins attract more and more competitors, who often obtain sales through lower price. The leader sees its market share eroding. To maintain leadership and discourage potential industry entrants, the leader then precipitates a short-term price war. Prices plunge below the marginal cost of small inefficient manufacturers, forcing them to exit the industry. Lower prices also increase industry sales, thereby giving the survivors a larger share of a larger pie. Late maturity can be peaceful so long as the leader does a good job of meeting customer wants and doesn't price too high.

However, the leader too often succumbs to temptation: Economies of scale and barriers to entry tempt the leader to keep prices high and margins growing.

Eventually, margins get so high that a current competitor or a new entrant starts a war with a low-price strategy and goes after the leader's market share. This time, the competitor who starts the war is prepared to hang in there. Since the market is fully penetrated, lower prices do not greatly increase volume. Furthermore, costs don't decline much when the industry is this far out on the experience curve. The result is inevitable: Price wars in late maturity lead directly to lower margins.

As the product evolves toward the commodity or decline phase, the low-price strategy dominates. The degree of war during this phase is influenced by the behaviors learned during late maturity. Industries that have developed a culture of war will continue to have poor margins. Those that have developed less aggressive cultures will do better. It's critical, then, that leaders learn how to influence the length and depth of wars during late maturity. There is a strategy, based on lessons learned from the "Price Promoter's Dilemma," that the leader can use to discourage war and to enforce peace.

The Price Promoter's Dilemma

Price competition takes many forms—automobile rebates and airline price wars, for example. Everyone is also familiar with price promotions and coupons from consumer packaged goods companies. Exhibit 8.4 shows the moves available to competitors in the price promotion game, along with the consequences of those moves. The first number in each cell represents the profit for Company #1 and the second number represents the profit for Company #2; only the relative values of the numbers are important.

Exhibit 8.4 **Discouraging war and encouraging peace: the dilemma of price promotion**

		COMPANY 2	
		LOW PROMOTION (COOPERATE)	HIGH PROMOTION (DEFECT)
COMPANY 1	LOW PROMOTION (COOPORATE)	+5, +5	−10, +10
	HIGH PROMOTION (DEFECT)	+10, −10	−5, −5

Consider the following characteristics of the various price promotion situations:
1. When both companies adopt a "cooperative" strategy of low price promotion, each has a good profit of 5 units.
2. Either company can increase its profits by 5 units (from +5 to +10) if it defects to a high promotion strategy and the other stays with the low promotion strat-

egy. Note, however, that this move lowers the competitor's profits by 15 units (from +5 to -10).

3. Finally, if one company defects from the low promotion strategy to the high promotion one, the other also has an incentive to adopt a high promotion strategy since it can reduce its losses from -10 to -5.

And that's the dilemma:

- On the one hand, both companies have higher profits in a "low-low" than in a "high-high" promotion environment. Peace is more profitable than war.
- On the other, each company has an incentive to go to war by defecting to the high promotion strategy, regardless of the competitor's strategy—since +10 is greater than +5 and -5 is greater than -10.

Hence, high promotion is the equilibrium, although it produces much lower profits for everyone. Indeed, analysis of scanner data by Information Resources Inc. shows that only 16 percent of trade promotions are profitable.

How can you break out of this unprofitable high-promotion equilibrium? The answer lies in a simple strategy, called "Tit for Tat," a demonstrated means of encouraging competitors to cooperate in a low-promotion strategy. Robert Axelrod[14] coordinated two promoter's dilemma competitions. In each round, leading game theorists submitted computer programs for their strategies for playing promoter's dilemma.

Fourteen people participated in Round 1. Each program played a series of 200 games with every other program. After Axelrod circulated the results of Round 1, 62 participants submitted programs for Round 2. This time, a random number of games, averaging 289, were played between each pair of contestants, for an average of 17,629 games for each program (289 x 61). In each round, Tit for Tat was the simplest of all the strategies submitted. Tit for Tat has just two rules:

1. Start off cooperating; adopt a low promotion strategy.
2. Do whatever your competitor did on the last move—cooperate if he cooperated; defect if he defected. Tit for Tat immediately rewards competitors who cooperate and punishes those who defect, thereby encouraging cooperative behavior from your competitors.

In both rounds, the measure of effectiveness was the total payoff over the entire number of games. Tit for Tat was the winning strategy for both rounds. However, Tit for Tat **lost or tied** each series of games. You don't "win" with Tit for Tat, if "winning" means coming out ahead of your competitor in any specific engagement.

Keep in mind that your objective with Tit for Tat, as it should be with all business warfare, is not to "defeat" your competitors; rather it is to maximize your own profits. Tit for Tat wins in the long run by evoking cooperative behavior from competitors. Tit for Tat is attractive for several other reasons:

- It's simple for the competitor to understand.
- It's "nice." You never defect first.
- It's immediately forgiving. You move back to the cooperate position on the

very next move after your competitor does.

- There is no need to keep your strategy secret. Tit for Tat is the optimal strategy against Tit for Tat itself.

However, don't apply Tit for Tat mindlessly. A danger with Tit for Tat is that it can spiral out of control. Competitors tend to perceive others' actions as more aggressive than their own—a distortion often made worse by the tendency of sales people to exaggerate threats from the competition. So, if you use Tit for Tat, respond with less that a 100 percent "tit" for your competitors' "tats." You should also consider quantitative monitoring of competitors' actions, so that your perceptions are checked against reality.

Tit for Tat is not a strategy for all seasons. It makes most sense during late maturity, when opportunities for increasing margins, best achieved with peace, are greater than they are for increasing volume, which can be achieved through war. Furthermore, intense competition can sometimes be good for you. Even in mature industries, the opportunity for volume gains sometimes exists. In that case, tough competition will lead to lower prices, higher quality, the demise of weak competitors, and the probability of market share gains for you.

Competition can be good for you in another way. Michael Porter[15] has found that extreme domestic competition leads to superior international performance. Companies that do well financially through "gentlemanly" competition at home tend not to be competitive internationally. Since global competition in every industry is more and more the norm, the peace fostered by Tit for Tat may weaken your ability to compete in the long run.

ALLIANCES AND "CO-OPETITION"

The power of alliances is illustrated by three strategies from the early days of personal computers.[16] Tandy tried to retain all of the profits from hardware and software sales, and follow-up service through its Radio Shack stores. Apple took a middle road. It controlled the computer design and operating system but encouraged independent software publishers, retailers, and training companies. IBM offered a completely open system by purchasing its central processor from Intel and its operating system from Microsoft.

Tandy's tight controls led to a fast start and out-sold Apple two to one in 1979. By 1982, however, Apple had sales of $583 million and a 25 percent lead over Tandy. The IBM with its open architecture, however, was the big winner. Despite a late introduction in 1981, by 1986 it reached industry leadership with sales of $5.65 billion. Eventually, it achieved dominance with a 90 percent market share.

The IBM PC offers two lessons. First, as we detail in this section, establishing a large number of partners offers superior potential. Second, as IBM learned too late, it's important to be the lead partner. Microsoft and Intel have achieved the first and third highest market capitalizations in the world by becoming the lead partners in PCs. IBM has lost money on its PCs for the last 10 years.

Micro-economics and much of the popular business press continue to focus on the battle for market share between individual companies. Many companies, however, have found that competition based on alliances provides a superior way to increase sales and profitability. Exhibit 8.5 shows that market structure is now two-dimensional: the traditional dimension of "number of competitors" and the new dimension of number of firms per competitor.[17] Let's look at why alliance strategies can add value in both static and dynamic environments.

Exhibit 8.5 **Alliances add a second dimension to market structure**

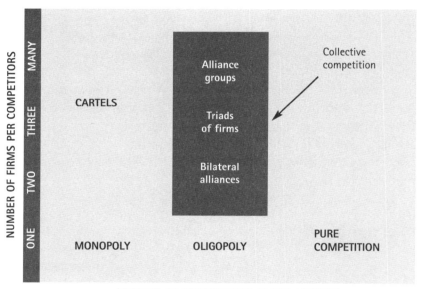

Alliance groups

Collective competition

CARTELS

Triads of firms

Bilateral alliances

MONOPOLY   OLIGOPOLY   PURE COMPETITION

NUMBER OF FIRMS PER COMPETITORS

ONE   TWO   THREE   MANY

NUMBER OF COMPETITORS IN THE MARKET

Alliances in Static Environments

Adam Smith's "division of labor" provides the basic rationale for alliances in a static environment.[18] Specialization leads to superior efficiency, which is why "focus" is one of the most important words in strategy today.

- In the early 1970s, Coors was the dominant brewer in the West. It also made all of its own cans. For a consumer product company of its size to vertically integrate into can manufacturing makes little sense. By 1990, it was spending 25 cents a case above the market price for its cans. Similarly, the Big 3 car companies are trying to spin off their parts manufacturing businesses so they can focus on their core competencies in designing and assembling cars.

- For small retailers and fast food companies, franchising offers superior benefits to both the franchisees and their parent companies. The franchisees bring entrepreneurial energy seldom found in corporate store managers while the parent provides brand building and strategic direction.

- Advanced Elastomers is a $500 million 50-50 joint venture which uses the natural resources of Exxon and the patents and technology of Monsanto. This much smaller startup, which created significantly greater value than either company could have generated alone, required a more entrepreneurial culture than either Exxon or Monsanto. A more appropriate culture was established by telling its people they could not return to the parent companies.

- Traditionally, suppliers are expected to jump through hurdles for their customers. "Partnering" requires that teams from the supplier and the customer work together as one company to optimize the total system. For important projects, partnering can produce breakthroughs in time, cost, and profits.

Alliances in Dynamic Environments

Static alliances often involve only two companies (or a lead company with many suppliers or many distributors). Exhibit 8.6 shows that the dynamic environments in high tech industries can involve hundred of stakeholders.[19] The richness of such alliances has led them to be called ecosystems.

A mature business ecosystem has a leader that provides industry standards. These standards provide value to customers by assuring compatibility across system components and over time. Leaders often generate amazing margins (e.g., 80 percent for Microsoft and 40 percent for Intel). The smaller companies in the ecosystem also benefit from the continuity of standards. Their diversity assures innovation and a complete product line to meet all customer needs.

Ecosystems produce a high level of accountability and competition. Cyrix, AMD, or Motorola would be quick to exploit the opportunity if the rate of innovation ever slowed down at Intel. The warfare between the Wintel ecosystem (Windows + Intel) and others (e.g., Oracle and Sun) is much more intense and effective in producing innovation and value to end users than the IBM hegemony of the 1970s.

"Co-opetition," the combination of cooperation to maximize long-term sales and profits and competition over its allocation, provides an economic structure for analyzing alliances. Two companies are "complementors" when the purchase of one company's product benefits the other company. Microsoft and Intel have no equity or legal link but are near-perfect complementors. Knowing that Intel is developing a next generation processor allows Microsoft to develop a next generation Windows operating system and Office Suite with additional features. Similarly, Intel has faith that there will be a market for its new processor because they know that Microsoft is developing more

---

Exhibit 8.6 **A business ecosystem**

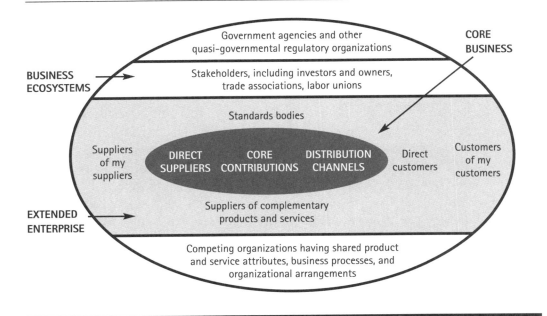

---

complex next generation software. The result is PCs have an expected life perhaps half that of cars.

Being in an alliance with a big company can be tough. Just ask anyone who supplies the Big 3 car companies or Wal-Mart about the unrelenting price pressures. Similarly, the franchisees of McDonald's and Anheuser-Busch know they are expected to meet high standards. Increasingly, however, companies must align themselves with other companies. Going head-on against Wintel or Wal-Mart is a lousy way to increase your net worth!

Conclusion

Virtually every industry today must compete in a global market. That reality has focused attention on the need to be competitor-driven in your strategy development, just as much as it is necessary to be customer-driven.

Sometimes, being competitor-driven means engaging in business warfare. The principles and strategies of military warfare can guide you in fighting your business foes. At other times, especially if you are the leader in a mature industry, your best competitor-driven strategy may be to encourage peace through Tit for Tat.

Most of the time in every industry, as many businesses in the United States and Europe have learned the hard way, you need a long-term strategic intent, a vision of where you intend to be 20 years down the road. This applies to both leaders' intent on fending off long-term challenges and smaller actors' intent on eventually achieving industry leadership.

Increasingly, companies are using alliances as a fundamental part of their strategy. It allows companies to focus on their own core competencies and to exploit the strengths of their allies to provide superior value to customers.

At all times, the key to business success is the development and execution of superior strategies—strategies that give you an unfair advantage

CHAPTER NINE

People-Driven Strategies and High Performance Cultures

Fred Smith, the CEO of Federal Express says, "Putting our people first allows them to take care of the customers, and if we do that in the right way, our customers will take care of us—completing a cycle that must be balanced as we move forward rapidly."[1] Southwest Airlines CEO Herb Kelleher says essentially the same thing, "Strategy has to work for employees, customers, and owners—in that order. If you do a great job of selecting, training, and motivating your employees, they will do a great job of wowing your customers. And satisfied customers are the best foundation for employee success."[2]

The Loyalty Effect[3], by Bain & Company consultant Frederick Reichheld, provides a six-step process that shows how employee-driven and customer-driven strategies fit together:

1. Develop a strategy that delivers truly superior customer value to a specific customer segment.
2. Focus all of your efforts on these target customers.
3. Earn customer loyalty with the right pricing policies, product lines, and service levels.
4. Find the right employees. Be selective. Look for people who share the company's values and have the necessary talents and skills.
5. Earn employee loyalty with compensation, incentives, training, benefits, and a positive working environment.
6. Gain cost and performance advantages through employee productivity.

The six steps are almost biblical. Companies must cast their bread upon the water and provide superior benefits to customers and employees before seeking superior financial performance.

The potential bottom-line benefits of superior customer-driven and people-driven strategies are amazing. Southwest Airlines, Wal-Mart, Tyson Foods, Circuit City, and Plenum Publishing have three things in common. They are in tough industries. They have solid people- and customer-driven strategies. And they increased their value an average of 18,360 percent in 1972-92.[4] Companies, which develop and retain employees, have greater stock price to book value ratios, some companies achieving $41,000 higher market value per employee[5] and five-year annual returns of 27.5% compared to 17.3%.[6]

While not citing actual numbers, there is other evidence that loyal employees add to the value of a company. Ernst & Young found that one of the eight most important measures which investors use in valuing a company is "attracting and retaining the very best people"[7]. Mercer Consulting found that over half of the participants in a study said that problems with attracting and retaining the right people led to poor customer service and loss of customers.[8] Finally, in a world-wide study, Andersen Consulting reported that 75 percent of executives surveyed believe that human performance is more important strategically than are productivity and technology. Eighty percent of executives surveyed believe that attracting and retaining people will be the number one issue in strategy by 2010. Most companies in fast-moving industries such as those having to do with the Internet, say that is the most important issue right now.[9]

While having valuable, loyal employees is important, company loyalty has been decreasing through the 1990s and is at all-time lows. In 1998, the workforce commitment index declined within virtually every industry, age group, income group, and job classification.[10] The same study found that over 25 percent of workers in the United States said they would leave their jobs for one paying 10 percent more. Over half would leave for a 20 percent pay raise.

In light of this, how can you build a workforce that is competent and loyal? The four sections of this chapter provide our answer to this question.
- Creating and maintaining a high performance culture,
- Getting the right people,
- Earning employee trust and loyalty, and
- Achieving superior results through people.

Exhibit 9.1 provides a framework for building the employee foundation for a high performance organization.

Exhibit 9.1 **The dynamics of creating competent, loyal employees***

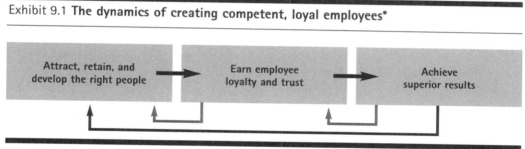

* Based on steps 4, 5 and 6 of *The Loyalty Effect*, discussed at the beginning of this chapter.

CREATING A HIGH PERFORMANCE CULTURE

Early writings on corporate culture—analysis-oriented rather than goal-oriented—emphasized the complexity of culture and the near impossibility of changing it. They implied that managers should work around the culture and the bureaucracy rather than try to change them.

"Overly simplistic" is about the nicest thing that can be said about these early views on the difficulty of changing corporate cultures. If you are the old Bell Telephone monopoly and you get deregulated, you'd better change your culture—in a hurry. If you are GM and paralyzed by bureaucracy, you'd better find a new CEO who can change your culture quickly. Jack Welch and Lou Gerstner did it at GE and IBM and gave those companies a whole new direction.

Characteristics of Healthy and Unhealthy Corporate Cultures

A basic assumption of the early writings on corporate culture was that strong cultures and financial performance went together. They were wrong! In a study of 207 companies, Kotter and Heskett[11] found that the strength of a culture is not as important as the type of culture. They had over 600 top corporate executives assess the strength of the cultures of companies in their industry. The result? **Very little correlation between cultural strength and return on average investment over 11 years.**

Of American companies known for strong cultures, IBM (before Lou Gerstner became CEO) most often comes to mind. While its strong culture may have contributed to its admirable performance in earlier decades, its values and behaviors hurt IBM during the very different competitive environment of the 1980s.

Kotter and Heskett identified certain cultural traits common to companies performing well and certain others common to those performing poorly. These traits are summarized in Exhibit 9.2.

Exhibit 9.2 **Healthy and unhealthy cultures**

	HEALTHY CORPORATE CULTURES	UNHEALTHY CORPORATE CULTURES
Core Values	• Managers are goal oriented, focusing on needs of customers, employees, and owners • Value leadership and change—to maintain fit between customers, competitors, climate, and culture	• Managers focus on themselves and their immediate work group or product more than customers or shareholders • Value orderly, risk-reducing management processes more than leadership
Common Behavior	• Strategy and performance drive decision making, reinforcing the goal-oriented, pragmatic culture • "Eyes on the future; hands on the present™" • Creating a desired future drives strategy and action • But achieving annual objectives is a commitment • Planning is top-down and bottom-up, and action oriented	• Political, insular, arrogant, centralized, bureaucratic • Subjective decision-making reinforces unhealthy culture • Strong bias against change stifles initiative • Planning is either top-down or bottom-up, and process oriented

Two fundamental values characterize all healthy, adaptive cultures: (1) a concern for satisfying the needs of all three key stakeholders (customers, employees, and owners), and (2) valuing change. The importance of these values makes sense. Customer wants must be the focus of all businesses. Employees are the mechanism for meeting customer wants. Failure to focus on owners can lead to giving all the benefits of success to customers and employees. And management must value change to counter threats and exploit opportunities.

How does a good culture come about? How does a company come to embrace these performance-enhancing values? More intriguing, how does a company lose them? Let's start with this last question first.

Kotter and Heskett found a pattern in the evolution of unhealthy cultures. Typically, such companies were often founded and led to early success by a dynamic and visionary entrepreneur. This leader's successful business strategy gained an early dominant market position. The company then hired managers to develop systems to manage its rapid growth. The eventual result was a management group with excessive focus on internal issues and too little focus externally on customers. Moreover, feeling that their way of doing things was the best way, the company's executives stuck too long with their strategy that no longer fit their competitive realities. The result was an unhealthy and unresponsive culture. The values and behavioral norms that once helped them reach the heights of success now gave way to a culture of arrogance, insularity, and bureaucratic inertia.

For these companies to develop a performance-enhancing culture requires a leader who can (1) convincingly show the need for change, (2) develop a successful new strategy, and (3) motivate others to help implement the new strategy. In the process, the leader begins to inculcate the two key values—concern for customers, employees, and stockholders, and acceptance of change. The firm's performance begins to improve, and the doubters and resisters in the organization slowly come around to the new way of doing things. Improved performance reinforces the values and behaviors, which further improves performance. The company spirals upwards.

Finally, maintaining a performance-enhancing culture requires three additional tasks of management:

1. Continuously communicate core values and behaviors in both words and actions,
2. Encourage leadership at all levels of the organizations, and
3. Aggressively implement the current strategy while adapting to a changing climate (i.e., success requires "eyes on the future and hands on the present™").

How Cultures Differ by Industry and Department

Many academics provide blanket statements on cultural aspects that lead to high performance cultures. "Egalitarianism is good (e.g., eliminate reserved parking spots, avoid excessive pay differentials)." Too often, these statements reflect the author's social ideology. Exhibit 9.3, based on the work of Deal and Kennedy[12], suggests that the culture for a company should reflect such variables as the riskiness of the industry and how slow or fast you learn of success or failure. Similarly, even within a company, the culture will be different in sales than accounting.

Deal and Kennedy advise that the best companies artfully blend the four types. Yet, the diagram suggests two additional conclusions:

Exhibit 9.3 **How corporate culture varies by industry and department**

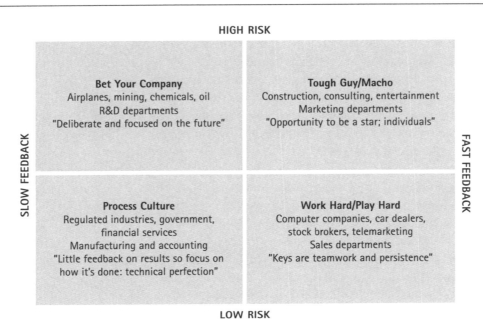

1. As with all elements of strategy, the right culture for your company depends on your specific situation. There is no single best corporate culture.
2. When your strategy changes (e.g., due to industry deregulation), consider what parts of your culture need to be emphasized and de-emphasized.

Assess Your Company's Current and Desired Culture

Arthur Andersen, based on its work with Baldrige National Quality Award-winner Wainwright Industries, has developed a simple, yet powerful tool for quantifying corporate culture.[13] Employees receive a survey which asks them to assign 40 items (Exhibit 9.4) into a forced distribution (Exhibit 9.5) indicating what they believe best characterizes the company culture as they **currently** see it. They are then asked to distribute the same 40 items in the same way, only this time representing what they want the **desired** company culture to be. Employees are told selections for the "desired" culture should be made so the resulting culture best meets the needs of all stakeholders, specifically:

- Values that lead to effective and efficient execution of their company's mission (since failure here will inevitably lead to poor organization performance, the loss of good people, and declining quality of work life), and
- Values that will allow the company to attract and retain good people because it meets their personal needs in the short- and long-term.

Exhibit 9.4 **Cultural characteristics of organizations**

ID#	CULTURAL CHARACTERISTICS	ID#	CULTURAL CHARACTERISTICS
1	We share a sense of purpose	21	We focus on long-term goals
2	We communicate openly and honestly	22	We adapt easily to new circumstances
3	We demonstrate trust in and respect for others	23	We strive to be a pioneer
4	We maintain high standards of excellence	24	We focus on continuous improvement
5	We develop knowledge and skills	25	We are quick to take advantage of opportunities
6	We expect to be rewarded for performance	26	We pursue aggressive goals
7	We accept different viewpoints	27	We compete with peers
8	We exceed customers' expectations	28	We are results-oriented
9	We pay attention to details	29	We focus on short-term competitive success
10	We punish failure	30	We work long hours
11	We focus on facts and figures	31	We are decisive
12	We pay attention to hierarchy and status	32	We seek personal success
13	We are reliable	33	We are team players
14	We use proven methods	34	We conform to the organization's image
15	We comply with directions and rules	35	We view co-workers as friends
16	We are organized	36	We help others grow and develop
17	We develop new products/services	37	We cover the mistakes of others
18	We are free to act independently	38	We expect long-term employment
19	We challenge the status quo	39	We avoid conflict
20	We anticipate customers' needs	40	We sacrifice for the good of the organization

Exhibit 9.5 **An instrument for quantifying corporate culture**

Place each ID # from the "Cultural Characteristics" page into a cell that shows how closely it reflects (name of Organization) as we are today.
• Only 1 ID # per cell
• Place each ID # in one cell
Most people have to cross out some initial entries until they are satisfied. Just make sure final selections are clear.

Most like Current Culture   **Least like** Current Culture

A	B	C	D	E	F	G

Importantly, the results of the culture survey (and especially the "desired" culture) should only be used as a starting point for discussion. People tend to agree with the results from the "current culture" analysis, although differences between results from senior management and lower levels of the organization provoke debate. The most valuable part of the process is deciding what future culture should be sought and how to move towards the desired culture. Exhibit 9.6 provides an excellent example of the end result of such a process.

Exhibit 9.6 **Culture and strategy for a chemical company**[14]

MARKET DEMANDS	CURRENT CULTURE	NEEDED CULTURE	CHANGE TOOLS USED
• New products • Low cost • High quality • Technical service • Rapid service • Multiple distribution points	• Entitled • Silo management • Slow • Inwardly focused • Reactive • Not innovative	• Sense of urgency • Teamwork • Innovative • Cost focus • Customer- market orientation	• Some of top team replaced • New incentive system installed • Select people changed at lower levels • Accountability systems installed • Strategic plan implemented

The rest of this chapter uses steps 4, 5 and 6 from *The Loyalty Effect* (see page 132) as a framework for designing employee-driven strategies to move towards the desired culture and become a high performance organization.

GETTING THE RIGHT PEOPLE

You have to have the "right" people to make your company really successful. That means you must attract, develop, fully utilize, and retain them. It also means separating people who prevent organizational success. But before all that, you need to define what "right people" means for your company.

Hiring Smart

Successful companies have determined both the functional/technical skills and the personal characteristics/interpersonal skills for success in their people.

- One has to thrive in a team atmosphere and be creative in order to work at Southwest Airlines.
- Grace & Company consultants must be SWANs: Smart, Work hard, Ambitious, and Nice.
- McKinsey & Company is more focused. They seek Baker Scholars, the top five percent academically of the Harvard Business School MBAs. Indeed,

Harvard and many other top tier universities have a similar singular criterion for their professors: world class publications.

- In addition to being able to work well on teams, Dell Computers tests candidates for tolerance for ambiguity and change and ability to learn rapidly.
- Enterprise Rent-A-Car has found that "Enterprise Quotient" (EQ), a measure of emotional intelligence, is more predictive of success than class standing. Hence, it weights leadership experience heavily in hiring decisions. The EQ consists of 15 situational questions which measure qualities such as self-awareness, persistence, and empathy.

Standard assessment tests are often remarkably effective in predicting employee performance. For example, high performing sales people share certain values, attitudes, and behaviors. Of the six values and attitudes measured by the Personal Interests Attitudes, and Values assessment (which measures an individual's values and what motivates them), 72 percent of the top sales people rank highest on "Utilitarian." Hence, seek sales candidates who are practical, results-oriented, and economically motivated.[15]

The most successful companies are picky. Southwest Airlines used to hire 10 percent of applicants. Their reputation as a great place to work now allows them to be twice as selective and hire only five percent of applicants. The reverse is also true. Companies that hire weak candidates tend to follow the downward spiral of poor performance, high turnover, bad reputation, fewer applicants, and ever more lax hiring criteria.

Productive cultures include high performance expectations. For example, new hires at Enterprise are expected to work ten hour days, and new hires at Dell Computers are given specific performance goals that they must reach within the first 30 days. Enforcing high performance standards has two benefits: it makes the company less attractive to underachievers and more attractive to overachievers.

Separating People When Necessary

In his 1991 shareholder letter, General Electric CEO Jack Welch described a two by two matrix for his executives: they either achieve their goals or don't, and they either follow GE's values or they don't. People who consistently fail to achieve their goals must eventually leave an organization to maintain its high performance culture. The tougher decision comes when people achieve their goals but do so in a way that weakens the culture. Eventually terminating such people may produce short-term problems but is essential for long-term success.

Cisco Systems takes a simpler approach. It trims the bottom five percent of its employees each year. The ones who go are those who do not add value (based on objective performance measures) or do not fit the culture.

DEVELOPING, RETAINING, AND PROMOTING PEOPLE

Hiring the right people is a challenge. Terminating those who don't work out is tough emotionally but simpler conceptually. The most complex challenge is developing people. It also pays the biggest dividends. Companies with a solid development reputation find it a lot easier to attract and retain the right people.

Training is the foundation. Put bluntly, with today's accelerating change and knowledge-based economy, a company must have a solid development program to ensure that long-term employees are competent. Federal Express is known as the "ultimate corporate university" and spends three percent of its total expenses on training. This is six times the amount at similar companies.

The key to management development, however, is challenging but achievable work. Exhibit 9.7 summarizes Mihaly Csikszentmihalyi's concept of "flow."[16] If skills are greater than challenges, boredom will create an uninspired, non-productive workforce. If challenges are greater than skills, anxiety will result and interfere with performance. The best companies provide increasing challenges within the employee's capabilities. The result is personal growth over time. The company benefits from superior employee performance. The employee benefits from personal satisfaction from a job well done, from continuously increasing capabilities, and growing compensation to reflect growing productivity.

Exhibit 9.7 **Creating "Flow"**

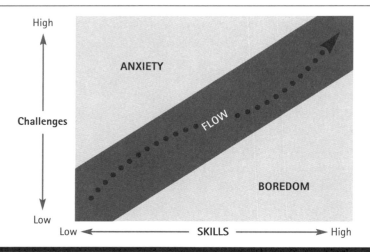

In the late 1990s, I went through five straight strategic planning programs in which "people issues" were the highest single priority. Too often, top management focuses on "lack of loyalty" by young workers as a major problem. Instead, with the right strategy and policies, that lack of loyalty is an opportunity. Many young employees make rational career decisions. They are excellent at balancing the trade-offs between pay, quality of worklife, development (for earning more in the future), and the company's future (for promotion opportunities). They will work for companies that offer the most rewards today and best opportunities for tomorrow. You can exploit their lack of loyalty by attracting and retaining the right people. All you have to do is (1) offer the most rewards today and opportunities for the future and (2) communicate that superior value so it is recognized.

EARNING EMPLOYEE TRUST AND LOYALTY

The 100 best companies to work for, as profiled in a *Fortune* magazine article,[17] do a great job of meeting the low and middle levels of Maslow's hierarchy of needs. There are frequent mentions of compensation and incentives; training and tuition reimbursement; casual days and other non-hierarchical policies; child care, flextime, and other family friendly policies.

People simply won't focus on their company's "high performance programs" until their basic needs are met. Companies must earn employee trust and loyalty before they can expect to achieve superior results through people. Here are seven basics for earning employee trust:

1. **Pay competitively:** Trans World Airlines found that people pay little attention to motivational programs when their compensation is below industry standards.

2. **Be people-oriented:** One of the glory eras of Anheuser-Busch, Inc. was 1977 to 1985, when it defeated Miller Brewing Company in "the beer wars." Under the leadership of CEO August Busch III and COO Denny Long, the stock increased 945 percent during those years. Busch focused on strategy, finance, and brewing. Long was marketing- and people-oriented. Occasionally, you will find a Sam Walton (Wal-Mart) or Herb Kelleher (Southwest Airlines) who excels at both hard and soft strategy. Usually, however, success requires the two complementary people. Make sure a very senior executive is people-oriented! (But, as Denny Long personally emphasized to me, also make sure there is a very senior executive who excels at "hard" strategy.)

3. **Earn employee trust on big issues.** CEOs who give speeches about employees being "our most valuable resource" lose all credibility when they unhesitatingly implement a downsizing program. Wainwright Industries began its transformation to an employee-driven strategy by making safety its number one priority in response to an employee survey.

4. **Listen and respond.** In 1996-97, Grace & Company began to lose good people. An employee survey isolated the sources of discontent. In response, Grace

hired a full-time human resource manager, instituted casual days, and modified fringe benefits. By early 1998, employee satisfaction was way up and turnover was way down. Use employee surveys as a foundation for improving satisfaction!

5. **Communicate, be visible, and share information:** Communications straight from top management is essential for bottom-up understanding, involvement, and commitment. Open-end interactions are especially valuable in keeping top management as well as employees informed. Wainwright Industries uses a simple philosophy about communication: "No secrets." As chairman Don Wainwright says, "If you try to hide vital information, you're wasting your money on training because people can't make sound decisions." People won't be successful and you can't hold them accountable if they don't have the information to do their job.

6. **Move towards egalitarianism and having fun:** This rule may not apply to all organizations (e.g., the military and justice system come to mind as exceptions). Yet, workers increasingly prefer less formal cultures and believe work should be enjoyable. Teamwork is also easier because interactions between people at different levels are easier and more honest. The culture of more and more high performing companies includes "having fun."

7. **Demonstrate integrity and commitment to company values:** The CEO is leader in word and deed. If top management suffers ethical lapses, many others will follow.

ACHIEVING SUPERIOR RESULTS THROUGH PEOPLE

Everything to this point has focused on creating a foundation for superior performance. You have crafted a compelling strategy that gives you an unfair advantage in meeting customer wants. You have hired and developed the right people. You have developed and implemented policies that build employee trust and loyalty. Achieving superior results requires one last step: Create an environment—with hard and soft incentives—that encourages everyone to work together to implement the strategy.

The sidebar discusses how Enterprise Rent-A-Car created a people-driven culture that is extremely entrepreneurial and straightforward. Each of its 4,000 locations is a profit center. The manager and assistant manager get a share of the profits. An assistant manager that does a great job will be in line to become a manager for the next location. Its people work hard but have fun in the process.

Enterprise Rent-A-Car's People-Driven Strategy

While Hertz, Avis and others fight over airport car rentals to business people, Enterprise Rent-A-Car dominates the market for people who need a rental car while their car is in the shop. This local car rental business is now 40 percent of the total market. *Forbes* magazine estimates that Enterprise founder Jack Taylor, who was a salesman at a car dealer before founding Enterprise, is worth $2.8 billion. Let's look at how its people strategies work for its employees and have led to marketing success for Enterprise.

Enterprise knows who they want to hire. Soccer captains, club members, and social chairs who are able to roll up their sleeves and be good team members are most likely to be happy and successful. Qualities like confidence, persistence, and social deftness are better predictors of success at Enterprise than IQ, GPA, and class rank. In search of ideal candidates, Enterprise has developed an "Enterprise Quotient" or EQ test of emotional intelligence. The EQ test uses 15 situational questions to measure such intangible qualities as self-awareness, persistence, and empathy.

Enterprise doesn't use a brute force approach to hiring. A 1999 *Business Week* cover story details how high tech firms are using huge pay increases, stock options, and even signing bonuses of BMW Z3 sports cars to attract talented programmers. It's refreshing to read that Enterprise attracts entry level employees by giving them the opportunity to make decisions early on and then rewarding them for performance. One 25 year old said his friends thought he was nuts to go with Enterprise for about $25,000 when they were starting at other companies for $10,000 more. Within 13 months, however, he was promoted to assistant branch manager with total compensation that could top $50,000.

New management trainees at Enterprise work hard. New hires spend 10-hour days working behind the counter, keeping the books, and delivering doughnuts or pizza to body shops and other referral sources. The work, however, can be fun. One trainee rented an ice cream truck to call on referral sources when the temperature reached 100.

Friendly competition produces results. In one location, a branch that wins a contest can spend a weekend day water-skiing and jet-skiing with its area manager. Other branches will have a "steak and beans contest." The losing branch has to buy and cook steak dinners for the winning branch. The losing branch eats beans.

Enterprise is entrepreneurial. Assistant managers and above receive a percentage of the profits from their office. Hence, Enterprise has maintained a small company feel as it has grown to over 35,000 employees.

Enterprise offers major opportunities. Promotions are based on merit, not tenure. With only 10 percent of its locations outside the U.S., Enterprise continues to offer decades of growth opportunities. Performance bonuses provide most of the compensation for assistant managers and above. Even CEO Andy Taylor has a base salary of only $35,000.

Supplies Network, which is discussed in detail in chapter 11, has a tougher challenge motivating people than Enterprise because it operates out of a single location. Within one year, each Supplies Network employee has clear quantitative departmental goals. To encourage teamwork, however, each employee is also measured by all "internal customers" (supervisors and above) on 13 inter-department goals. To receive the maximum bonus and pay increase, the employee must achieve their quantitative goals and score above 85 percent on the teamwork measures. Such clear accountability works. Supplies Network grew from $10 million in 1990 to $100 million in 1998.

In addition to clear hiring and development criteria and policies that build trust and loyalty, companies that achieve superior results through people share four other characteristics:

1. Clear quantitative performance measures and incentives. (Many high performance companies also have teamwork and "soft" incentives, although some sales organizations and companies such as Nucor Steel do not.)
2. Company-wide information sharing (which may or may not extend to "open book" financials).
3. Clear, frequent performance feedback.
4. Rewards based on performance—not tenure or politics. People are held accountable.

What gets measured and rewarded gets done. Think through exactly what behaviors you want to encourage. Develop performance measures and link them to recognition and rewards.

Conclusion

Linking solid market-driven strategies with solid people-driven strategies is the foundation for financial success. A growing profit pool then provides the opportunity to reward all key stakeholders. As shown in Exhibit 9.1, positive feedback then leads to greater trust and loyalty from employees and greater ability to attract and retain the right people. You have a solid foundation for even greater success tomorrow.

In the first few years of a new strategy, management should focus on changing behavior rather than directly changing the culture. People will change behavior in response to recognition and rewards. Explicitly trying to change beliefs and culture in the early stages only creates frustration and delays action. John Kotter places changing the culture as dead last in his eight step process for leading change.[18] To prevent relapse, a CEO must eventually explicitly identify the counterproductive aspects of the old culture. But do so only after superior results from the new behaviors make the benefits of the new culture clear.

We have now examined in depth every element of your strategy. You should now have a good feel for your competitive realities and strategic alternatives. But the strategic thinking process to this point is necessarily complex, and complex strategies simply don't work. They don't motivate people and don't get implemented. The next chapter shows how to move from complexity to simplicity. It starts the process of moving from top-down strategy development towards bottom-up understanding and commitment ... and aggressive implementation of a strategy that gives your company an unfair competitive advantage.

CHAPTER TEN

Vision, Mission, and Key Moves

There's nothing new about vision and mission statements. It's hard to think of any great historic movement or cause that did not rely on a motivating mission statement in one guise or another. Jesus' Sermon on the Mount, Luther's Ninety-Five Theses, the American Revolutionaries' Declaration of Independence, Abraham Lincoln's Gettysburg Address—these and many other public expressions of purpose, strategy, and underlying values moved followers of these grand movements to victory.

Great accomplishments flow from powerful visions. In recent years, more and more CEOs have become sensitive to that fact. Those who strive to make their companies great have developed formal mission statements.[1]

Yet, most mission statements are worse than useless. These committee-written documents were designed to make the company sound good to all stakeholders but were taken seriously by none. By glorifying the company as it exists, such mission statements made change more difficult. Why should we change if we are already so great? A mission statement has value only if it is a goal-oriented manifesto for the future.

In 1975, Bill Gates developed a vision that provided motivation and direction for Microsoft that lasted 24 years: "A computer on every desk and in every home." Due to the rise of the Internet and non-PC hardware such as the Palm Pilot and TV sets, however, Microsoft president Steve Ballmer crafted a new vision in mid-1999: "Empower people through great software anytime, anyplace and on any device." This vision basically provides a business definition guiding Microsoft's continued domination of software:

- Customer: People (everyone, and not just in the U.S.),
- Customer want: To be empowered ... anytime, anyplace and on any device, and
- Mechanism: Great software.

Today, however, too many vision and mission statements simply "don't grab people in the gut and motivate them to work for the common end," in the words of two astute students of mission statements.[2] James Collins and Jerry Porras quote several examples of such banality, cited anonymously to protect the guilty. Here's just one of those that missed the mark:

> We provide our customers with retail banking, real estate, finance, and corporate banking products which will meet their credit, investment, security and liquidity needs.

Every mission statement should possess at least two characteristics. First, it must be brief. Second, it must inspire. Hence, style is as important as content. Think of the mission statement as the marketing campaign for your strategy. Just as an advertisement should not be a laundry list of your product's benefits or attributes, a mission statement should not be page after page of business babble. An effective ad concentrates a product's attributes into a single, simple, memorable concept that moves people to action. So it is with a good mission statement.

As we will detail later in this chapter, an effective mission statement has two parts:

- A memorable two to six word "vision" that grabs people in the gut, and
- The "public strategy," a few sentences that describe how people will work together to achieve the vision and how achieving the vision will benefit all key stakeholders.

The mission statement process includes four basic steps, each discussed in separate sections of this chapter:

1. Using idealized design to move from complexity to simplicity,
2. Drafting the mission statement,
3. Developing the three to five key moves and broad action plans for achieving the vision, and
4. Getting bottom-up understanding, involvement and commitment to the strategy.

THE CREATIVE LEAP: IDEALIZED DESIGN

"Simplicity" is the ninth law of war in chapter 8. Yet, the strategy process so far has been complex. Such complexity was required so the strategy works for employees, customers, and owners at each step of the strategy development process. The time has come to move strategy from complexity to simplicity.

"Idealized design," a creative process developed by Russell Ackoff,[3] can help your organization make the creative leap to an ideal alternative. It moves an organization from the constraining thought, "It can't be done," to the liberating and empowering thought, "Yes, we can do that." The outcome will be your final vision and the public statement of your strategy.

The Reference Forecast: Unfreezing the Organization

Inertia is the great enemy of effective new strategies. Thus, before you can design a desired future, you must "unfreeze" your organization from the fetters of the status quo. You can "unfreeze" an organization by developing a "reference forecast" showing that current strategies will lead to ruin or, at a minimum, performance far below potential.

Unfreezing the organization is easier to do if current results are clearly unacceptable. It was not hard for Lee Iacocca to convince Chrysler in 1980 or Lou Gerstner to convince IBM in 1995 that the need for drastic change was upon them. Imminent bankruptcy at Chrysler and a 70 percent decline in IBM's stock made the case convincingly. However, it's far wiser, even if much more difficult, to make that convincing demonstration before performance has turned to disaster.

How do you bring an organization to see the need for change? The management of one preeminent R&D organization struck right at the values and pride of its employees. Its researchers thought of themselves as the best of the best—until management proved to them that they had not come up with a real breakthrough in 40 years. They had actually made only incremental improvements in performance, reliability, and costs of existing products. Clearly, the organization was performing far below its perceived potential.

During the 1980s, some perceptive CEOs used the threat of corporate raiders to convince their companies that they needed to change their ways. Some less perceptive CEOs had their ways changed for them—by corporate raiders.

Sometimes, business leaders generate a "quasi-crisis" by amplifying weak signals that point to the need to improve. One way of doing this is to plan for the worst-case scenario. The Japanese heavy equipment manufacturer Komatsu did this when they budgeted on the basis of worst-case exchange rates, using 115 yen to the dollar, for example, when the actual rate at the time was 145 to the dollar.

Top management can often use selective measurements of costs and quality compared to those of competitors. Declining customer satisfaction scores, for example, can show that a new strategy is needed—and needed now, since the difficulty in closing the gap between you and your competitors increases exponentially with delay.

Whatever your method, you have to prove the need for change. Only then will you be able to unfreeze the organization and begin the process of moving it to a new strategy.

Designing the Desired Future

The next step in idealized design is to develop a consensus on a challenging but achievable vision of a desired and exciting future. Here's how:

Focus on ends. At this stage, your sole focus should be on ends. Insist that all discussion of the means needed to achieve the ends be totally off limits for the time being. There's a very practical reason for this. It's far easier to get consensus on a vision than on actions needed to realize the vision. Every proposed action will be countered with a hundred excuses why it won't work.

However, once people agree upon a vision and become excited about it, they will figure out how to achieve it. They'll make short-term sacrifices for greater long-term benefits, and they'll spend less time and effort defending turf and building empires as they work together to achieve the vision.

Design for today. Visualize where you would like to be today—not five or ten years from now. Focusing on the present forces everyone to really understand and address customer wants. If you focus on the future, the process is likely to degenerate into a forecasting session, which will open the door to all sorts of disagreements and distractions that pull you away from the task of designing your ideal company.

Abolish self-imposed constraints. Since idealized design requires breakthrough thinking, you want no limits on creativity. These can be real and imagined policies, organizational systems and structures, investments in plant and equipment, and so forth. These constraints will hold you back from the creative leap needed to move people to extraordinary achievements.

The only acceptable constraints are the laws of physics. So, blow the system up—that is, have everyone assume that the entire system was destroyed and that they have total freedom to design, from scratch, a new system as it should be.

Idealized design can produce extraordinary results because it frees individuals and organizations from the constraints that have held them to only incremental improvements at best. There are three specific reasons for this:

1. The resulting vision leads to **quantum leaps in benefits** to customers, employees, and owners.
2. The vision excites people and stirs them to give a **100 percent effort.**
3. **Teamwork** increases because everyone is focused on the same objective.

Like all other steps in Cycle 1, idealized design depends on the others. For example, if American railroad executives in 1910 had subjected their strategy to idealized design, they could then have seen their business definition as transportation. That simple modification in business definition would have enabled them to think clearly and creatively about how the newest technology—trucks—fit into their strategy. They would have later been receptive to thinking about the place of airplanes in their strategies.

THE MISSION STATEMENT

At this point in the Cycle 1 process, you have arrived at a near-final seven to 10 year vision and strategy for the organization. Most of the analyses and strategy documents, however, are in a confidential form inappropriate for distributing to the public and in an analytic form unsuitable for guiding and motivating your organization.

Hence, you should articulate the essence of the strategy through a succinct, instantly understandable form that stirs the blood of everyone in the organization. That form is the one-page mission statement. In practice, mission statements vary, but the best all strive to convey the organization's mission through two elements:

1. The vision, and
2. The public strategy.

The Vision

The vision is a simple and eloquent distillation of the strategy and corporate culture. Limit it to two to six words to make it memorable. Unlike the timeless ("100 years") credo or purpose of the company, the vision states a seven to 10 year mission. It concentrates the formal and abstract statements of business definition, role, strategy, and culture into an energizing goal that impels everyone in the organization to superior execution of the strategy.

For those reasons, the vision should connect the objectives of the firm to the personal values of its members. That's why truly effective expressions of vision do not refer to purely financial targets or shareholder value. Frankly, shareholder value is too abstract and impersonal to inspire the rank and file. However, by tapping into personal values, to use Peters' and Waterman's terminology, you can "achieve extraordinary results through ordinary people."[4]

Visions typically fall into one of four types:
- Targeting,
- Common enemy,
- Role model, and
- Internal transformation.

Targeting Visions: A targeting vision states a concrete goal. An excellent example is President Kennedy's 1962 challenge to NASA to "send a man to the moon and bring him back safely by 1970." Henry Ford's target "to democratize the car" led beautifully into his business definition of making cars for everyone instead of just the wealthiest five percent.

Qualitative targeting visions are more motivational, but quantitative ones are more precise and measurable. Robert Galvin launched two successive targeting visions at Motorola. In 1984, he set an internal yet customer-driven target of "six sigma quality," that is, fewer than 3.4 defects per million. As the company approached that target, he set another target of reducing "cycle time" between order placement and delivery, and between product concept and commercialization by 90 percent within five years.

By setting a second target even before the full achievement of the first, Galvin avoided a common problem with targeting visions: What do you do next, after you've reached your target? Lacking a follow-up vision, NASA has floundered since successfully fulfilling its man-on-the-moon mission.

Common-Enemy Visions: Common-enemy visions are powerful motivators. They can mobilize a company just like a war can mobilize a nation. This approach has worked twice for Nike, first in dislodging Adidas from its leadership position in athletic shoes and next in regaining leadership after Reebok took over first place.

In 1979 Yamaha publicly declared its intention to overtake Honda in Japan's motorcycle market. Honda responded with one of the most vivid common-enemy visions ever—"We will beat, squash, slaughter Yamaha." Honda's employees did just that, and within the year Yamaha conceded defeat and publicly apologized to the Japanese people for being so arrogant as to think it could beat Honda.

One of the problems of common-enemy visions is the enduring mind-set it can create. After Nike defeated Adidas, the company had no enemy and drifted, allowing competitor Reebok to sneak into first place. Only then, with a new enemy, did Nike become energized and regain the lead. Nike seems to respond best only when there is an enemy. Pepsi-Cola's vision of beating Coke led to a U.S. market share almost equal to Coke's by the mid-1980s. This warfare, however, destroyed U.S. profits for both soft drink makers until Coca-Cola again achieved clear leadership in the 1990s. Mindlessly applied, common-enemy visions can cause people to forget that the purpose of business is to maximize one's own profits and not to beat a competitor.

Role-Model Visions: Small, young companies with high aspirations frequently adopt a role-model vision, which provides guidance on corporate culture as well as strategy. The role-model vision of Giro Sport Design, a start-up bicycle products company, is "to be a great company by the year 2000—to be to the cycling industry what Nike is to athletic shoes and Apple is to computers." This conveyed some important and motivating messages—Giro would be innovative and it would allow both employees and customers to achieve their full potential.

During the early 1980s, the real estate firm Trammell Crow set out to become "the IBM of the real estate industry." With that vision, the company strove to become a strong No. 1 through customer service and also be a great place to work. This vision points to a danger with role-model visions—which is the role model itself. Clearly, Trammell Crow's vision was more appropriate and inspiring in the early 1980s than in the early 1990s.

Internal-Transformation Vision: Internal transformation is often the vision of an older company in need of rejuvenation. GE is a classic case. After a targeting vision of becoming No. 1 or No. 2 in all its businesses during the first half of the 1980s, Jack Welch articulated an internal-transformation vision of becoming "a big company/small company hybrid," which he explained as follows:

In addition to the strength, resources and reach of a big company, which we have already built, we are committed to developing the sensitivity, the leanness, the simplicity and the agility of a small company.[5]

Welch set out to eliminate the "tentacles of bureaucracy" and to institutionalize specific anti-bureaucratic processes and values as part of the company's structure and culture.

The Public Strategy

The public strategy section of the mission statement further explains and amplifies the vision. Inspiration and motivation are still the keys, but the public strategy is also explanatory. It states the objectives of the organization and outlines its strategy, wrapping them up in the values and behavioral norms of the organization.

First, a word of warning: The traditional mission statement—with the words "Our Mission" at the top followed by 20 or so bullets of objectives, strategies, and responsibilities in MBA jargon—simply does not work! I have never known an employee at any level (including the CEO) who could provide any recall from one.

Instead, use the "vivid description" approach proposed by Collins and Porras. Everyone remembers the two to six work vision at the top. And they remember key elements of the brief paragraph or half-page public strategy, which describes how everyone in the company will work together to achieve the vision.

The vivid description usually paints a compelling picture of an ideal future. It should present "a vibrant, engaging, and specific description of what it will be like when the mission is achieved," Collins and Porras suggest. "It provokes emotion and generates excitement."[6] Let's look at three examples of vivid description mission statements.

Exhibit 10.1 **The mission statement of Giro Sport Design**

The best riders in the world will be using our products in world-class competition. Winners of the Tour de France, the World Championships, and the Olympics Gold Medal will win while wearing Giro helmets. We will receive unsolicited phone calls and letters from customers who say, 'Thank you for being in business; one of your helmets saved my life.' Our employees will feel that this is the best place they've ever worked. When you ask people to name the top company in the cycling business, the vast majority will say, 'Giro.'"[7]

A "vivid description" such as Giro's is not only a statement of business definition and generic strategy, it also helps define and reinforce the corporate culture. That makes it especially valuable to a young company whose culture is in the early formative phases.

Eckert Family Farms is a St. Louis institution where people pick apples with their children or grandchildren or pick the best tasting peaches they have ever had. The vision tells employees that their job is not to prune trees or operate a cash register. Instead, it tells them they are on-stage, and their job is to create memories for guests that will last for years and decades. Basically, the Eckert mission statement says they want to be "the Disney of family farm markets," the one all of their competitors will try to emulate. After taking prospective summer employees through this mission statement, most high schoolers elect to work for Eckert's rather than flip hamburgers at a fast food stand.

Exhibit 10.2 **The mission statement of Eckert Family Farms**

CREATE COUNTRY MEMORIES
Above all else, we are farmers. The Eckert Family Farm began in 1837. We have always believed in hard work and unquestionable integrity.

We will create lasting memories for our customers when they visit our farms. We will create a country experience through wholesome family fun, superior quality products, and friendly service.

Individuals are important to us. Our work place will foster outstanding performance and personal satisfaction.

We will become the example all other farm markets wish to emulate.

Exhibit 10.3 **The mission statement of Albers Manufacturing**

Albers—The First Name in SysFab™

We, the people of Albers, are the foundation of its strategy and success. Working together, we will delight—not just satisfy—our internal and external customers, make Albers the first name in SysFab™, and create both deep satisfaction and maximum security for our families and ourselves.

Being the first name in SysFab™ requires that we focus on Systems Integration and Metal Fabrication. Using our quality systems, we will provide superior product quality, delivery timeliness, solutions, responsiveness and value.

Commitment to this vision will lead to high sustainable growth, superior business performance, and recognized leadership in SysFab™.

Exhibit 10.3 presents the mission statement of Albers Manufacturing, a high quality company which was recognized by *Industry Week* magazine in 1999 as one of the 25 best small manufacturing companies. As reflected by SysFab, a word it created, Albers' specialty is the intersection of **sys**tems integration and metal **fab**rication. Just the vision and first paragraph have several points worth noting:

- The vision of being "the first name in SysFab" has several meanings. Albers is the creator of the term. With a name beginning in A, Albers is first alphabetically. Most importantly, Albers wants to be first in every business aspect: market share, growth, quality, top of mind awareness, etc.
- The opening, reminiscent of the U.S. Constitution, says that the mission statement reflects the beliefs and commitments of all the people of Albers, not just top management. It also reflects the shift towards employee-driven strategies.
- The commitment to delighting, rather than just satisfying, customers reflects the huge difference in follow-up sales and profits from being a "five" rather than a four on a five-point overall customer satisfaction scale.

Exhibit 10.4 summarizes the key elements of a good mission statement.

Exhibit 10.4 Key elements of a mission statement

- Have a two to six word, instantly understandable, motivating vision at the top,
- Reflect components of your top-down strategy,
- Motivate everyone in the organization to work together for a common purpose,
- Target employees as the primary audience (although it should also be meaningful to customers, suppliers, and stockholders),
- Contain a challenging but attainable goal (NASA's "Man on the moon by 1970"), and
- Contain a timeless guiding philosophy (Merck's "In business of preserving and enhancing human life"; Disney's "To make people happy").

DEVELOPING KEY MOVES AND BROAD ACTION PLANS

The mission statement provides a clear vision of what you want to achieve. It does not, however, provide enough detail so each department can develop strategies for achieving the vision. The last step in top-down strategy development is for the management team to develop the three to five key moves and a few broad action plans for each key move.

The rules for developing the key moves are simple:

1. Each key move should be essential if the organization is to achieve its vision.
2. Fully implementing the key moves should lead to achieving the vision.
3. All employees should spend at least 80 percent of their discretionary time and resources on the key moves.
4. The key moves (together with the broad action plans for each move) should provide sufficient direction so senior executives can develop compelling strategies for their departments consistent with the corporate vision and strategy.

If your overall strategy is to be a low-cost provider, then you should focus on activities that lead to cost advantage for you—things that improve internal efficiencies or reduce materials costs. For differentiation, you would need to focus on marketing— to research what customers want and to help them understand how your features add value for them. Differentiation might also require R&D to develop differentiated products and services for which customers will pay extra.

The following key moves helped Jack Welch grow the market value of General Electric from $14 billion when he became CEO in 1981 to over $500 billion in late 1999. The first key move (which changed over time) focused on internal transformation. The second two focused on two specific product-markets that accounted for 80 percent of the profit growth of GE.

1. Internal transformation
   - 1981-86, **Acquisitions and divestitures:** To become #1 or #2 in market share in a coherent set of industries. Welch's actions and annual shareholder letters in his first five years as CEO focused completely on restructuring GE so it had the potential to win. During that time he sold or closed down over $10 billion and acquired over $20 billion worth of companies.
   - 1986 to Mid-1990s, **Change the culture:** Kill bureaucracy. Become as lean and fast as a small company while exploiting GE's size and resources. Use Economic Value Added to focus on shareholder value.
   - Since mid-1990s: Focus on **cost reduction** via TQM, selling solutions instead of products and services, and move to the Internet era.
2. GE Capital Corporation.
3. International.

The key moves concept also works for small companies that want to become large. The following key moves are for DeMoulin Brothers, a $20 million company that is the clear leader in the $50 million marching band uniform industry. The key moves are designed to help it achieve 50 percent market share and to use its core competencies to achieve leadership in closely related industry niches.

1. Manufacturing operations flexibility.
2. New product niches.
   - Accessory products for the current industry niche.
   - Using the same technology to enter niches with similar characteristics but different customers.
3. Alignment of sales reps and the company.
4. Grow company value through mergers and alliances, information systems, and financial planning.
5. Top management planning/teamwork.

The American Red Cross St. Louis Area Chapter developed the following five key moves. The first two key moves reflected its desire to change its culture to become more team-oriented both internally and externally. The other three moves focus on achieving an aggressive growth BHAG.

1. Work together as a team.
2. Develop win-win partnerships.
3. Achieve clear leadership in priority programs.
4. Communicate our value.
5. Grow financial and human resources.

My clients' key moves nearly always include people or culture issues, marketing, and at least one external product-market opportunity for growth. Many clients also

---

Exhibit 10.5 **Two key moves and their broad action plans for a building sub-contractor**

Key Move 1: REDUCE COSTS (per dollar of revenue). Reduce general & administrative costs X%, labor costs Y%, and material costs Z% in four years.
- Driven by information technology.
- G&A: Replace weak performers and limit staff growth as volume increases (not absolute cuts).
- Operations: Improve, reduce, or eliminate processes as necessary (engineering, warehousing, etc.).
- Field labor: Planning, procedures, productivity, training.
- Materials/Tools: Partnering with suppliers, blanket order pricing.

Key Move 2: MARKET DEVELOPMENT.
- Target one more design/build general contractor and 1 or 2 more general contractors.
- Call on a high growth territory once per week.
- Free up a rising young star to make more sales calls.
- Hire a new salesperson in the next year.
- Analyze three specific new niches to enter (and determine niches to avoid).
- Do customer satisfaction surveys after every project and annually.

include internal cost reduction (or TQM or reengineering program), information technology, mergers/acquisitions, or partnering as a key move.

After the three to five key moves are developed, the management team develops a few broad action plans for each key move. The action plans must reflect your company's capabilities. For example, after the management team developed 37 action plans, the chief operating officer said it simply wasn't feasible; they simply couldn't hold themselves accountable for implementing more than 15 projects. The initial list then represented a great starting point for developing the final list of 14 projects.

Exhibit 10.5 presents examples of the action plans for two key moves of a large building sub-contractor.

GETTING BOTTOM-UP COMMITMENT

With completion of the mission statement and key moves, you move from strategy development to implementation. So far, the process has been heavily top-down. Effective implementation, however, requires bottom-up participation to gain the commitment of the entire organization. To gain that commitment and to develop a more realistic final strategy, you need to involve all levels and functions of the organization in reviewing and revising the draft strategy. Only then is it "final."

The strategy review process begins with long employee communications meetings. For small companies, a single meeting may suffice. Fortune 500 companies will require many meetings with perhaps 200 employees at each meeting. The meetings have four parts:

1. **The strategy presentation.** First, communicate the need for a new strategy. People will not be interested in a new strategy until they clearly understand the current gap between potential and performance and the adverse consequences of failing to change. Going through some of the analyses and showing how the BHAG is achievable and benefits employees, customers, and owners lays the foundation for the mission statement.

2. **Presentation of the draft mission statement and key moves.** Take them through each phrase and sentence. Explain that the final vision and strategy are going to be the road map for decisions and actions for the next seven to 10 years. The people in the room are going to be the ones responsible for implementation. If it is on-target, they will have an unfair advantage and prosper. Otherwise, they will be swimming upstream and struggling.

   Mention that each department will be developing its own strategies consistent with the overall strategy. Don't cover the broad action plans. Instead, tell them preliminary ideas have been developed on implementation but will be revised significantly to reflect the inputs from people at all levels.

3. **Open the session for questions.** Done right, this part will go as long as the

presentation. It gives the management team the opportunity to explain the need for change and the rationale for the new strategy. The interaction allows real understanding to occur. If necessary, ask questions of the audience. Is there anything in the mission statement that sounds like bull? Is there anything off-target? Most difficult, is there anything we have left out and needs to be included?

4. **Discuss next steps.** Tell them to send any additional ideas for the strategy (and especially the mission statement) in writing in the next two weeks. At that point, the management team will be meeting to make final revisions based on ideas from these meetings. Outline the time table for Cycles 2 and 3. Frankly discuss the importance of developing challenging but achievable individual goals and then holding everyone accountable for implementation. Finally, remind them of the benefits to everyone of successfully implementing the strategy and achieving the vision.

We recommend that the review process involve all employees. Many companies, however, include everyone in the in-depth presentation and discussion of the strategy but only include the salaried people in the development of bottom-up strategies and plans. Keep in mind, the more people understand and are involved in strategy development, the more committed they will be in its implementation.

Comments and suggestions from the bottom-up review process should find expression in the final mission statement. If senior management is doing its job and is in touch with employee values and behavior, the final product will be little different from the draft version, and the changes should improve the final version. However, if employees see the review process as a rubber-stamp farce, the whole Cycle 1 process will have been a waste of time.

Conclusion

You have now completed Cycle 1 of the Three-Cycle Strategy Process. You have (1) a business definition, (2) BHAG, (3) generic strategy, (4) customer, competitor, and people analyses, (5) mission statement, and (6) key moves and broad action plans.

The mission statement is your organization's charter for the next seven to 10 years. Its power and effectiveness during that time depend mostly on how you and your senior management use it. The key is to **use it;** don't let it die from neglect. It should guide all annual plans and functional strategies and frequently find its way into both public statements and private conversations by executives. Tie performance evaluations to it, particularly those of higher-level executives and managers. With the help of Cycles 2 and 3 (departmental strategies and detailed bottom-up action plans), these things should happen naturally and easily if the CEO and senior management are truly committed to the vision and strategy.

Now that the strategy is in place, Cycles 2 and 3 will drive implementation of the strategy that will help you beat competitors in meeting customer wants.

CHAPTER ELEVEN

Strategy Implementation

A 1994 survey[1] asked planning professionals to rate 13 items on "importance for effective strategy implementation." As shown in Exhibit 11.1, the seven most important scales indicate that top management must do two things well to implement strategy successfully:

1. Develop a clear, constant vision and a compelling (but adaptive) strategy for achieving the vision (the two scales with the highest scores), and

2. Create an environment—through hard and soft incentives—that encourages everyone to work together to achieve the vision (the next five scales).

Exhibit 11.1 **The keys to effective strategy implementation**

7 = Very Important

	IMPORTANCE	
STRATEGY DEVELOPMENT	6.49	1. Constancy of purpose by top management
	6.16	2. Allow mid-course corrections
	6.04	3. Reward performance
	5.89	4. Use data and information systems
STRATEGY IMPLEMENTATION	5.88	5. Compare performance to plan
	5.78	6. Set individual responsibilities
	5.62	7. Use multi-functional, multi-level teams

If management does these two tasks well, then people at all levels can work together to 100 percent of their abilities. Since the five "strategy implementation" scales are so fundamental, let's re-order and re-phrase them:

- Make sure each person has clear goals (6),
- Compare each person's performance to those goals (5),
- Reward (positively or negatively) based on performance (3),
- Have people work together, and base some rewards on the performance of the team and total organization (7), and
- Make sure people have solid information for making decisions (4).

Top management has responsibility for strategy development but implementation is bottom-up. While everyone must work together to implement strategy, it only happens when top management creates the right incentives and then holds everyone accountable.

OVERVIEW OF STRATEGY IMPLEMENTATION

Top management leaves the strategy development process full of energy and optimism. The vision is exciting. The strategy exploits the company's core competencies and competitors' weaknesses. The path to implementation—based on the three to five key moves and broad action plans for each key move—seems clear and feasible. Enthusiasm builds with the employee communications meetings as most of the people at all levels welcome the vision of growing sales and profits benefiting all stakeholders.

All too often, however, that initial energy fades. Trying to develop detailed implementation plans requires skills that few in the organization possess. People at all levels are almost relieved when they move back from the stress of change to fighting fires. Yet, they know that failure to implement the strategy will eventually carry a huge cost.

This chapter provides a Three-Cycle Process, summarized in Exhibit 11.2, that makes implementation work. Chapters 4 to 10 took you through the details of Cycle 1: strategy development. This chapter shows how you can overcome the challenges of implementation:

- Resolving organization and people issues after Cycle 1,
- Developing departmental strategies in Cycle 2 (the missing link in effective implementation),
- Using detailed performance measures and action plans in Cycle 3 to link individuals with both strategy and resource allocation, and
- Using the Three-Cycle Process annually.

Exhibit 11.2 **The Three-Cycle Strategy Process**

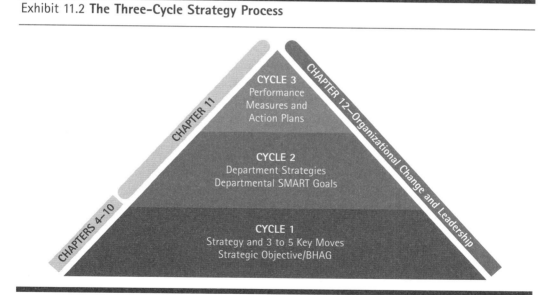

Each of the three Cycles involves goals (BHAG in Cycle 1, SMART goals in Cycle 2, and performance measures in Cycle 3). Each Cycle involves strategies and action plans for achieving the goals. And each Cycle requires that organizational and people issues be addressed. It's obviously easy to make implementation too complex. Here's how to simplify the process and avoid the classic problem of focusing on the rituals of the planning process rather than leading change: After you go through the mechanics of strategy implementation, try to identify the very few elements that are truly essential for driving implementation in your company. It's analogous to the Cycle 1 strategy development process: It's very important to go through the complexity of chapters 4 through 9, but then it's equally important to dramatically simplify the strategy to the mission statement and key moves of chapter 10. Use the Enterprise sidebar (chapter 3) and Supplies Network sidebar (below) as guides.

Strategy Development and Implementation at Supplies Network

I have never seen a company do the two challenges in Exhibit 11.1 better than Supplies Network in Chesterfield, MO. Its results support the validity of that 1994 survey. Supplies Network's sales were less than $10 million in 1990 when IBM set it up as a wholesaler of computer imaging supplies—toner, ink, ribbons, film, paper, magnetic media, and other disposable items. Since then, its annual growth of almost 40 percent produced 1998 sales of $100 million. Plans to expand from one to six distribution centers should accelerate annual growth to 50 percent, producing revenue of $500 million by 2002.

The success of Supplies Network began with management frustration. As a dealer of supplies to businesses, they were frustrated by their wholesale suppliers' lack of dependability and integrity. Wholesalers would assure them that products were in stock and would be delivered the next day while knowing the promises could not be kept. Supplies Network developed a customer-driven vision—to be low cost **and** the most dependable computer supplies wholesaler in the country. Low cost means 9 percent overhead while much larger competitors have overhead of 21 or 22 percent. Dependability includes a 96 percent fill rate on orders. Delivering both low cost and great service requires careful planning and great execution. Supplies Network delivers through people, incentives, and management systems.

As with other companies, people are increasingly the foundation for its business success. Supplies Network is perpetually interviewing. They hire whenever they find a great addition. All of their turnover has come from hiring a marginal person because they "needed a body." Average sales tenure is five years, amazing for an eight year-old company.

Many supplies wholesalers hire part-timers who don't understand the products they are selling. Supplies Network hires full-time, degreed, financially motivated, experienced sales people. Supplies Network tests all sales candidates to make sure they fit the profile of its most successful sales people: extroverted, so they will pick up the phone and initiate the conversation; impatient, so they will ask for the sale; non-conformist, so they will creatively solve customers' problems.

Measurement and incentive systems are the second foundation for Supplies Network's success. All employees of more than one year have performance goals based on their job and department. Purchasing is measured on both order fill rates and inventory turns, so they will focus on both customer satisfaction and working capital. Accounting is measured on closing the books and producing operating reports by the tenth working day of each month, plus the number of end-of-year adjustments.

Dysfunctional "silos" could develop if people were only rewarded for the performance of their own department. Hence, each person is also evaluated by internal customers on 13 teamwork measures such as integrity, attitude, professionalism, interpersonal relations, productivity, initiative, independence, reliability, and leadership. Most employees receive monthly performance feedback and quarterly bonuses if they meet their goals. The big rewards come to those who meet their annual goals and score above 85 percent on the 13 teamwork measures. They receive the maximum pay increase, receive membership in the performance club, and go with their spouses to the annual first class, four-day vacation in the Bahamas or Cancun.

Soft incentives are essential for developing team solutions. People from purchasing and customer service go on a sales call. Customers are brought in to meet with the support staff. Sales people refer to "our" customers to gain support from the staff. Staff wear "I made a difference" and "I love my customers" pins.

Even the best, most motivated people cannot deliver low costs and delight customers without solid management systems, the third key to success. Supplies Network has invested millions of dollars in hardware and software to develop a system to support its expansion plans. Its interactive website allows customers to do anything a salesperson can do—place an order, check the status of an order, get training on a product, etc.

With great execution of a solid business strategy, Supplies Network reaps the rewards of having an unfair advantage over its competitors.

RESOLVING ORGANIZATION AND PEOPLE ISSUES

Organizational Structure

Since the 1950s, Harvard Business School has followed the Strategy ⟹ Structure ⟹ Systems paradigm. First develop the **strategy.** Then develop the organization **structure** that works best in implementing the strategy. Finally, develop the **systems** and policies. This paradigm still makes sense. During Cycle 1 you have developed a clear vision of your company and you have seen your management people in action. Now is the time to make sure you have the right organizational structure. Stripping away all the complexity, there are three basic organization structures: entrepreneurial, functional, and corporate (or divisional).

In the **entrepreneurial** structure, individuals may have titles and responsibilities but people have multiple responsibilities and decisions are made as needed. It works well and is even essential for very small companies. Communications and decision making, however, suffer as the company becomes larger and more complex.

The **functional** organization has strong expertise in each traditional department such as operations, sales, and finance. It is the natural next step after an organization reaches a few million dollars in revenue or more than 100 or so people. The structure may remain viable as single product companies grow by creating new departments (e.g., human resources) or separating a department into two parts (e.g., sales and marketing, or finance and accounting). Bureaucratic problems that emerge with size include departmental "silos" (that slow information flow and action) and a decline in innovation and entrepreneurial culture.

The **corporate or divisional** organization is divided into business units (which often report to the chief operating officer) and staff departments (which report to the CEO). It is very desirable when a company participates in more than one product market. Indeed, even a company with a homogeneous product such as Enterprise Rent-A-Car benefits by treating each of its 4,000 locations as a profit center and each region as a business.

- If your company has grown dramatically, it may be time to move from an entrepreneurial to a functional organization or from functional to a divisional structure.
- Try to make the organization more entrepreneurial. Hence, even if you have a single product line, you may want to emulate Enterprise and make each location a profit center or use performance measures and incentives like Supplies Network.
- Most new strategies strive to make the organization move faster and be more innovative. Hence, large organizations should try to eliminate hierarchy (which may require new information systems, performance measures, and incentives).
- Perhaps the importance of international sales or product quality warrants the separation of the company into domestic and international divisions or the movement of quality from the operations department to a separate department reporting to the president.
- Large organizations should also focus more of their energy on their core competencies. Is it time to sell businesses that don't fit your business definition? Is it time to divest vertical integration and establish partnerships or alliances with others in the value chain? Should you outsource your information systems?

People Issues

As you change the structure, make sure you have the right people in each slot. Consider doing "assessments" of both your top management people and your next generation of leaders to get the right people in each key position. I am amazed at the power of the right assessment package as used by a talented consultant to identify strengths and weaknesses of your people. Before hiring such a consultant, however, get references so

you can ask other companies how effective the consultant was in the following ways:
- Identifying senior people who were bound to fail because they were in positions that required abilities they simply did not possess.
- Identifying other senior people who will sabotage the organization's new strategy,
- Identifying next generation leaders who should be given greater challenges (and guidance on how to make the change to improve odds of success), and
- Identifying challenges the management team as a whole will face because of their combined skill set and culture.

Classify each manager as A, B, C, or D based on their abilities and their commitment to the new strategy. Get rid of Ds fast. Let Cs know they have to improve. Make sure that your top management team includes only As and strong Bs who are committed to the new strategy. A key responsibility of your top management is to identify and fix resistance and competency problems quickly. About a fourth of managers will strongly resist change. One of the major regrets of CEOs is failure to make such changes early. To make these changes easier, have severance and early retirement packages in place early in the program.[2]

Skipping the organization and people step is a prescription for disaster. You have to have the right people in the right organizational structure to win the great game of business. Clydesdales are great at pulling a beer wagon but will come in last in the Kentucky Derby. And even the best Thoroughbred will lose if it doesn't have the right jockey and the right training.

Time Table for Implementation

Exploit the energy that comes from Cycle 1. Insist on action at the same time you are developing Cycles 2 and 3. I recommend that each senior executive identify a problem to get rid of and an opportunity to exploit each month between the end of Cycle 1 and the end of Cycle 3. Then celebrate these wins. Each such victory will convert more people to the new vision. Eventually, the people who simply don't believe in the new strategy or can't change will leave and can be replaced with people who believe in the strategy and have the right skills and experience.

To maintain momentum and a sense of urgency, minimize the time between the end of Cycle 1 and the presentation of departmental strategies. Keep it less than two months for small companies and less than four months for the Fortune 500 (to allow for more in-depth use of internal and external consultants).

Get the Order of Implementation Right

During the strategy development process, key moves are developed without completely thinking through their interactions. Before the departmental strategies are presented, the management team must determine which key moves should be implemented first in order to provide a solid foundation for the others. The importance of "order of implementation" is reflected in the identical sequence of key moves by Anheuser-Busch under August Busch III and Coca-Cola with Roberto Goizueta, as shown in Exhibit 11.3. Both were market leaders that were facing a challenge from a strong No. 2—Anheuser-Busch from Miller Brewing and Coca-Cola from Pepsi-Cola. Both of these new CEOs saw an opportunity to protect their leadership positions and gain market share through aggressive marketing. Their first step was to staff up internally, putting in place a new senior management team, and beefing up the marketing function. Next, each transformed and strengthened its wholesaler and bottler network. Only then did it roll out new products and a new marketing mix to customers.

Exhibit 11.3 **The importance of order of implementation**

PHASE	ANHEUSER-BUSCH AND COCA-COLA
New CEO	Anheuser-Busch in the mid-1970s and Coca-Cola in 1980
New strategy	Significantly accelerate market share through aggressive marketing
Strategy implementation	1. Staff up internally (new senior management and increased marketing) 2. Transform the wholesaler/bottling system 3. Introduce new products (e.g., Bud Light and Diet Coke)

Making massive changes in the distribution system was easier after the parent company demonstrated its commitment internally to major change. The odds of success of a major new product strategy are much higher if supported by large marketing budgets and aggressive management teams from both the parent company and distribution system.

Prioritization and order of implementation are also important in providing guidance to developing departmental strategies and individual action plans in Cycles 2 and 3. By clearly stating that the first two key moves are the company's priority for the first year, the department heads can make sure that their strategies and detailed action plans do not give significant attention to the other key moves until later years. Failure to observe this caveat can lead to an avalanche of proposed action plans in year one that wastes a great deal of time at all levels to prioritize and prune.

Cycle 1 Lays the Foundation for Cycle 2
Involving the entire senior management team in Cycle 1 leads to a superior strategy. It also leads to their ownership of and commitment to the strategy. The communication

and implementation of Cycle 1 then gets the direct reports of each senior executive involved. Done right, Cycle 1 lays the foundation for departmental strategies.

CYCLE 2: DEPARTMENTAL STRATEGIES AND SMART GOALS

Possible Strategy Elements for Departments

The last 20 years have seen an explosion of powerful strategy concepts. The opportunity is that many of these tools have great potential. The threat is that department heads may seize on a tool that does not fit with the overall corporate strategy at the expense of less sexy tools that are essential for successful strategy implementation. That's one of the benefits of the Three-Cycle Process. Cycle 1 provides guidance on what departmental strategies make sense and the review process of Cycle 2 ensures that the departmental strategies will fit together. Let's look at some of the strategy concepts that can provide the foundation for departmental strategies.

- **Finance:** Chief Financial Officers can directly impact shareholder value through acquisitions. They create an environment for others to increase shareholder value through such performance measurement and incentive systems as open book management, The Balanced Scorecard, stock options at all levels, and pay for performance.

- **Information technology:** In the early and mid-1990s, the largest companies spent hundreds of millions of dollars each for Enterprise Resource Planning systems (ERPs) from SAP, Oracle, PeopleSoft, and Baan. Now, IT departments are shifting their infrastructure budgets to Internet-based e-commerce solutions, which promise to transform industry after industry.

- **Marketing:** The 30-second television ad was the key tactical marketing weapon from the rise of TV in the 1950s through the mid-1980s. Today, Promotion/advertising is the least important of the 4 Ps of marketing (Promotion, Price, Product, and Place/distribution). The "graying of the population" makes value (the combination of Product and Price) more important than a glitzy ad. Even more importantly, distribution has moved from the least important to the most important marketing variable. This trend began with the rise of Wal-Mart in the 1980s. The move to e-commerce is now creating new distribution channels which threaten to eliminate many traditional retailers and distributors, as reflected in the market capitalizations of Amazon.com and Charles Schwab compared to Barnes & Noble and Merrill Lynch.

- **Operations:** Quality programs and reengineering allowed companies to get costs down and quality up from 1980 to the mid-1990s. Now supply chain management, partnering with suppliers, and outsourcing are allowing companies to cut time and costs. Mass customization allows firms to exactly meet the needs of customers (and increase loyalty by dramatically increasing switching costs).

- **Human resources:** HR departments in the most successful companies have moved from the bureaucratic executors of downsizing programs to the CEO's partner for growth. They are responsible for helping senior executives attract, develop, and retain the best people and help implement policies for getting everyone to work together.

Department Strategies Are the Missing Link

The fatal flaw in many implementation programs is moving directly from the key moves to action plans. Departments find it easy to develop a long list of proposed actions. But implementing the action plans from all of the departments would result in a lot of action and expense with only weak linkage to the original strategy. It's a classic case of not being able to see the forest for the trees.

Instead, each department needs to establish its "SMART" goals (discussed next) and strategies for achieving these goals on a single piece of paper. (Of course, backup pages can provide detail if desired.) This simplicity is essential so the CEO and other department heads can clearly see if the department's strategy has any major gaps that impact their plans. The lack of detail is not a big issue because individuals will present their detailed action plans (consistent with departmental strategies) in Cycle 3. Using that single page, the department head should be able to discuss how:

- The recommended strategy elements are consistent with the company's key moves and implementing them will result in achieving the department's SMART goals,
- Achieving the SMART goals will result in his or her department doing its share in achieving the company's short-term goals and long-term BHAG and vision, and
- The strategy elements are necessary and reasonably cost-efficient.

As reflected by the variety of strategic tools discussed in the previous section, developing a departmental strategy is not easy. Indeed, I believe that each department should go through departmental strategic planning in much the same way as top management developed the overall strategy (and with many of the same benefits):

- Using outside consultants often provides broad perspective and helps produce a focused strategy in a reasonable period of time.
- Involving all of the senior people in the department leads to real understanding of the company's overall strategy and the department strategy.
- Helping to develop the department strategy leads to better individual performance measures and detailed action plans in Cycle 3.
- Most importantly, each department produces a better strategy.

Departmental SMART Goals

To be acceptable, departmental goals must (1) lead directly to the three to five key moves and (2) be "SMART:" **S**pecific, **M**easurable, **A**chievable, **R**esults-oriented, and **T**ime-based.

- **Specific:** Goals must be specific so people can understand clearly what is required. Avoid platitudes like "become the best" and to "be the industry leader." They're meaningless and breed cynicism that undermines commitment. Specific goals must be focused on the vision and strategy.
- **Measurable:** Without a measure, we don't know if or when we have reached a goal. People don't know what is expected or them or how well they are doing.
- **Achievable:** A goal should be challenging but realistic in order to be taken seriously. For example, Texas Instruments suffered in the early 1980s because it set unachievable targets.
- **Results-oriented:** State the goal in terms of results, not activities or processes. For example, set goals like "zero errors in filling customers' orders," rather than "send all employees to quality assurance seminars." Sending all employees to quality assurance doesn't ensure zero errors in filling orders. The result of zero errors is what counts.
- **Time-based:** "Better late than never" no longer works in most business situations. If a customer wants a product by Tuesday and you don't have it ready until Friday, the customer is going to go to your competitor. So, set deadlines. Otherwise, a goal loses urgency and doesn't command the attention of those responsible for achieving it.

The importance of SMART goals cannot be overstated. In a benchmark study, Monsanto found that challenging, quantitative, externally-oriented goals are a key to effective planning.[3] David Garvin of the Harvard Business School came to the same conclusion in his study of manufacturing quality. In a comparison of Japanese and U.S. manufactures of room air conditioners, he found that only three of 11 U.S. manufacturing plants set specific annual targets for reducing field failures. These three cut their service call rates by more than 25 percent. The others showed little or no change.[4]

The CEO should combine all of the company's SMART goals on one piece of paper (see Exhibit 11.4). Moreover, all direct reports should know it is in the CEO's top desk drawer. Making their achievement a major source of discussion (and positive or negative rewards) at performance review time, the CEO communicates that SMART goals are a commitment.

In Cycle 2, the SMART goals sometimes drive departmental strategies and sometimes the strategies take precedence. For example, the Internet is such a major event that developing a compelling e-commerce strategy would come before developing final marketing goals. The goals set for the Purchasing Department of Supplies Network (Exhibit 11.5), however, drove department strategies that would never have been suggested otherwise.

Exhibit 11.4 **Illustrative SMART goals for a company**

STAKEHOLDER*	MEASURES (FOR ILLUSTRATION ONLY)	PERSON RESPONSIBLE	BASELINE 1997	1998	1999	TARGET 2000	2001	2002
Owners	Net income ROI Acquisitions							
Customers	Customer satisfaction Market share Sales Sales from new products							
The Company	Productivity Quality measures Cycle time Information systems							
Human Resources	Employee satisfaction Turnover Suggestions Management development							

* Note that these measures focus on the three key stakeholders (employees, customers, and owners) plus the company. This reflects the breakthrough work done by Kaplan and Norton on using a "balanced scorecard" of performance measures.[5]

Example of a Department Strategy: Purchasing at Supplies Network

As shown in Exhibit 11.5, Supplies Network has SMART goals for every department. For confidentiality reasons, the specific numbers are disguised or excluded.

The three goals for Purchasing are designed to achieve customer satisfaction (96 percent in-stock), cash flow (low inventories), and profitability (profit margin). The goals are very aggressive to achieve the company BHAG of being world class and ranked in the top three in revenue by 2002.

Initially, Purchasing may argue that it is unfair or even impossible to have both excellent in-stock performance (which requires high inventory) and above average inventory turns (which, by definition, means low inventories). Once the CEO makes it clear that (1) the goals are non-negotiable but (2) funds are available for implementing breakthrough strategies for achieving the goals, then the following elements of a departmental strategy can emerge:

1. Develop solid inventory management and forecasting systems (software, hardware, and trained employees).
2. Develop information systems that allow you to track inventories and usage rates with major customers so you can forecast demand more accurately.
3. Partner with a few key suppliers so they get additional volume and you get preferred pricing, solid information, and rapid response to prevent projected shortages.

Exhibit 11.5 **Departmental goals for Supplies Network**

PURCHASING	CREDIT
• Fill rate: 96 percent by volume next day • Inventory turns: 14 versus industry average of 12 • Margin: 12% profit margin	• Days of sales outstanding • Bad debt percent • Credit releases
CUSTOMER SERVICE	SALES
• Open transactions past 10 days • Resale certificates 100% • Freight claims past 30 days	• Gross profit objective • New account target • Product line discipline goal
DISTRIBUTION CENTER	INFORMATION SERVICES
• Picking & receiving accuracy • Same day shipping • Package quality • Productivity • Cycle count accuracy	• 100% operational hours • 30 minute response help desk • Meet project deadlines • Maintain acceptable system speed
ACCOUNTING	MARKETING
• Month closed 10 working days • Cash application completed 4 of 5 days • 100% of eligible trade discounts taken	• Production deadlines • Accuracy • Project turnaround • Co-op funds past 90 days

Finally, Purchasing can negotiate on the time required to achieve the ultimate goals. Because information systems are an essential element for achieving the in-stock and inventory goals, these SMART goals might call for little improvement in year 1 and then closing the gap 50 percent in year 2 and 100 percent in year 3. An analysis of spot versus long-term purchasing contracts might indicate that 40 percent of the profit margin SMART goal can be achieved in year 1 and then increase to 100 percent attainment by year 5.

Implementation of Cycle 2

Strategy implementation requires bottom-up understanding, involvement, and commitment. Hence, communication and discussion of the strategy to all employees should be conducted shortly after the conclusion of Cycle 1. Immediately after the communications meeting, each department head should begin working with his or her reports to develop the departmental strategy and SMART goals.

For a small or mid-size company, the one- or two-day Cycle 2 meeting should come within 60 days of the completion of Cycle 1 to avoid loss of momentum. The heart of the meeting is the presentation, discussion, and modification of one-page strategies from each department head. The people who helped develop the department strategy should attend their department's presentation so they can better understand management's concerns and answer any questions that arise. The CEO and department heads should not approve a strategy until they believe it is at least an eight on a 10-point scale based on the following criteria:

- It reflects the Cycle 1 strategy (i.e., the department's strategy and SMART goals are consistent with the company's strategy, BHAG, and key moves).
- It has year one priorities consistent with the corporate key moves for year one.
- It is consistent with strategies of other departments (e.g., provides outputs to meet their needs, and does not overlap excessively or require infeasible outputs from them).
- It is feasible (given the department's requested resources) and reasonably cost effective.

A department strategy that is completely inconsistent with the new strategy is a red flag. Be "tough on the issue" and "easy on the person." Quickly replace the department head if assessments, performance, and past behavior indicate he or she simply does not have the ability or the commitment needed for the new strategy. Promote a talented young person or bring in a person from the outside with the right abilities, experience, and values. Such moves demonstrate a new cultural value of accountability that helps attract the right people, encourage others to leave, and then get everyone to work together to achieve the vision.

Involving the entire department in Cycle 2 leads to their understanding of and commitment to the department strategy. Done right, Cycle 2 prepares them for Cycle 3, where the focus is developing detailed individual performance measures and action plans.

CYCLE 3: PERFORMANCE MEASURES AND ACTION PLANS

Preparation of Individual Plans

Immediately after approval of the departmental strategy, the department heads must provide direction to their direct reports for developing their individual plans. I recommend a one or two-hour staff meeting for kicking off the process. The meeting begins with reviewing the approved department strategy and SMART goals and discussion of strategies from other departments that impact your department. The two key elements of the meeting are:

1. Providing broad guidance on the performance measures expected of each person so the department can achieve its SMART goals, and
2. Outlining the Cycle 3 time table and individual responsibilities leading up to submission of each individual action plan on the standard action plan form.

The goal of Cycle 3 is to link each person's activities to both (1) achievement of the company's vision and strategy and (2) the budgeting/resource allocation systems. The action plan form must be designed to provide this linkage. Exhibit 11.6[6] outlines such a form.

Exhibit 11.6 **Contents of a Cycle 3 action plan form**

---

1. Name and brief project description:
2. Identify which corporate key moves it is linked to (allocating 100 percent):
   - Key Move: _____ _____ %
   - Key Move: _____ _____ %
   - Key Move: _____ _____ %
   - Not related to Key Moves ___%. (Include a brief rationale for the project if above 40%)
3. Which department SMART goals benefit from this project?
4. Person responsible:_____ Others involved: _____
5. Cost $_____Budget line item:_____
6. Due date:_____
7. Interim steps (and connection to other action plans)

Cycle 3 Action Plans Meeting

The Cycle 3 action plans meeting allows senior management to (1) obtain detailed understanding of each department, (2) obtain modifications to action plans that are off-target, and (3) see the key people in each department in action. Each department head begins the presentation with a one-page review of the department's strategy and another page or two that lists the individual projects and how they fit with the department strategy. The direct reports then present each of their action plans. The specifics of the plan from the form should be covered quickly. Most of the time is spent understanding the strategic value of the project, how it fits with other projects, and its feasibility.

The CFO develops budgets and projections after all of the departmental action plans are tentatively approved. Final adjustments to achieve acceptable business performance are a lot easier if a list of "desirable but not essential" projects, people, and pricing decisions are kept during the planning process.

Cycle 3 produces performance measures and detailed action plans from each manager and supervisor. For example, the purchasing manager's strategy at Supplies Network would lead to detailed action plans (and interim goals) for developing computer systems, selecting and training appropriate staff, and establishing close relationships with key suppliers and customers. Cycle 3 assures that detailed action plans reflect departmental SMART goals and the key moves of the company. By including the resources necessary to implement these action plans, Cycle 3 also links strategy with the annual budgeting process.

Throughout the Three-Cycle Process, top management should consciously identify and change systems, policies, and individuals that are obstacles to change. Department heads should advise their people of the benefits of each such action in implementing the new strategy. With the approval of Cycle 3 action plans, each person is empowered and strongly encouraged to begin aggressive implementation.

Management should recognize and encourage major actions, then celebrate and reward successes. Equally important, participants in hard fought defeats should be given additional challenges instead of being punished.

THE ANNUAL PLANNING PROCESS

Using the Three-Cycle Process of business strategy, department strategy, and individual plans annually after year one makes a great deal of sense since it keeps the strategy fresh and goal-oriented. Other benefits include departmental coordination and the opportunity for senior managers to see junior people in action. Importantly, the process requires much less time and effort after year one.

Cycle 1 continues to make sure that the company has identified the threats and opportunities on the horizon and has solid strategies in place. The Cycle 1 meeting usually focuses on one or two major new issues and then reviews the key moves and major action plans for each key move. Some years no key move will change but the broad action plans will change significantly each year. The second major benefit of the meeting is providing direction to the department heads.

While Cycle 1 is the focus in year 1, Cycles 2 and 3 are the focus in later years. The overall company strategy is becoming clearer so the key to success is now implementation through effective department strategies and tactics.

Avoid the huge bureaucratic rain dances that flourished through the 1970s. Ban scripted presentations and PowerPoint presentations since their focus on style over content dramatically limits interaction. Just as Lou Gerstner banned overhead foils to force interaction when he became CEO of IBM, you may want to severely limit the allowed number of foils. Most importantly, management should use the meetings to make decisions, and then implement the decisions throughout the year.

Use the meetings to ensure accountability. Require that each Cycle 2 and Cycle 3 presentation begins with a comparison of SMART goals or performance measures from the previous year versus actual performance. The big benefit is to make people commit to their goals and discourage them from setting goals they are unlikely to achieve, not to embarrass them.

The Three-Cycle Process drives change and prevents complacency. Major changes in the strategy (short of a complete revision) are especially called for when the BHAG is close to achievement. Top management must then reinvigorate the process by developing a new BHAG and one or more new key moves to drive its success. Celebrate and reward the participants for the victory in round 1, but raise the hurdle and provide new hard and soft incentives so everyone continues to work together in round 2.

Conclusion

The Three-Cycle Strategy Process takes you from the development of a vision and mission to the pragmatics of delivering results. It allows you to respond to threats and to take advantage of opportunities. While Cycle 1 uses the qualitative tools of strategic thinking, Cycles 2 and 3 also rely on the quantitative goals of proactive "predict and prepare" planning. Quantitative targets and measurements give you control over your organization. People devote time and effort to achieving quantitative goals since their compensation and careers are directly tied to measurable results.

In Cycle 1, top management makes sure the strategy is on-target and provides direction for developing departmental strategies. In Cycle 2, each department then develops bottom-up strategies, which senior management can fine-tune. The resulting bottom-up action plans in Cycle 3 have three extremely important characteristics:

1. They focus each person on projects that are coordinated with other projects,
2. Cycles 1 and 2 help ensure that each Cycle 3 project has the potential to produce superior payoffs to the company, and
3. Cycle 3 leads to an implicit contract between each person and senior management: If you give me the requested resources, I will implement the specific programs and achieve specific results, which will then entitle me to specific rewards.

The "top-down, bottom-up" nature of the Three-Cycle Process produces superior payoffs to all levels of the organization and to all of its stakeholders.

CHAPTER TWELVE

Leading Change and
Results–Based Leadership

The first 11 chapters provide a proven approach to develop and implement a strategy that gives your company an unfair advantage. But the real objective is producing superior performance that benefits employees, customers, and owners. This concluding chapter addresses two final questions that link strategy with superior results:

- How does strategy fit into a broader framework for producing lasting major change in an organization?
- What are the critically important leadership tools so a CEO can effectively lead strategic change?

Both the title of this chapter and the content of the two sections draw heavily from two exceptional books: *Leading Change* by John P. Kotter[1] and *Results-Based Leadership* by David Ulrich and others.[2]

LEADING MAJOR ORGANIZATIONAL CHANGE

Strategic planning plays a major role in effective organizational change. Yet, the focus of strategy and organizational change are very different. Strategy focuses primarily externally, on customers and competitors. The focus of organizational change is internal.

Strategy is based on "hard" business concepts. Finance, marketing, production, and R&D/new products were all ranked more important than human resources in a 1994 survey of what drives strategy and what should drive strategy.[3] The "soft" social sciences have always provided the theoretical foundation for organizational change. Indeed, the three-part "unfreezing, changing, and refreezing" process of organizational change developed by psychologist Kurt Lewin[4] in the 1940s continues to have a strong following:

1. **Unfreezing:** The company must recognize that the old way of doing things is no longer viable and that major change is necessary. Two dramatic ways of communicating the need for change are presented in the sidebar on page 22. Ackoff's use of a reference forecast (page 149), which shows the status quo leads to disaster, is a more rigorous approach for unfreezing an organization.
2. **Changing:** The company must develop a new vision, and a strategy and implementation plan for making the vision a reality. The vision must produce major benefits to all stakeholders. The strategy must reflect the competitive and environmental realities. The implementation plan must be feasible. Finally, employees at all levels must have ownership and commitment to it.
3. **Refreezing:** Once the new strategy and new behaviors are producing superior results, the new attitudes, practices, and policies must be institutionalized. The "new rules" provide a framework for goals, behavior, and rewards.

This three-step approach to organizational change is very similar to the process of changing scientific paradigms developed by Thomas Kuhn.[5] A great deal of conflict occurs between the advocates of a new scientific theory and those committed to the old paradigm. After a rush of breakthrough work and major changes in a short period of time, the basic elements of the new order of things emerges. Then, everyone in the scientific community works together to produce smaller, evolutionary changes over a longer time period.

Kanter *et al.*[6] take a more sophisticated approach to organizational change by looking at three types of organizational participants in the change process. Top management "change strategists" are responsible for deciding when the strategy must change and developing the new vision and strategy. Middle management "change implementors" manage the day-to-day process of change. They must develop the detailed action plans and make sure that the strategy is fully understood, resistance is overcome, and the action plans get implemented. Lower level "change recipients" determine whether change will stick. Exhibit 12.1 presents some of the key elements for obtaining bottom-up support for major change.

Exhibit 12.1 **Requirements for obtaining support for change from "strategy recipients"**

SUPPORT FOR CHANGE INCREASES IF MANAGEMENT ...	SUPPORT FOR CHANGE DECREASES IF ...
• Clearly demonstrates the problems and high costs associated with the status quo • Develops a compelling strategy and implementation plan • Makes sure that all stakeholders benefit significantly if the vision is achieved • Communicates all aspects clearly	• Too much is done to people and too little done by them • Decisions are sprung without background • Too many things change at once • Change requires too much work • People are insecure about their jobs or their competence in the new environment • People don't trust management

KOTTER'S EIGHT STEPS FOR LEADING CHANGE

Exhibit 12.2 **Kotter's eight steps for leading change***

1. Establish a sense of urgency
2. Create a guiding coalition
3. Develop a vision and strategy
4. Communicate the change vision
5. Empower broad-based action
6. Generate short-term wins
7. Consolidate gains and produce more change
8. Anchor new approaches in the corporate culture

* Kotter uses slightly different phrasing in his March–April, 1995 *Harvard Business Review* article and his 1996 book, both titled *Leading Change*. The phrasing above comes from an interview Marilyn Norris and I did with him in *Strategy & Leadership*, January–February 1997), pp. 18–22. The descriptions of the eight steps borrow from all three sources.

John Kotter's eight steps are the best I have seen for making major change in an organization (see Exhibit 12.2). Following these steps greatly increases the likelihood of successful change. Skipping any of these steps or doing them in a different order causes major problems.

1. **Establish a sense of urgency:** Many people fear and hate change. Quite simply, major change in an organization seldom happens until most people believe the pain of not changing is greater than the pain of changing. Kotter claims that well over 50 percent of the companies he has watched have failed in this first phase. Top management must do a superb job of documenting and communicating the need for change to "unfreeze" the organization.

   Examine the market and competitive realities. Identify and discuss crises, potential crises, or major opportunities. Eliminate obvious examples of corporate excess (e.g., company planes and catered lunches). Change won't occur where there is complacency.

2. **Create a guiding coalition:** Major change seldom happens unless the CEO and, eventually, line executives are advocates. A renewal program may begin with just one or two people, but no one person has the credibility, expertise, and skills necessary to provide the necessary leadership. Pull together a group with enough power to lead the change, and urge them to work together as a team. Change requires a committed, capable, energetic top management team. Replace those senior executives who are clearly opposed to change or incapable of leading change in their area of responsibility.

3. **Develop a vision and strategy:** Provide a vision that gives the change effort direction and motivates people. Set a BHAG that requires great effort and produces great benefits. Provide clear direction but be general enough to allow individual initiative and flexibility. Make sure that the strategies for achieving the vision are compelling. Keep the vision and strategy simple. Complex strategies fail because they can't be communicated, don't motivate, and simply aren't implemented. Kotter's rule of thumb: If you can't communicate the vision to someone in five minutes and produce both understanding and interest, you are not yet done with this step 3.

4. **Communicate the change vision:** Even top notch CEOs often under-communicate the new strategy by an order of magnitude. Use every vehicle possible to get the message out—big and small meetings, memos, company newsletters, formal and informal interactions. Use symbols, logos, banners, T-shirts, jackets, and hats. Top-down communications must be followed by bottom-up questions and involvement.

   Actions are the most visible form of communications. Make sure senior executives act in ways consistent with the new values and strategy. Otherwise, cynicism goes up and the willingness of "implementers" and "strategy recipients" to make sacrifices for the new strategy plummets.

5. **Empower broad-based action:** Get rid of obstacles to change. Change systems or policies that seriously undermine the vision. Remove key people who

oppose the new strategy or only give it lip service. Emphatically encourage risk-taking and non-traditional ideas, activities, and actions. Make sure that people aggressively implement their action plans once they are approved in Cycle 3.

6. **Generate short-term wins:** Make sure that each department heads identifies "low hanging fruit"—problems to get rid of and opportunities to exploit— immediately after Cycle 1. Then have them systematically create short-term wins. Recognize and reward people who make the wins possible. Each positive action builds momentum and turns doubters into advocates.

   The need for action is one of the reasons that line executives must be involved in planning for change. Too often, staff people develop elaborate strategies that fail to produce tangible results for a year or even longer. The resulting loss of momentum can kill even a solid strategy.

7. **Consolidate gains and produce more change:** After a year or two of long hours and the stress of constant change, clearly positive results begin to emerge. People begin asking when they can celebrate their achievements. Beware of the pre-mature celebration! Too often, people view it as a victory celebration. Once a war has been won, it's hard to get the troops back on the field. Soon, change comes to a halt, and the "old ways of doing things" re-appear. Don't let it happen!

   Instead, use increased credibility to change all systems, structures, and policies that don't fit together and don't fit the transformation vision. Hire, promote, and develop employees who can implement the vision. Reinvigorate the process with new projects, themes, and change agents. Push responsibility and accountability down. Institutionalize change by creating leaders at all levels of the organization.

   If the BHAG is in sight, consider developing a new BHAG and changing two or three of the key moves to support the new approach. Review the performance measures and incentives to make sure that everyone benefits from accomplishing the new goals.

8. **Anchor new approaches in the corporate culture:** Changing beliefs and culture is hard. Hence, the early stages of the change process should focus on getting results by changing performance measures and behaviors. Failure to institutionalize the new behaviors, however, leads to relapse into the old ways. Sometimes that only occurs after the CEO who revitalized the company retires and is followed by a person who embodies the company's "traditional values."

   To avoid such relapse, the last step in leading lasting change is to explicitly link the improved results to specific behaviors and values. The mechanism may be formal presentations from the CEO to the Board and to employees, which are then reprinted and distributed as booklets. Each old cultural value may be contrasted with a new value. The old value may be honored for its contributions in the past. But the CEO can then drive a stake through it by detailing its corrosive impacts when the competitive environment changed. The CEO then begins institutionalizing each new cultural value by detailing how it fits with the current competitive realities and the results it has produced. With a history of success, people are willing to accept new beliefs.

How do Kotter's eight steps fit with the Three-Cycle Strategy Development Process? The next two paragraphs show where we cover each of Kotter's steps. Yet, as pointed out at the beginning of this chapter, the organizational change literature takes a softer, people-centered approach. We strongly advocate that someone on the senior management team take responsibility for the softer side of strategy. They should use Kotter's book (as well as *Results-Based Leadership*, which is covered in the next section) in developing people-driven strategies.

Only Kotter's step 3 explicitly focuses on strategy. Yet, his steps 1 and 2 are a lot easier to accomplish because this book provides confidence that a solid vision, strategy, and implementation plan can be developed. CEOs become more willing to launch major change initiatives. Similarly, the rest of the management team is more willing to join the guiding coalition for change once they trust the strategy process.

The last part of chapter 10 addresses communication of the Cycle 1 strategy and initiating the process of getting bottom-up involvement and commitment (step 4). Chapter 11 focuses on bottom-up implementation, including empowering broad-based actions and generating short-term wins (steps 5 and 6). Step 7 basically advocates something just short of a complete strategy review rather than a simple three-cycle annual planning process. While chapter 9 discusses corporate culture, we do not address many of the issues in Kotter's final step.

RESULTS-BASED LEADERSHIP

Neither strategy nor leadership is essential when things are stable and change occurs slowly. Strategy is only needed when the pace of change is faster than people can adapt using informal methods. Similarly, leaders are only needed when changing conditions require different behaviors from organizations. Peter Drucker's 834-page magnum opus *Management,* which came out in 1973, only has three references to leadership, and all three basically equate leadership with top management. The oil shock of 1973 and the rise of globalization, which accelerated in the 1970s, however, mark the transition to an era of accelerating change. The subsequent creation of a "leadership" industry is not surprising.

John Kotter does a nice job of distinguishing the roles of managers and leaders.[7] Through the 1970s, the terms were interchangeable, except leaders were higher in the organization. In the 1980s, they were thought of as being on opposite ends of a continuum, with an organization being managed or led. In the 1990s, however, people realized that management and leadership are not a trade-off. Instead, they are two separate dimensions, and both are very important. That is why high performance companies often have a CEO who is 80 percent leader and a COO who is 80 percent manager. The leader has eyes on the future and focuses on how things must change. The manager has hands on the present and ensures that daily commitments are handled effectively.

The leadership literature since 1980 is huge. Some is excellent while much is truly awful. Prior to 1999, my one firm belief was no Adam Smith or John Maynard Keynes had developed a compelling leadership paradigm. *Results-Based Leadership*[8] by University of Michigan professor Dave Ulrich and consultants Jack Zenger and Norm Smallwood, however, is immensely readable and provides a compelling structure. It is the one leadership book for CEOs who want to achieve dramatic results. Its only weakness is looking at the leader in isolation and omitting the roles of the environment and followers.

Much of the leadership literature focuses on four sets of attributes of successful leaders: setting direction, demonstrating personal character, mobilizing individual commitment, and building organizational capability (see Exhibit 12.3). *The Balanced Scorecard*[9] demonstrated that long-term organizational success requires results in four areas: employees, company capabilities, customers, and investors. Ulrich emphasizes that effective leadership requires both attributes and results: leadership = attributes x results. The equation states that the complete absence of attributes (e.g., "Chainsaw" Al Dunlap of Sunbeam) or zero focus on results leads to disaster:

- Attributes without results produces leaders with talent and good character who don't meet their goals, and
- Results without attributes produce only short-term, unsustainable results.

Exhibit 12.3 **A framework for leadership attributes**

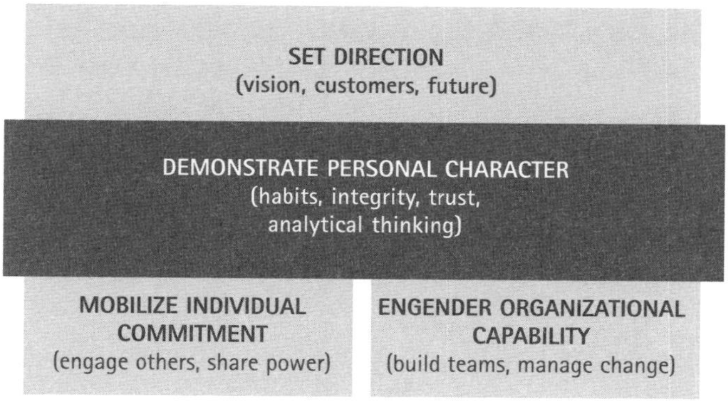

Reprinted with permission from *Results-Based Leadership* by Dave Ulrich, Jack Zenger, and Norm Smallwood. © 1999 by Harvard Business School Press. p. 7.

Leadership Attributes

Pages 8 to 13 of Ulrich break the following four attributes of leaders into 89 bullets based on 44 different publications.

Setting Direction

Setting direction is the role of the leader as chief strategist. As Warren Bennis says, "The indispensable first quality is a guiding vision, a clear idea of what he wants to do. All the leaders I know have a strongly defined sense of purpose. And when you have an organization where the people are aligned behind a clearly defined vision or purpose you get a powerful organization."[10] Setting direction has three dimensions:

1. Understand external events: Focus strongly on customers, form networks outside of the company, and see new possibilities.
2. Focus on the future: Visualize the business through the customer's eyes, operate from a set of inspiring core values and beliefs, and articulate a tangible vision and strategy.
3. Turn vision into action: Create a climate of success by inspiring a shared vision, aligning performance with the vision, and enlisting others to achieve the vision.

Mobilizing Individual Commitment

Getting everyone in the organization to become as passionate for achieving the vision as senior management requires superior people skills. If the CEO's strength is in the analytical, hard strategy areas, make sure that someone else on the top management team focuses on these attributes. Building collaborative relations with all levels requires a love of people, promoting cooperative goals, and trust. Cheerleading, supporting, and encouraging are more important than judging, criticizing, and evaluating.

Share power and authority and strengthen others by sharing information and eliciting participation. Ask questions and listen rather than telling and directing. Use a variety of approaches so you get the best out of each person. Like FDR during the depression and Churchill during World War II, use language to touch the heart, generate emotion, and create confidence, courage, optimism, and a conviction that the future will be better.

Building Organizational Capability

Built to Last[11] details nine ways in which 18 visionary companies differ from 18 less visionary competitors (e.g., IBM vs. Burroughs and Procter & Gamble vs. Colgate). With reinvestment, a dollar invested in the general stock market at the beginning of 1926 would have grown to $415 by the end of 1990. A similar investment in the visionary and less visionary companies would have grown to $6,356 and $995, respectively. The first key difference was the founders of the visionary companies focused on building organizational capability. They were decidedly less charismatic than the founders of the less visionary companies. Like the writers of the U.S. Constitution, they concentrated more on architecting an enduring institution than on being great individual leaders.

Leaders build organizational capability in four ways:

1. Build organizational infrastructure: Align the organization structure with the strategy. Develop formal leadership capable of integrating the key moves needed to achieve your vision. Form ad hoc leadership within each key move. Provide advocacy and resources for continuous improvement.
2. Leverage diversity: Fully utilize people, regardless of race, gender, ethnic origin, or culture. Advocate partnering and collaboration. Resolve conflicts diplomatically. Do not fear strength in subordinates.
3. Design human resource systems: Build, maintain, and consciously promote a clearly articulated, stimulating culture.
4. Make change happen: Be a change agent. Challenge the status quo. Initiate change rather than reacting to external pressures. Experiment and take risks. Learn from both successes and failures. Relentlessly provide customers with better products or services. Use teams so others become involved in change.

Demonstrating Personal Character

Warren Bennis[12] says that a leader's character is a tripod with three elements: ambition and drive; competence and expertise; integrity and moral fabric. Major weakness in any of the three elements causes the tripod to topple:

- An ambitious leader without competence and integrity is a demagogue.
- A person with competence but without integrity and drive is a technocrat.
- Someone with ambition and competence but without integrity is a destructive achiever.

Ulrich lists three somewhat different dimensions of personal character:

1. Live values by practicing what is preached: Lead by example and live the values of the organization. Submit to the mirror test, and find comfort with the person you see.
2. Have and create a positive self-image: Combine self-confidence and humility. Be perceptive in the realities of the world and with individuals and groups. Exhibit extraordinary levels of motivation to enable group members to go through the pain of learning and change.
3. Possess cognitive ability and personal charm: Have an open mind and be receptive to information and broad business knowledge. Act with integrity. Learn from mistakes and be open to criticism. Deal effectively with complex, ambiguous, and even contradictory situations.

"What Managers Can Learn from Manager Reagan"[13]

A 1986 article on President Reagan (before the Iran-Contra affair) provides fascinating insight into the person known as "The Great Communicator." It is interesting to try to classify Reagan's 13 leadership characteristics into Ulrich *et al.'s* four dimensions of leadership. My attempts place most of the points into multiple dimensions. Those that don't fit easily are consistent with Kotter's eight steps for leading change.

1. Strong vision but constantly, skillfully compromises.
2. Translates his vision into a simple agenda with clear priorities that legislators, bureaucrats, and constituents can readily understand.
3. Constantly recalculates balance between idealism and realism—demonstrates a realization that his goals are achieved not overnight but slowly, day by day, year by year.
4. Message to his team and the public is consistent and upbeat.
5. Sets priorities. Departments and agencies must fit funding requests to his blueprint.
6. Painstaking in choosing subordinates but otherwise avoids details.
7. Set of criteria for hiring—loyalty not just to Republican Party, but to Reagan and his program.
8. Selects people who are on his wavelength, delegates to them, doesn't interfere as long as the policy is being carried out.
9. Encourages staff people to speak their minds.
10. Decisions, at least on major matters, are fast and firm.
11. Expects his aides to fall in line once a decision has been made.
12. Facilitates change by taking tension out of situations. He ends even the most serious meetings with a funny story and staffers go away smiling.
13. Maintains credibility. Through the several disasters, he went to the public with a relatively full account.

Leadership Means Results

Next to integrity and ethics, results are the most important requirement for effective leadership. Achieving permanent results, however, requires a "balanced scorecard" across four areas: the organization and the three key stakeholders of employees, customers, and investors. The last section pointed out the importance of building the organization for long-term success, while the early chapters showed that effective strategy must benefit all three key stakeholders.

The four leadership dimensions in Exhibit 12.3 allow you to achieve balanced results in both the short-term and long-term. Moreover, positive results for employees and the organization provide the foundation for continuous improvement in customer loyalty and financial performance. A "virtuous cycle" results since the larger profit pool provides additional opportunity to further strengthen employees, the organization, etc.

The results a person wants to achieve should determine leadership attributes to focus on and which leadership development programs make sense. Ulrich gives the following examples of following a leadership attribute to strengthen with "**so that** ... a particular goal can be achieved":

- Improve the interpersonal skills of a shift supervisor **so that** the people on the shift feel comfortable approaching him when they have suggestions for improvement and they can beat the budget by five percent each month.
- Delegate more **so that** people feel committed to the job, as reflected by a 25 percent reduction in absences and sick days.

Employee Results: Investing in Human Capital

Human capital = capability x commitment. Capability includes each employee's technical knowledge and abilities. But it also includes interpersonal social skills and sensitivities. Having people who know how to work together effectively directly impacts productivity. Management must identify which capabilities to strengthen to achieve the vision, and then increase capabilities through the "six Bs":

- Buy: Turnarounds often involve replacing 75 percent of the senior management within 18 months.
- Build: Through on-the-job development programs, short courses, and elaborate management development programs.
- Benchmark: So people adapt "best practices" from other companies.
- Borrow: Use consultants for specific engagements (and make sure that their capabilities are transferred to internal people).
- Bounce: Remove the weakest five percent or so of employees each year.
- Bind: Make sure that today's leaders and tomorrow's stars (as well as key technical experts at all levels) have clear incentives to stay.

While capability reflects people's potential, commitment measures what percent of that potential they actually deliver. Commitment increases dramatically when management develops the right BHAG and demonstrates commitment leadership attributes (e.g., listen rather than tell, and cheerlead and encourage rather than criticize).

Organization Results: Creating Capabilities

Companies that have the information systems and culture to work together better across departmental lines, to out-innovate, and to move faster than competitors are the big winners in the last 20 years and will widen their lead in the future. Industry leaders get a bigger payoff and the industry laggards pay a bigger price in the Internet era. I'm writing this on December 31, 1999. Qualcomm's stock has increased 2,422 percent this year and reached a market capitalization of $60 billion because of its CDMA standard for digital wireless phones.

Analyze your key processes and reengineer those that aren't working. It's not hard to identify troubled computer, human resource, new product development, production, and sales and marketing systems. Start with the one system that is most linked to your key moves. Give it the internal and external resources necessary for success so that it builds momentum.

Combining capabilities can produce huge synergies. Combining the capability to **develop a strategy** that gives an unfair competitive advantage is infinitely more valuable when combined with the capability to **implement a strategy** (e.g., by holding people accountable for their departmental SMART goals and individual performance measures).

Customer Results: Building Loyalty

To produce long-term results, leadership must eventually focus externally. The most effective strategies focus on identifying the right customer segment, exactly understanding their wants, and designing the 4 Ps of marketing to exactly meet those wants. Similarly, the most effective BHAGs focus on beating competitors or achieving daunting sales results.

Customer satisfaction surveys are a proven way of measuring how well you are doing and suggesting what changes are necessary to increase customer loyalty.

Investor Results: Building Shareholder Value

Doing a solid job of increasing human capital, growing organizational capability, and building customer loyalty makes it a lot easier to produce solid financial results. But a lot of times a football team fails to score a touchdown after getting to the 10 yard line. Investor results require that leaders reduce costs, increase volume, and demonstrate that superior performance is likely in the future.

Most of the cost reduction programs of the last 20 years have paid a high price by destroying employment commitment. As a result, fewer than half of all reengineering programs have produced projected results. The key is to get every employee to act like an owner. Open book management and stock purchase plans provide knowledge and hard incentives for aligning employees with company goals. When significant job reductions are needed (e.g., during a turnaround or after a merger), it's best that the reductions be done fast and as humanely as possible. Also, combine the cost reduction programs "for surviving" with a future growth plan "for thriving."

Since 1995, most large companies have shifted from cost reduction to revenue growth as the primary driver of profit growth. Too many, however, have demanded growth without investing in the human capital, organization capabilities, product attributes, or marketing communications needed for sustainable growth. Quite simply, a completely different leadership focus and corporate culture is required for growth. The good news is that a growth culture is much more conducive to employee commitment and high performance.

Management equity is the final and most important element in producing investor results. General Electric's market capitalization grew from $14 billion to over

$500 billion in the 18 years since Jack Welch became CEO. At the same time, leaders who left GE have produced remarkable results at other companies. The stock of The Stanley Works grew twice as fast as the S&P 500 after John Trani became CEO. The stock of McDonnell Douglas grew 298 percent in the three years between Harry Stonecipher becoming CEO and when it was acquired by Boeing. Stanley Gault proved the GE magic twice. First, he produced legendary results at Rubbermaid. He then grew the stock of Goodyear at almost twice the S&P 500 rate in his five years as its CEO. The rules for such success are easy:

- Develop solid strategies and implement them by holding people accountable for stretch goals,
- Develop leaders at all levels who exhibit both leadership attributes and a commitment to results, and
- Create a great stock from a great company by maintaining consistent revenue and earnings growth and never surprising Wall Street.

Final Observations on Leadership
Results Are the Litmus Test for a Leadership Practice

Ulrich notes that using results as the litmus test for judging a leadership practice will increase your performance. The slow but steady demise of "command and control" tactics is due to the demonstrably superior results in quality, innovation, and productivity from "communication and commitment" approaches. Similarly, flatter, less hierarchical structures are replacing bureaucratic organizations because they attract more entrepreneurial people and produce better results. Three forces are accelerating the conversion to these more productive organizational forms and leadership styles:

1. Tougher competition and a less forgiving stock market force companies to take the difficult steps needed to achieve their potential.
2. The shift to growth rather than cost reduction and to more dynamic and people-driven strategies requires leadership tactics that develop and fully utilize human capital.
3. The intolerance of Generation X for bureaucracy combined with the shortage of skilled people due to the strong economy means that only companies with people-friendly policies will be able to attract and retain the best people—who are increasingly the key success factor for growth.

Beware of the Five Temptations of a CEO

Most people make it to CEO because they have demonstrated solid management capabilities and produced solid results. But once they make it to the top, some seem to shift their focus from producing results to preserving their status. Consultant Patrick Lencioni shows how this occurs and the consequences for both the CEO and his company in *The Five Temptations of a CEO: A Leadership Fable.*[14]

The cause of this shift in focus is simple. Many people are motivated by personal gain in dollars, power, and status to make the sacrifices required to reach the top. Once there, they maintain this personal focus. They act as though the best way to stay at the top is to focus their energies on maintaining their position. They are wrong. CEOs who fail to produce results have increasingly short tenures at organizations of all types.

Exhibit 12.4 presents the five temptations of a CEO and simple recommendations for overcoming them. While "results" is the first temptation, the CEO must really completely reverse the order. Results occur only if the CEO has overcome the other four temptations.

Exhibit 12.4 **The five temptations of a CEO**

OVERCOMING THE FIVE TEMPTATIONS	RECOMMENDATIONS FOR AVOIDING THE TEMPTATIONS
1. Choose results over status	Make results the most important measure of personal success, or step down from the job. The future of the company you lead is too important for customers, employees, and stockholders to hold it hostage to your ego.
2. Choose employee accountability over popularity	Work for the long-term respect of your direct reports, not their affection. They aren't going to like you anyway if you fail, and they must deliver on their commitments if the company is to produce predictable results. You can't hold them accountable unless you provide clear performance expectations and feedback on results.
3. Choose clarity over certainty	Take decisive action rather than always waiting for more information. Change plans and explain why if your decisions are wrong. The only real cost to you of being wrong is loss of pride. The cost to the company of not taking the risk is paralysis.
4. Choose conflict over harmony	Tolerate discord. Encourage your reports to argue their positions passionately. Guard against personal attacks but not to the point of stifling important interchange of ideas.
5. Choose trust over invulnerability	Demonstrating integrity and the leadership attributes of personal character is the foundation for trust. Improve strategy development and implementation by actively encouraging your people to challenge your ideas.

Conclusion

In the mid-1990s, senior executives of a struggling retail chain sat in a room discussing their many woes. With them was an outsider, who suggested that they might wish to reconsider their strategy since the rise of a powerful new competitor had fundamentally changed the competitive equation. They listened respectfully, but then told him they would do fine if only their store managers would meet sales targets. What they really needed, they said, was to put more pressure on the store managers.

Less than a year later, this company declared bankruptcy—no doubt, although the announcement was silent on this, all because of the failure of the store managers. Neither the quality of management nor their strategy seems to have had anything to do with it.

Superior management is the **only** way to turn around a business decline, the only way to increase a company's long-term growth rate, the only way to achieve long-term objectives. Level changes in price or in advertising, for instance, only produce level changes in sales. But superior management creates an environment in which everyone in the company works together to achieve their full potential. Superior management causes the organization to make superior decisions every day up and down the line, and this leads to continual level increases in sales month after month, quarter after quarter, year after year.

Superior management is both a cause and a consequence of superior strategy—strategy that results in intelligent adaptation to change and serves the interests of all stakeholders—shareowners, customers, and employees alike. Often, superior strategy causes the change. Whether it's Henry Ford's redefinition of the automobile business early in the century, or the industry standards of the Wintel ecology at the end of the century creating a combined market capitalization of Microsoft and Intel approaching a trillion dollars, superior strategy can change the rules and give you an unfair competitive advantage.

At other times, external competitive or climate forces change the rules, and you need a new strategy appropriate to the new conditions. Failure to develop one means your eventual decline as competitors fill the strategy void. This is a lesson many companies must take to heart so they transform themselves and thrive in the Internet era.

Whatever the era and whatever the industry, whether you force change or whether change is forced upon you, superior strategy is the only way you will win in the real world—by creating an unfair competitive advantage that benefits employees, customers, and owners.

ENDNOTES

CHAPTER 1

1. Frederick F. Reichheld, *The Loyalty Effect: The Hidden Force Behind Growth, Profits, and Lasting Value* (Boston: Harvard Business School Press, 1996).
2. Survey of 254 middle managers. Based on Russell L. Ackoff, *Creating the Corporate Future* (New York: John Wiley & Sons, 1981).
3. Darrell Rigby, "Strategic Planning Tools," presented at the International Conference of The Planning Forum, 1994.
4. Paul Romer, "The New Economy," presented at the International Conference of Strategic Leadership Forum, 1999.
5. Henry Mintzberg, *The Rise and Fall of Strategic Planning* (New York: The Free Press, 1994).
6. "Survey of U.S. Business," *CFO Magazine,* Spring, 1996.

CHAPTER 2

1. Robert A. Burgelman and Andrew S. Grove, "Strategic Dissonance," *Harvard Business Review,* January-February 1996.
2. See Russell L. Ackoff, *Creating the Corporate Future* (New York: John Wiley & Sons, 1981), pp. 101-103.
3. This example is based on a presentation by Tom Fleming, president of Supplies Network. See chapter 11 for a more detailed discussion of strategy implementation at Supplies Network.
4. This discussion is based on talks by Russell Ackoff.

CHAPTER 3

1. Michael Porter, *Competitive Strategy* (New York: The Free Press, 1980), p. 4.
2. Similarly, paying millions for a strategy from a leading strategy firm can be counter-productive. Few executives will aggressively argue with a McKinsey & Company strategy. A strategic planning process that begins with a tentative strategy costing 99 percent less may lead to a better final strategy.
3. At the time, I was president of a strategy consulting firm. After the strategy was completed, I joined Grace as principal and director of their business consulting group.

CHAPTER 4

1. Derek F. Abell, *Defining the Business: The Starting Point of Strategic Planning* (Englewood

Cliffs, NJ: Prentice-Hall, 1980), p. 5. Abell provides the approach to business definition used in this chapter.

2. Theodore Levitt, "Marketing Myopia," *Harvard Business Review,* July–August 1960, pp. 45–56.
3. B. Joseph Pine II and James H. Gilmore, *The Experience Economy* (Boston: Harvard Business School Press, 1999), p. 21.
4. Clayton M. Christensen, *The Innovator's Dilemma: When New Technologies Cause Great Firms to Fail* (Boston: Harvard Business School Press, 1997).
5. See Robert D. Buzzell and Bradley T. Gale, *The PIMS Principles: Linking Strategy to Performance* (New York: The Free Press, 1987).
6. These examples come from William S. Birnbaum, *If Your Strategy Is So Terrific, How Come It Doesn't Work?* (New York: American Management Association, 1990), pp. 112–13.
7. See Arthur Thompson, Jr., and A.J. Strickland III, *Strategy Formulation and Implementation* (Plano, TX: Business Publications, Inc., 1983), pp. 255–57.

CHAPTER 5
1. See Chapter 10 for discussion of motivating missions.
2. James C. Collins and Jerry I. Porras, *Built to Last: Successful Habits of Visionary Companies* (New York: Harper Business, 1994), p. 94.
3. *Ibid.,* pp. 111–12.
4. Jim Collins, "Turning Goals into Results: The Power of Catalytic Mechanisms," *Harvard Business Review,* July–August 1999, pp. 71–80.
5. GE and McKinsey & Company may have been the first to refine the BCG matrix planning approach, but they were not alone. A.T. Kearney, Royal Dutch Shell, and others developed various refinements, all similar to the GE Business Strength-Industry Attractiveness Matrix. PIMS grew out of a research project initiated by General Electric in the early 1960s. Top management was continually faced with "hockey stick" forecasts from business units claiming that incremental investments would produce high incremental returns. In an effort to identify businesses that could benefit from additional management and capital and those that could not, GE's planners sought to develop a regression model to determine the "par" or expected ROI given a business' controllable and uncontrollable variables. This work led to the initial PIMS pilot project at the Marketing Science Institute at Harvard in 1972. In 1975 the Strategic Planning Institute was founded to conduct the ongoing PIMS research. See Robert D. Buzzell and Bradley T. Gale, *The PIMS Principles: Linking Strategy to Performance* (New York: The Free Press, 1987), chapter 3, for background and an overview of PIMS. The discussion of PIMS presented here is based on this excellent book.
7. Exhibits 5.4 and 5.5 were adapted from Buzzell and Gale, *The PIMS Principles,* pp. 69, 87, and 146.
8. Adrian J. Slywotzky and David J. Morrison, *The Profit Zone: How Strategic Business Design Will Lead to Tomorrow's Profits* (New York: Times Business, 1997).

CHAPTER 6
1. Michael Porter, *Competitive Strategy* (New York: The Free Press, 1980), chapter 2.
2. Michael Treacy and Fred Wiersema, *The Discipline of Market Leaders* (Reading, MA: Addison-Wesley, 1994).
3. For a discussion of PLC and its criticisms, see Steven P. Schnaars, *Marketing Strategy: A Customer-Driven Approach* (New York: The Free Press, 1991), chapter 12.

4. Geoffrey Moore, *Inside the Tornado: Marketing Strategies from Silicon Valley's Cutting Edge* (New York: Harper Business, 1995).
5. See Derek F. Abell, "Strategic Windows," *Journal of Marketing,* July 1978, pp. 21-25.
6. This Exhibit is based on Michael Porter, *Competitive Strategy* (New York: The Free Press, 1980), pp. 40-41.

CHAPTER 7

1. Ries' and Trout's thinking on positioning is presented in their classic book, *Positioning: The Battle for Your Mind* (New York: Warner Books, 1981).
2. This Exhibit is based on George S. Day, *Market Driven Strategy* (New York: The Free Press, 1990), p. 102.
3. Dennis H. Gensch, Nicola Aversa, and Steven P. Moore, "A Choice-Modeling Market Information System That Enabled ABB Electric to Expand Its Market Share," *INTERFACES,* January-February 1990, pp. 6-25.
4. For an excellent discussion of geodemographic systems and other sophisticated new market research systems, see David J. Curry, *The New Marketing Research System* (New York: John Wiley & Sons, 1993). Chapter 13 discusses PRIZM and the other major geodemographic systems.
5. George Day, *Market Driven Strategy,* p. 103.
6. *Health Marketing News,* Market Opinion Research, Detroit, Mich., Fall 1988.
7. The statistical technique used is called multidimensional scaling. The input data could be different types of survey results. For instance, the researchers could ask respondents to grade hospitals on a five-point scale (1 = very weak, 5 = very strong) on each of the 16 services. Or they could rank the hospitals from best to worst on each of the 16 services. See David A. Aaker, ed., *Multivariate Analysis in Marketing: Theory and Application* (Belmont, CA: Wadsworth Publishing Co., 1971).
8. Trout and Ries, *Positioning,* chapters 12 and 13.
9. Marketing materials from Maritz Inc., St. Louis, Missouri.
10. Clayton M. Christensen, *The Innovator's Dilemma: When New Technologies Cause Great Firms to Fail* (Boston: Harvard Business School Press, 1997).

CHAPTER 8

1. Michael Porter, *Competitive Strategy* (New York: The Free Press, 1980).
2. Col. John R. Elting, U.S. Army, Ret., *The Super-Strategists* (New York: Charles Scribner's Sons, 1985).
3. Al Ries and Jack Trout, *Marketing Warfare* (New York: New American Library, 1986).
4. Philip Kotler and Ravi Singh, "Marketing Warfare in the 1980s," *Journal of Business Strategy,* Fall 1980, as reprinted in Roger A. Kerin and Robert A. Peterson, eds., *Perspectives on Strategic Marketing Management* (Boston: Allyn and Bacon, Inc., 1983), pp. 67-81.
5. Robert Axelrod, *The Evolution of Cooperation* (New York: Basic Books, Inc., 1984).
6. Gary Hamel and C. K. Prahalad in "Strategic Intent," *Harvard Business Review,* May-June 1989, pp. 17-30.
7. Adam Brandenburger and Barry Nalebuff, *Co-opetition* (New York: Currency Doubleday, 1996).
8. James F. Moore, "Predators and Prey: A New Ecology of Competition," *Harvard Business Review,* May-June 1993, which won the McKinsey award as the best *HBR* article of 1993.

9. See Elting, *The Super-Strategists*, pp. 323-31.
10. The concept of "strategic intent" was brilliantly developed by Gary Hamel and C. K. Prahalad in "Strategic Intent," *Harvard Business Review*, May-June 1989, pp. 17-30. My discussion draws heavily on this article.
11. For a discussion of Savin's entry into the photocopier market, see George L. Farr, "Developing New Game Strategies," a talk before the American Marketing Association's 1983 Strategic Planning Conference, Chicago, April 19, 1983.
12. Hamel and Prahalad, "Strategic Intent," p. 24.
13. See Hamel and Prahalad, "Strategic Intent," pp. 23 and 25.
14. Robert Axelrod, *op cit.*, pp. 27-69.
15. Michael Porter, *The Competitive Advantage of Nations* (New York: The Free Press, 1991), pp. 69-89.
16. This example is taken from James F. Moore, *op cit.*, p. 77.
17. Benjamin Gomes-Casseres, *The Alliance Revolution: The New Shape of Business Rivalry* (Cambridge, MA: Harvard University Press, 1996), p. 7.
18. This example is taken from Gomes-Casseres, *ibid.*, p. 2.
19. James F. Moore, *The Death of Competition: Leadership & Strategy in the Age of Business Ecosystems* (New York: HarperCollins, 1996), p. 27.

CHAPTER 9

1. Holly Threat, "Measurement is Free," *Strategy & Leadership*, May-June 1999, p. 19.
2. Paraphrased from a presentation by Herb Kelleher to the St. Louis Association for Corporate Growth in 1995.
3. Frederick F. Reichheld, *The Loyalty Effect: The Hidden Force Behind Growth, Profits, and Lasting Value* (Boston: Harvard Business School Press, 1996), p. 303.
4. Jeffrey Pfeffer, *Competitive Advantage Through People: Unleashing the Power of the Work Force* (Boston: Harvard Business School Press, 1994).
5. Brian Friedman, James Hatch, and David Walker, *Delivering on the Promise: How to Attract, Manage, and Retain Human Capital* (New York: The Free Press, 1998).
6. Linda Grant, "Happy Workers, High Returns," *Fortune*, January 12, 1998.
7. Jonathan Low and Tony Siesfeld, "Measures that Matter: Wall Street Considers Non-Financial Performance More Than You Think," *Strategy & Leadership*, March-April 1998.
8. Rob Duboff and Carla Heaton, "Employee Loyalty: A Key Link to Value Growth," *Strategy & Leadership*, January-February 1999.
9. John Byrne, "The Search for the Young and Gifted: Why Talent Counts," *Business Week*, October 4, 1999.
10. David L. Strum, "Workforce Commitment: Strategies for the New Work Order," *Strategy & Leadership*, January-February 1999, p. 7.
11. John P. Kotter and James L. Heskett, *Corporate Culture and Performance* (New York: The Free Press, 1992).
12. Terrence E. Deal and Allan A. Kennedy, *The New Corporate Cultures* (Reading, MA: Perseus Books, 1999), pp. 12-15.
13. I wish to thank Les Landes of Landes Communications for bringing this tool to my attention. This culture instrument is part of Arthur Andersen's Accelerated Corporate Evolution[SM] (ACE) Workshop. Call Jay Fedora of Arthur Andersen at (314) 425-9241 for more information. This instrument may not be used without the written permission of Arthur Andersen.
14. Adapted from C. Davis Fogg, *Implementing Your Strategic Plan* (New York: AMACOM, 1999), p. 239.

15. From a 1999 presentation by Bill Bayer to the St. Louis Sales & Marketing Executives on "Building a World Class Sales Force." The PIAV is a registered product of TTI © 1990–1999, All rights reserved.

16. Mihaly Csikszentmihalyi, *Flow: The Psychology of Optimal Experience* (New York: Harper & Row, 1990) p. 74.

17. "The 100 Best Companies To Work For In America," *Fortune,* January 11, 1999, pp. 118+.

18. John P. Kotter, *Leading Change* (Boston: Harvard Business School Press, 1996).

CHAPTER 10

1. Two of the best works on mission statements are by James C. Collins and Jerry I. Porras, "Organizational Vision and Visionary Organizations," *California Management Review,* Fall 1991, pp. 30–52. Comments on mission statements in this chapter rely heavily on that article. A somewhat more accessible update is "Building Your Company's Vision," *Harvard Business Review,* September–October 1996, pp. 65–77.

2. Collins and Porras, "Organizational Visions and Visionary Organizations," p. 31.

3. Russell Ackoff, then of The Wharton School, developed the idealized design approach, which he has applied to dozens of organizations, including some of America's largest corporations. Ackoff's *Creating the Corporate Future* (New York: John Wiley & Sons, 1981) presents his theory of interactive planning; chapter 5 deals with idealized design. Ackoff *et al.'s A Guide to Controlling Your Corporation's Future* (New York: John Wiley & Sons, 1984) is a "how to do it" guide to interactive planning. Michael Hammer's concept of "reengineering" is similar to idealized design. See Hammer, "Reengineering Work: Don't Automate, Obliterate," *Harvard Business Review,* July–August 1990, pp. 104–12.

4. Thomas J. Peters and Robert H. Waterman, Jr., *In Search of Excellence* (New York: Harper & Row, 1982), p. 239.

5. Quoted by Collins and Porras, "Organizational Vision and Visionary Organizations," p. 46.

6. *Ibid.,* pp. 46–47.

7. *Ibid.,* p. 49.

CHAPTER 11

1. William C. Finnie, "The State of Strategy," *The Real World Strategist,* December 1994, p. 3.

2. The sections on organizational structure and people issues borrow liberally from *Implementing Your Strategic Plan: How to Turn "Intent" Into Effective Action for Sustainable Change* (New York: AMACOM, 1999) by C. Davis Fogg.

3. Private communication, 1993.

4. David A. Garvin, "Quality on the Line," *Harvard Business Review,* September–October 1983, pp. 65–75.

5. Robert S. Kaplan and David P. Norton, *The Balanced Scorecard* (Boston: Harvard Business School Press, 1996).

6. From a form developed by Linda Bryant, president of Financial Focus (private communication).

CHAPTER 12

1. John P. Kotter, *Leading Change* (Boston: Harvard Business School Press, 1995).
2. Dave Ulrich, Jack Zenger, and Norm Smallwood, *Results-Based Leadership* (Boston: Harvard Business School Press, 1999).
3. William C. Finnie, "The State of Strategy," *The Real World Strategist*, December 1994, p. 4.
4. The discussion of Lewin's approach is taken from *The Challenge of Organizational Change* by Rosabeth Moss Kanter, Barry A. Stein, and Todd D. Jick (New York: The Free Press, 1992), pp. 9, 375.
5. Thomas S. Kuhn, *The Structure of Scientific Revolutions,* 3rd ed. (Chicago: University of Chicago Press, 1996).
6. *The Challenge of Organizational Change, op cit.,* pp. 376–82.
7. Bill Finnie and Marilyn Norris, "On Leading Change: A Conversation with John P. Kotter," *Strategy & Leadership,* January-February 1997, p. 21.
8. Dave Ulrich, Jack Zenger, and Norm Smallwood, *Results-Based Leadership* (Boston: Harvard Business School Press, 1999). This section borrows liberally from this book.
9. Robert S. Kaplan and David P. Norton, *The Balanced Scorecard* (Boston: Harvard Business School Press, 1996).
10. Marshall Loeb, "Where Leaders Come From," *Fortune,* September 19, 1994. p. 241.
11. James C. Collins and Jerry I. Porras, *Built to Last: Successful Habits of Visionary Companies* (New York: Harper Business, 1994).
12. Loeb, *op cit.,* p. 242.
13. Summarized from "What Managers Can Learn from Manager Reagan," *Fortune,* September 15, 1986, pp. 33+.
14 Patrick Lencioni, *The Five Temptations of a CEO: A Leadership Fable* (San Francisco: Jossey-Bass, 1998).

INDEX

Get a Head Start on Crafting Your Company's Future

○ **YES,** I would like to receive free materials on the Three-Cycle Strategy Development and Implementation Process:

   ○ My company's management team has **more than five** people.

   ○ My company's management team has **five or fewer** people.

○ **YES,** I also want _____ copies of *Hands-On Strategy: The Guide to Crafting Your Company's Future,* 2nd edition, at $24.95 each, plus $3 shipping and handling per book (Missouri residents please add $1.80 sales tax per book.) Deduct 25% for orders of five or more.

NAME

COMPANY   INDUSTRY

ADDRESS

CITY   STATE   ZIP

PHONE   E-MAIL

○ My check, payable to **The Finnie Group,** for $ _____ is enclosed.

Please complete this form and return it with your payment to:
Hands-On Strategy
The Finnie Group
12501 Glencroft Drive
St. Louis, MO 63128